Psychology and Medicine

Psychobiological Dimensions of Health and Illness

DONALD A. BAKAL

TAVISTOCK PUBLICATIONS

To my parents

For Janice, Jeff, and Chris

First published in Great Britain in 1979 by
Tavistock Publications Limited
11 New Fetter Lane, London EC4P 4EE

Printed in Great Britain by
J.W. Arrowsmith Ltd, Bristol

ISBN 0 422 77010 8 (hardback)
ISBN 0 422 77020 5 (paperback)

British Library Cataloguing in Publication Data

Bakal, Donald A
  Psychology and medicine.
  1. Medicine and psychology
  2. Clinical psychology
  I. Title
  610'.1'9   R726.5

  ISBN 0-422-77010-8
  ISBN 0-422-77020-5

PSYCHOLOGY
AND MEDICINE

Donald A. Bakal, Ph.D., is Director of the Headache Research Unit at the Ambulatory Care Centre of the University of Calgary Medical School and Associate Professor in the University of Calgary Department of Psychology. He received his doctorate in psychology in 1971 from the University of Manitoba.

Contents

epilogue

a new perspective   249

1

Medicine: Body and Mind

Psychology is rapidly becoming an integral part of modern health care delivery systems. This trend is reflected in hospitals and medical schools by the appearance of new programs with labels such as *holistic medicine*, *behavioral medicine*, and *environmental medicine*. Medical and nursing students, in increasing numbers, are also looking to psychology for concepts and techniques that will enhance their understanding of health and illness. The material contained in this book represents a direct effort to develop this interest. Throughout the chapters, theoretical and practical concepts from psychology are examined for their relevance to the understanding of some of the most frequent and serious health problems encountered in general practice and hospital clinics.

A number of writers have observed that disease patterns in Western industrialized countries have shifted dramatically over the past 150 years. Communicable diseases such as smallpox, cholera, and typhus have been largely brought under control, whereas disorders such as coronary heart disease and hypertension have increased dramatically during the same period. Some researchers believe that health disorders with a large psychological component constitute 30% of the complaints now seen by physicians in general practice. Other guesstimates have ranged as high as 60% to 90%. Surveys of populations have revealed that 50% of the respondents report suffering from at least one psychosomatic symptom (headache, gastrointestinal complaints, hypertension) on a regular basis (Schwab, Fennell, & Warheit, 1974). Individuals with psychosomatic complaints are often

The author gratefully acknowledges the support he received from the University of Calgary, Killam Resident fellowship, while writing this book.

labeled as "problem patients" by medical practitioners because their disorders are believed to represent the outcome of mental and physical disturbances that can neither be diagnosed nor treated by modern technological medicine.

This book examines health and illness from a psychobiological perspective. This perspective by no means represents an argument against the significance of biochemical variables in understanding disease. On the contrary, the material presented is intended to complement the existing biochemical knowledge of disease. Furthermore, the psychobiological perspective does not imply that illness can easily be reversed by the adoption of some naïve mind-over-matter philosophy. Many illnesses are associated with structural damage and require chemical or surgical intervention. At the same time, however, the presence of structural damage does not rule out the possibility that psychological variables were critical in precipitating the disorder. The conditions that maintain a disorder need not be the same as the conditions that led to the disorder. Thus, although psychological manipulations may not be effective in curing an established disorder such as heart disease, the same manipulations may be effectively used to reduce the overall incidence of heart disease through the implementation of preventive medicine programs.

Another important aspect of the material that follows is that the presence of organic damage in a patient should never be taken as a sign that psychological variables are now unimportant, for psychosocial stimuli may play a major role in maintaining or aggravating disorders associated with tissue damage. For example, it has been demonstrated that patients recovering in coronary care units often show remarkable changes in cardiovascular activity in response to unnoticed social stimuli. Figure 1-1 shows the change in cardiovascular activity that occurred with the routine taking of a patient's pulse. The data were obtained from a 72-year-old female who had been admitted to the hospital following complaints of shooting pain in her right side (Lynch, Thomas, Mills, Malinow, & Katcher, 1974). An electrocardiogram revealed that her heart was missing one ventricular beat for every two atrial beats (called a 2:1 AV block). The pulse taken by the nurse (stimulus) led to a dramatic change in the original heart rhythm irregularity (response). The authors provide another example in which an intermittent AV block disappeared during the taking of the pulse and reappeared as soon as the nurse left the coronary care unit. The proper care of the patient demands that health professionals recognize the possibility that such unnoticed reactions may occur in any hospital setting, whether involving intensive care or during a routine medical examination.

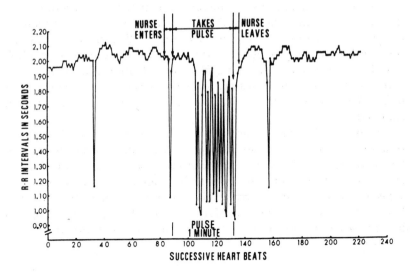

Figure 1-1   Effect of pulse taking on heart rate of patient with 2:1 block. Heart-rate data are plotted such that 2:00 equals a heart rate of 30, while 1:00 equals a heart rate of 60, and so forth (Lynch, Thomas, Mills, Malinow, & Katcher, 1974). Copyright © 1974 by The Williams & Wilkins Co., Baltimore. Reprinted by permission of the publisher and J. J. Lynch.

Paradigm Shift in Medicine

All of us, whether students, educators, physicians, nurses, or patients, believe in a particular philosophy that affects our understanding of human behavior and illness. Even when we try to be "objective" about some situation or person, our perceptions are colored by the philosophy of life that we hold. In science, this philosophy is known as a paradigm. A paradigm is like a supertheory that actually extends beyond a particular problem being investigated by a scientist. In fact, the paradigm adopted often determines how the scientist will solve the problem. For example, behaviorism and psychoanalysis represent two powerful paradigms in psychology. A patient with a psychological complaint will be seen from totally different perspectives by behaviorists and psychoanalysts. A behaviorist will see the patient as emitting responses to an environmental stimulus, whereas the analyst will see the same responses as reflecting unconscious conflicts. Both models are the creations of theoreticians and therefore are not necessarily correct or incorrect in some absolute sense.

Because theoreticians are members of particular societies, their theories of human behavior and of health and sickness are influenced by the very societies in which they live. An excellent illustration of the relationship between societal values and theory is Freudian psychology. Freud attributed major significance for understanding human behavior to the sexual instinct—a view which is not widely held today. Did Freud misperceive the situation or has the situation changed?

Consider the state of affairs that existed at the time Freud was treating his patients and developing his elaborate theories. Sexual behavior during the Victorian era was to be reserved for reproduction and was not to be enjoyed. Even sexual fantasies were regarded as signs of sickness. In order to appreciate the situation, examine the following quotation provided by Maddi (1976). The quotation, written by a physician in 1901, was taken from a book for mothers with young children:

> Teach him that these [sexual] organs are given as a sacred trust, that in maturer years he may be the means of giving life to those who shall live forever.
>
> Impress upon him that if these organs are abused, or if they are put to any use besides that for which God made them—and He did not intend that they should be used at all until man is fully grown—they will bring disease and ruin upon those who abuse and disobey those laws which God has made to govern them.
>
> If he has ever learned to handle his sexual organs, or to touch them in any way except to keep them clean, not to do it again. If he does, he will not grow up happy, healthy and strong.
>
> Teach him that when he handles or excites the sexual organs, all parts of the body suffer, because they are connected by nerves that run throughout the system, this is why it is called "self-abuse." The whole body is abused when this part of the body is handled or excited in any manner whatever.
>
> Teach him to shun all children who indulge in this loathesome habit, or all children who talk about these things. The sin is terrible, and is, in fact, worse than lying or stealing! For although these are wicked and ruin their soul, yet this habit of self-abuse will ruin both soul and body.
>
> If the sexual organs are handled it brings too much blood to these parts, and this produces a diseased condition; it also causes disease in other organs of the body, because they are left with a less amount of blood than they ought to have. The sexual organs, too, are very closely connected with the spine and the brain by means of the nerves, and if they are handled, or if you keep thinking about them, these nerves get excited and become exhausted, and this makes the back ache, the brain heavy and the whole body weak.

It lays the foundation for consumption, paralysis and heart disease. It weakens the memory, makes a boy careless, negligent and listless.

It even makes many lose their minds; others, when grown, commit suicide.

How often mothers see their little boys handling themselves, and let it pass, because they think the boy will outgrow the habit, and do not realize the strong hold it has upon them! I say to you; who love your boys—"Watch!"

Don't think it does no harm to your boy because he does not suffer now, for the effects of this vice come on so slowly that the victim is often very near death before you realize that he has done himself harm. (p. 280)

After reading this excerpt, it is not difficult to see why Freud was so preoccupied with the sexual motive. The important point, however, is to appreciate how existing values affected the nature of Freudian theory.

Dualistic Thinking

Until very recently, the dominant paradigm in medicine has been that the mind and body are separate entities. This philosophical position was first proposed by René Descartes in the seventeenth century (and hence is known as Cartesian dualism). Descartes believed that mind and body were two distinct entities and that each was subject to different laws of causality. Dualism was very strong in Western society in preventing acceptance of the fact that psychological and physical disease are closely related. Some scientists believed that the mind-body issue could be solved simply by denying it was an issue. Others believed that, inasmuch as it is unknown how anxiety, depression, or stress could cause a migraine attack, an ulcer, or elevated blood pressure, it was best to ignore the problem for the time being.

One important factor that has contributed to the desire to describe humans either in purely physical or in purely psychological terms is the high degree of specialization that exists in science. Specialization has become a fact of life in all professions. The complexities of all disciplines make it difficult for anyone to understand his or her own discipline and impossible to fully understand other related disciplines. Although specialization is necessary, it is important to remember that each specialty has a particular way of viewing things. Thus a biochemist will view illness from a molecular level while a psychologist will see the same illness from a behavioral perspective. There is nothing inherently wrong with specialization. The problem begins when the specialists attempt to generalize from their particular model to include all aspects of human functioning.

Victor Frankl (1969), an existential psychiatrist, uses the following analogy to illustrate the distortion that occurs when a human is viewed from either a purely biological or a purely psychological perspective (Figure 1-2). A cylinder projected out of its own three-dimensional space with lower horizontal and vertical dimensions results in two new dimensions with different properties. In the one case, the result is a circle; in the other case, a rectangle; and in both cases, something is lost. Similarly, if a human being is projected into a purely biological frame of reference or entirely into the frame of reference of psychology, the same limitations occur. In one case, the outcome is physical data; in the other, psychological or behavioral data; yet in both cases, the psychobiological perspective is lost.

Disease is most often described solely from the biological perspective. It often goes unrecognized that the term *disease* is simply a label that describes biological phenomena and that it is not a real thing (Harlem, 1977). *Pneumonia*, for example, is simply a word and not an entity by itself. Bacteria such as the pneumococcus exist in nature, but pneumonia does not. Pneumonia is a condition involving the entire person and not a condition that can be found in nature independent

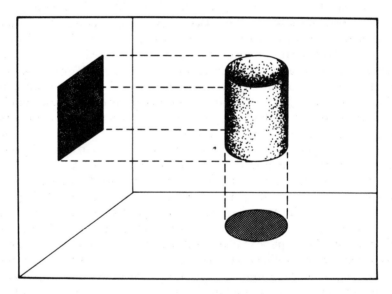

Figure 1-2   Projection of cylinder out of its three-dimensional space to form a circle and a rectangle; in both cases, something is lost (Frankl, 1969). Copyright © 1969 by Hutchinson Publishing Group Limited. Reprinted by permission of the publisher.

of the person. This is an important observation, for it makes us realize that we are always dealing with ill people and not with diseases. The disease label simply facilitates our ability to deal with the patient's illness. Failure to recognize this point can make it difficult to retain a patient-centered approach. Quite often health professionals come to view patients as consisting of nothing more than a conglomeration of parts, some working and some not. The following quotation provided by an intern making rounds illustrates this tendency:

> Both hernias were doing fine; the gastrectomy was already eating; the veins were okay and walking; and neither hemorrhoid had managed a BM [bowel movement]. The disease paraded verbally out of me, unattached to personal names or thoughts. (Cook, 1972, p. 146)

Not all medical scientists are willing to accept the importance of psychological variables in disease. On the contrary, many of these individuals argue that there should be an all-out effort to disentangle the organic elements of disease from the psychosocial aspects of human misery. From this perspective, disease and psychosocial behavior are independent phenomena. They also believe that at some time in the future a complete understanding of both behavioral and medical disorders will come from the identification of underlying biochemical and neurophysiological processes. This strictly biomedical view of health and illness is widely held throughout the Western world (Engel, 1977), illustrating again the close relationship between the beliefs of the larger society and scientific thought.

Will it be possible some day totally to reduce the explanation of human functioning to the biological level? Returning to the analogy of the cylinder, this becomes a meaningless question because it is like trying to determine whether it is possible to reduce the characteristics of a circle to the characteristics of a rectangle. Psychological states undoubtedly have a physiological substrate, but at the same time they are not likely to be totally explainable at the physiological level. Kety (1960) provided the following example to illustrate what he believes is the irreducible nature of conscious phenomena:

> When we look at the clear sky on a crisp autumn day, a remarkable sequence of physiochemical changes is set in motion, no less remarkable because it is commonplace. Today we can describe many of them, and we have every right to assume that some day we may be able to describe them all—from the light of a specific wavelength impinging on our retina, through the chemical and physical conversions there, to its emergence along the optic pathways as a series of specific signals in spe-

cific fibers. We shall trace these signals through the neuron pools in the great visual relay stations to certain portions of the visual cortex. We shall, I hope, someday be able to trace accompanying impulses through association pathways in the reticular system and in other areas of cortex, and if we are fortunate, we shall watch these ramifying impulses or their progeny converge in the motor centers of the brain in just the proper temperospatial arrangement to actuate the muscles which will say, "How blue the sky is today."

Where, pray, in that sequence is the sensation of blueness? It is neither wavelength, nor nerve impulse, nor spatial arrangement of impulses; it is not necessary to any of these processes and, though dependent on many of them, is explained or even described by none. It is richer and far more personal. (p. 1861)

Kety's insightful theoretical description is becoming a reality in medicine, where the division between mind and body is quickly dissolving.

Psychobiological Approach to Illness

The change in paradigm that is sweeping medicine is reflected in the current diversity of medical research. Historically, medical research has been identified with studies of the physiology and biochemistry of systems underlying disease. The disease itself was viewed as a "thing" or condition that operated independently from psychosocial variables. Now medical research has expanded to include also the psychological and social determinants of health and disease. Possibly the most significant change is that researchers from different disciplines are now recognizing the necessity of examining the *interrelationships* between social, psychological, and physiological determinants of health and disease (Lipowski, 1977). The recognition that variables of very different levels of abstraction (social, psychological, physiological) interact is also resulting in a change in the classification of illness. Traditionally, illness has been viewed as *psychosomatic, hysterical (conversion reaction), or organic in origin.*

Psychosomatic Disorders

Psychosomatic disorders are defined as "physiological dysfunctions and structural aberrations that result primarily from psychological processes rather than from immediate physical agents like those involved in the organic disorders" (Lachman, 1972). The psychological processes are listed as frustrating circumstances, conflict situations, and emotion-provoking situations. The physiological changes involved are those that accompany normal emotional states, but in this case the changes are much more intense. The changes are usually associated with the autonomic nervous system, which is the portion of the nervous system that controls smooth muscles, heart, blood vessels, glands, and other internal organs. Notice that the above definition states that organic changes do take place. The symptoms are real. This is important because many people have believed that a physical symptom induced by psychological factors cannot really be serious— certainly not as serious as the same symptom induced by physical factors. For example, the belief that emotionally triggered asthma is "fake asthma" has been found among both the relatives and physicians of patients suffering from this disorder. Purcell, Weiss, and Hahn (1972) gave an example of a family practitioner who referred a patient suffering from asthma to a psychiatrist on the basis that "it can't really be serious since everybody knows this patient's asthma is all psychic." The same reasoning is behind the commonly used phrase "it's all in your head" to describe ailments with no obvious organic basis. This kind of thinking illustrates the difficulty many people have in giving the same significance to psychological variables as they do to physical variables in understanding the cause of illness.

At one time only a few specific illnesses were labeled as psychosomatic, these being bronchial asthma, essential hypertension, neurodermatitis, peptic ulcer, rheumatoid arthritis, thyrotoxicosis, and ulcerative colitis. All of these disorders are mediated by the autonomic nervous system. The problem discovered in trying to isolate illnesses that are psychosomatic from illnesses that are not is simply that few illnesses, if any, have either an "emotional" or a "physical" cause. The majority of illnesses are multifactorial in origin, having both psychosocial and physical causes. In this sense the label "psychosomatic" is misleading and should be abandoned.

Conversion Reaction Disorders

Conversion reactions (also called hysterical disorders) are characterized by the onset of an illness symptom, which usually involves a loss or alteration of a sensory or motor function. The symptom usually appears very suddenly and the individual cannot remember what was happening at the time the symptom appeared. Thus the individual may suddenly develop a tremor, paralysis of a limb, or the loss of vision. Malmo (1970) described a young girl named Anne who after having many angry disputes with her mother finally left home but, upon returning, began to complain of fainting, dizziness, and buzzing in the ears. Then one morning she awoke to find herself totally deaf.

A conversion reaction disorder is not associated with tissue damage, although its continued presence may lead to organic changes (muscular atrophy, permanent stiffness). The disturbance is purely at the cortical level. The patient with a conversion reaction disorder is often capable of functioning, in spite of the disorder. For example, patients with bilateral blindness are still capable of walking about freely without harming themselves or bumping into things:

> A young woman complaining of total blindness in both eyes asked for a glass of water. It was placed on her bedside stand, precariously balanced on the edge so that the slightest touch would send it crashing to the floor. When told to reach out for it, she stared vacantly ahead and with her hand felt all around the periphery of the glass. So accurate and delicate were her movements that she exactly outlined the circumference of the glass without once touching it and then, in disgust, asked that it be handed to her since she could not find it. (Nemiah, 1975, p. 1215)

Conversion reaction disorders are usually interpreted as solving a problem for the individual at the unconscious level. The word *conversion* refers to an intrapsychic process whereby an unacceptable fantasy or impulse is converted into bodily sensation or feeling. In the case of Anne, mentioned above, her psychiatrist thought her deafness represented an unconscious wish to be free from her mother's nagging voice. Conversion reaction disorders may occur during extreme periods of stress in individuals not considered to be psychologically maladjusted. Such symptoms commonly appear during periods of intense grief:

> In a group of 12 "normal, healthy" women, who were under study during a time their husbands were dying of cancer, 3 developed a symptom similar to what they observed their husbands were experiencing. The symptoms of chest pain, hoarseness, and weakness of the right arm and leg, respectively, were similar to those experienced by their husbands with cancer. The conversion symptoms came at a time when their husbands were making more demands for care than these women could meet. None of these women had had conversion symptoms in the past, and even though they considered it an extremely inopportune time to get sick, all of them were judged to have been psychologically relieved by the appearance of a somatic symptom which allowed them to ask for help. With the onset of the symptoms, all 3 considered themselves ill and sought medical advice. All 3 reported that they had reached the

end of their psychologic endurance in trying to please and care for their dying husbands. There was nothing more they could do to make their husbands more comfortable and less symptomatic. In one way or another all 3 experienced the fleeting awareness of conflict over the wish that it would all be over soon. In each case the conflict over the wish was symbolized by the appearance of a symptom indicating an identification with the suffering of the dying spouse. The symbolic suffering protected them from having to take any further responsibility or action as far as it concerned the suffering. The symbolic suffering then served to protect them from a conscious awareness of their aggressive wishes toward their husbands. (Schmale, 1969, p. 1878)

Historically, conversion reaction and psychosomatic disorders have been distinguished primarily on the basis of the anatomical structures involved and the presence or absence of motivational variables. Conversion reaction disorders were assumed to involve only sensory and motor systems, whereas psychosomatic disorders were assumed to involve only the autonomic nervous system. Motivational variables, although considered central to the onset of conversion reaction disorders, were not considered significant in influencing the onset of psychosomatic disorders.

Recent evidence is leading to a blurring of the distinction between conversion reaction and psychosomatic disorders. Conversion reaction symptoms are not necessarily restricted to sensory and motor systems. Fainting, nausea, and vomiting are observed in conversion reaction disorders, and these symptoms are mediated by the autonomic nervous system (Barr & Abernathy, 1977; Nemiah, 1975). In fact, over the past 60 years there has been a subtle shift in the kind of conversion reaction disorders seen in the clinic. Fewer and fewer cases of classical paralysis and blindness are appearing, whereas the incidence of symptoms mediated by the autonomic nervous system is increasing. This may reflect an increasing sophistication in the populace's understanding of anatomy, physiology, and psychology. That is, glove anesthesia (paralysis from the wrist down), which is anatomically impossible, may for this very reason no longer be "chosen" as an appropriate symptom. Any nervous system structure may become involved in a conversion reaction, just as long as that structure and the associated symptom are capable of representing an intrapsychic compromise.

The distinction between conversion reaction and psychosomatic disorders in terms of the presence or absence of motivational variables is also no longer valid. Motivational variables are not always present in conversion reaction disorders nor are they necessarily ab-

sent in psychosomatic disorders. The term *motivational* has been used
in the past to refer primarily to unconscious conflict resolution within
the Freudian framework, but it is quite possible that sensory symptoms are under the control of environmental stimuli. Recent research
also suggests that the autonomic nervous system may be controlled by
motivational variables as well:

> This fact removes the main basis for assuming that psychosomatic
> symptoms involving the autonomic nervous system are fundamentally
> different from those functional symptoms, such as hysterical symptoms,
> that involve the somatic nervous system; it allows scientists to extend to
> psychosomatic symptoms [a] type of learning theory analysis . . . ; it
> means that psychosomatic symptoms can be reinforced by the full range
> of rewards, including escape from aversive stimulation, that are fre-
> quently described by psychiatrists as secondary gains. For example, one
> child's mother may habitually allow him to escape from unpleasant situ-
> ations ("You're sick and can't go to the dentist today") when he looks
> pale, but another child's mother may allow him to escape whenever he
> shows signs of gastrointestinal distress. One might expect the two chil-
> dren to learn to be predisposed to different types of psychosomatic
> symptoms. But such learning, if indeed it does occur, need not rule out
> innate differences. In stressful situations in which any symptom of ill-
> ness is likely to be rewarded, the symptom to which a person is innately
> predisposed is the one most likely to occur, be rewarded, and thus be
> strengthened additionally by learning. To date, the foregoing discus-
> sion is theoretical speculation, but it may provide a point of departure
> for fruitful clinical research. (Miller, 1975, p. 361)

What is important then is not the difference between conversion reaction and psychosomatic disorders but the fact that both classes of
disorder might to some extent represent learned responses. Furthermore, these disorders, once firmly established, might lose their symbolic significance and become habitual responses with a life of their
own. That is, gastrointestinal complaints in childhood and associated
reinforcement might lead to the development of a hypersensitive gastrointestinal system that is excessively responsive to stress in adulthood.

Organic Disorders

The traditional view holds that *organic disorders* are caused by
parasites, toxic substances, or other pathological agents. A few years
ago, psychological variables were not considered to be significant with
respect to organic disorders. What disorders are organic? Again there
is no answer to this question although there certainly have been arguments. Some investigators believed (and continue to believe) that

asthma and hypertension are organic disorders while other investigators believed that they are psychosomatic disorders. Ignoring for a
moment the problem of definition, the evidence continues to accumu-
late in support of the position that virtually all disorders are susceptible to psychosocial influences. The list includes disorders such as hay
fever, asthma, tuberculosis, heart failure, coronary artery disease,
emphysema, hypertension, arthritis, and ulcers.

Even the most formidable of all diseases, cancer, may be influenced by psychological variables. A common theme in the literature is
that cancer patients suffer from an inability to express emotions and
as children lacked a close relationship with their parents. Thus, instead of discharging their feelings openly, these patients have directed their tensions inward and in some way upset immunological
body systems, which resulted in cancerous changes. The evidence in
support of this theory is very poor (Marcus, 1976). It is mentioned
only to illustrate the extent to which psychology is being implicated in
illness.

Little support can be offered for the continued use of the terms
conversion reaction, *psychosomatic*, and *organic* as labels for distinct
classes of illness. It is likely that all illness is determined by environmental, psychological, and physiological variables. At the theoretical
level, a tricky conceptual issue remains to be solved in that we do not
always understand how these different variables interact to produce
illness. For example, stress may lead to heart disease but we cannot
explain how this happens. For this reason, many medical researchers
continue to concentrate their efforts on identifying dysfunctions in
regulatory and immunological systems that they feel are the basis of
disease. In time our understanding of how these physiochemical systems interact with psychological events will increase. Even now, there
is no question that the psychobiological model is critical to the understanding of the patient and his illness. At the beginning of the chapter, there was an example of how subtle psychosocial stimuli may
influence existing heart disease. One immediate lesson that is reinforced in the following chapters is that the presence of organic damage does not rule out the need to understand the patient's behaviors
and environment.

Ladinos

Some cultures have long recognized the significance of incorporating
all aspects of human functioning into their understanding and treatment of health and sickness. For example, in the Ladinos, a group of
people living in the highlands of Chiapas in southeastern Mexico, one

finds a view of health and illness that integrates psychological, social, and physical variables (Fabrega & Manning, 1973). Emotional, personality, and social processes are considered to have significance equal to that of biological processes in the onset and recovery from illness.

The occurrence of illness represents evidence that the afflicted individual's strength, or *consistencia* has been overrun or depleted. The term *consistencia* includes physical as well as psychological attributes. The individual's personality, or *caracter*, along with his intelligence, education, and previous experiences also contribute to illness and to his ability to cope with illness. The *consistencia* of the individual and his personality form a base line of vulnerability to disease in general.

The Ladinos consider excessive emotions as being capable of precipitating illness:

> Emotions can actually be ranked as to their pathogenicity, and it is also possible to associate causally illness types with each of the various emotions. Inspection of the list of emotions that are described as pathogenic indicates that pleasantness or unpleasantness are not critical factors. Rather, their amount and persistence in the individual across time appear to be critical. Emotions and feelings are viewed as inevitable, but when present they should be discharged (in action, talk, or thought) or neutralized (as with alcohol) so that the body at no one time or during any one interval carries an excessive load. For emotions, when present in this way, are seen to have deleterious bodily extensions. Related to the pathogenicity of the emotions is the importance that Ladinos ascribe to types of interpersonal situations. Arguments, separations, envious coveting, love triangles, intensely satisfying exchanges, etc., all have medical relevance precisely because they give rise to excessive feeling. The personality types or "caracters" assume relevance here since they reflect an individual's habitual mode of conducting and responding to interpersonal situations. (Fabrega & Manning, 1973, p. 228)

Interpersonal events are important because illness to one member of the group influences the behavior of other members—just as the behavior of the group influences the sick member. The group, for example, can antagonize the sick member and produce further debilitation or can provide emotional support necessary to abate the illness. Surprisingly our culture seldom recognizes the medical significance of these variables.

The Ladinos do not ignore physical causes of disease. Genetic factors, pathogenic microorganisms, and physiological dysfunctions are considered important. These factors, however, are considered to enhance susceptibility to disease rather than to cause the illness. The major triggers of an illness are viewed within the context of emotional and interpersonal variables. The issue is not so much which variables are more or less important but, rather, that this model of disease includes aspects of personality, social relations, and biological functioning, all of which operate in an interdependent fashion.

Mental illness is also treated in a holistic fashion. These people truly believe the statement, "Mental illness is like any other illness." They do not censure an individual for having an affliction of the mind rather than the body because the mind-body distinction is not made in the first place. Attacks of depression, anxiety, or paranoia are considered to have emotional, interpersonal, and physical components operative in a fashion similar to "physical" illness.

It might be instructive to examine what happens when one of these individuals is treated by a specialist in Western medicine:

> When a ladino visits a physician he experiences an orientation to his problem that is markedly different from his own. A "modern" view that fractionates the native holistic and integrated view of the disease is encountered. For there he is probed in a very precise and intensive way about his body (its appearance, function and sensations) but not about his feelings, moods, dispositions, and social relations. Little confidence and trust can be placed in procedures and strategies that stem from a framework and orientation that is judged as highly formal and mechanistic, especially when these procedures are coordinated by an impersonal individual who appears uninterested in the varied personal and social goings-on which are believed to cause alterations in bodily states and in fact give these their significance. For the ladino patient, one result of having his medical problems reduced in this fashion and of receiving interpretations about bodily matters that are not only discordant but frequently viewed as insufficient and simplistic is skepticism, alienation, and a lack of compliance with medical regimens. (Fabrega & Manning, 1973, p. 235)

Cultures such as the Ladinos', although far behind in modern technological medicine, are capable of teaching us much about the dangers of segmentalizing the patient and illness into mental and physical components.

Personality and Disease

A tremendous amount of energy and effort has been expended over the past 50 years toward identifying personality characteristics believed to be characteristic of patients with particular afflictions. Thus asthmatic patients were thought to have distinctive personality traits as were hypertensive patients, migraine patients, and many other patient groups. Where did this notion come from? Why was the belief in personality and disease so pervasive? The answers to these questions come with an understanding of Freudian psychology. Freudian ideas had a powerful influence on early efforts to link psychological constructs to disease processes. Freud represents the first modern theorist to emphasize that physical disorders may occur when an individual cannot discharge his emotional impulses in some acceptable fashion.

According to Freud, a definite relationship existed between an individual's personality and the manner in which the individual dealt with emotional and instinctual impulses. In fact the adult personality is characterized by the kinds of defense mechanisms an individual uses. The habitual use of certain defense mechanisms becomes established very early in life, usually by the end of the 5th year. Why the emphasis on the first 5 years? According to Freud, it is during these years that each of us passes through several critical stages of psychosexual development (oral, anal, and phallic). Each stage is defined in terms of a central conflict that must be resolved before the child can pass on to the next stage. For example, the oral stage is characterized by strong feelings of dependency. Problems arise when the mother, possibly because of hostile feelings toward the infant, is unable to gratify the oral tensions and associated psychological needs.

Psychiatrists were quick to apply this kind of reasoning to their psychosomatic patients. The best representative theory of this approach is the *nuclear conflict* model, which states that the presence of specific unconscious conflicts may lead to the presence of specific psychosomatic complaints (Alexander, 1950). That is, each psychosomatic ailment is the outcome of a central, or nuclear, emotional conflict. In general terms, unconscious feelings of hostility are believed to trigger cardiovascular disorders (migraine headaches, hypertension), whereas unconscious feelings of dependency or desires to be loved are believed to trigger gastrointestinal and respiratory disorders (ulcers, asthma). The model is depicted schematically in Figure 1-3. Conflict over the expression of aggressive impulses or feelings of dependency leads the individuals to use a variety of defense mechanisms to ward off unconscious awareness of such emotions. Moreover, the specific defense mechanisms adopted lead to the appearance of specific personality traits that the analyst can then use to identify the conflict.

With hypertension, migraine headache, and other cardiac disor-

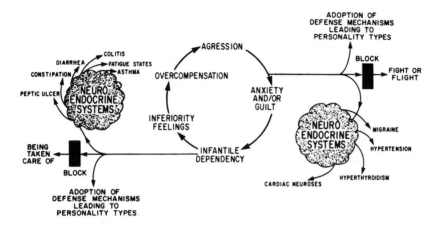

Figure 1-3   Nuclear conflict theory of disorders (Alexander, 1950). Figure is reproduced from *Psychosomatic Medicine* by Franz Alexander, M.D., with the permission of W. W. Norton & Company, Inc. Copyright 1950 by W. W. Norton & Company, Inc. Copyright renewed 1978.

ders, the central conflict has to do with the inhibition or repression of self-assertive hostile impulses. Because the impulses are repressed or inhibited, the corresponding behavior (aggression) is never consummated. In other words, although the physiological processes have been activated for aggression, they are not brought to action and the individual remains in a state of physiological preparedness. The situation for individuals suffering from hypertension was depicted as follows:

> The damming up of his hostile impulses will continue and will consequently increase in intensity. This will induce the development of stronger defensive measures in order to keep pent-up aggressions in check. . . . Because of the marked degree of inhibitions, these patients are less effective in their occupational activities and for that reason tend to fail in competition with others, so that envy is stimulated and their hostile feelings toward more successful competitors is intensified. (Alexander, 1950, p. 150)

Some clinical descriptions of hypertensives are in agreement with the nuclear conflict theory. Essential hypertensives have been described as: (a) more susceptible to anger, resentful, jealous, and oversensitive; (b) driven into anger more quickly than the average person; and (c) unable to cope with rage in that they are too insecure and frightened of retaliation to attack those who anger them (Buss, 1966). The generality of the description, however, remains questionable, as does its therapeutic usefulness. One might find such characteristics in some hypertensive patients, but one might find other negative (or even positive) emotions to be associated with hypertension.

Peptic ulcers and asthma are the best examples of disorders associated with emotional withdrawal. The term *peptic ulcer* refers to both gastric and duodenal ulcers. An ulcer is a lesion of the mucous lining of the stomach or of the duodenum. In the human, ulcers are most frequently duodenal. Such ulcers are quite common, but in many instances they are "quiet," causing no pain or distress, and are, therefore, unnoticed and unreported. However, ulcers often cause severe pain, and when they perforate, serious internal bleeding results, which can cause death. Alexander (1950) hypothesized that such patients invariably suffer from the same conflict, that is, dependence versus independence, which has its genesis during the oral stage of development.

The ulcer patient, it is assumed, has an unconscious wish to be loved and cared for like an infant. These feelings are not recognized by the ego because, if they were, the individual would experience guilt and shame because of the infantile nature of the wishes. To avoid awareness of the conflict, the ulcer patient uses defense mechanisms such as reaction formation and overcompensation. The nature of the defensive structure is inferred from the ulcer patient's personality, which is thought to be characterized by pseudoindependence (reaction formation) and driving ambition (overcompensation). Following are three caricatures of ulcer-prone patients to indicate how those underlying dependent wishes may be organized:

Pseudoindependent. In this type of patient, underlying dependent needs may be largely or completely denied and an opposite facade presented. These patients appear to be highly independent, self-reliant, aggressive, controlling, and overactive. The men present caricatured hypermasculine (by culturally bound definitions) identifications. Such persons ridicule the necessity for rest, relaxation, and vacations and are contemptuous of those they consider weak and dependent. In Western society these characteristics are peculiarly in keeping with success in the business and professional world. The interpersonal relationships of these patients are controlling, rather than warm. By dominating or controlling behavior, they force others to provide their wants and in this way succeed in keeping unconscious the resulting gratification of their

dependent needs. The spouse, for example, is likely to be the long suffering, self-denying provider, and the patient sees himself as powerful
and self-sufficient.

Passive-dependent. The underlying dependent needs are overtly
expressed and to a considerable degree are conscious. These persons,
some of whom may be fairly successful, are outwardly compliant, passive, ingratiating, and eager to perform for others, yet they are also
clinging and dependent and may even be demanding in a passive-
aggressive way. They tend to get into social and interpersonal relationships in which they can depend on a nurturing figure or a paternal,
supportive social organization. The men may show strong feminine (by
culturally bound definitions) identifications.

Acting out. In these patients the dependent needs are taken care
of by blatant acting out and by insistent demanding. These are, psychologically speaking, the most immature patients; their character is
marked by the infantile trait of "I want what I want when I want it,"
even if gratification involves asocial, antisocial, or criminal behavior that
disregards the needs and rights of others and society. Irresponsible,
with little investment in achievement, they may drift from job to job and
are often unemployed. Addiction, tobacco, alcohol, and drugs is common. In their relationships they are parasitic and without considera-
tion of others. (Engel, 1975, p. 1641)

Until very recently, these notions were so firmly entrenched in
the psychoanalytic literature that, even if ulcer patients did not manifest the above-mentioned characteristics, the implication was that
they were simply using different defense mechanisms. For example,
one group of investigators found that over half of their ulcer subjects
failed to manifest personality traits that were reflective of conflicts
over dependency impulses. Rather than question the classical theory,
however, they suggested that these patients were simply manifesting
their unconscious oral motives in a more subtle manner (Weiner, H.,
1973).

Some clinicians continue to take the theory as correct and simply
look for what they think "should be" in the patient's dynamics according to the illness. Thus, if the therapist knows that the patient is suffering from ulcers, he is likely to probe for patient feelings of need to
be loved or taken care of. Such feelings might be identifiable in most
individuals, whether they be sick or healthy. Moreover, if feelings of
dependency or hostility are not apparent to the patient, it would be a

serious mistake to assume that such feelings must, therefore, be repressed and operating from the unconscious. A few years ago, a student who in fact suffered from hypertension listened to my presentation of the nuclear conflict theory and then asked why he was not
aware of his latent hostility!

A Study of Psychosomatic Specificity

Alexander recognized the possibility of subjective bias in his clinical observations, and in 1968 he published, along with French and
Pollack, a study that minimized this danger. He attempted to establish
whether psychiatrists who were familiar with his theory would be able
to diagnose patients correctly solely on the basis of clinical interview
data. The study involved interviews with 83 patients, each with one of
seven illnesses. The disorders and the theoretical expectation of the
associated conflict are as follows:

1. *Bronchial asthma.* Excessive unresolved dependence upon the
   mother.
2. *Eczema.* Showing the body in order to obtain attention, love,
   and favor (exhibitionism).
3. *Rheumatoid arthritis.* Repression of rebellious tendencies.
4. *Ulcerative colitis.* Frustrated hope of carrying out an obligation
   and frustrated hope in accomplishing some task.
5. *Duodenal ulcer.* Frustration of dependency needs.
6. *Essential hypertension.* Conflict over expressing aggressive impulses.
7. *Hyperthyroidism.* Fear of death, development of phobias related
   to this fear.

Each disease was represented by at least five patients of each sex.
Clinical interviews were recorded and edited to remove references to
the underlying diseases and then submitted to psychoanalysts who
were familiar with the nuclear conflict theory. As there were seven
categories of disease, the probability of an analyst being correct by
chance alone was 1/7, or 14%. Although the judges were above chance
in their diagnoses, the percentages were generally below 50%. Thus
the study did show a weak relationship between specific conflicts and
specific diseases.

The outcome of the Alexander et al. study is typical of the majority of studies that have attempted to identify specific personality corre-

lates of disease. Some patients manifest pathological personality traits whereas many others do not. Moreover, the presence of pathological personality traits or emotions is not predictive of specific illnesses. Emotions and personality traits involving resentment, frustration, depression, anxiety, and helplessness are the most frequently reported antecedents, regardless of the disorder (Luborsky, Docherty, & Penick, 1973).

These findings parallel a situation that has been recognized in the mainstream of personality research. Personality constructs are poor predictors of human behavior. What difference would it make if efforts to identify relationships between personality, unconscious conflicts, and disease were stopped? Many researchers feel that it would make no difference whatsoever inasmuch as such relationships have generally failed to increase our understanding of the etiology and treatment of the disease.

Behavior versus Symptom

The stimulus-response approach to behavioral and physical disorders represents an alternative to the personality-disease model. Emphasis is placed on the environmental, psychological, and physiological processes that currently maintain a physiological or behavioral disorder. This approach stands in direct contrast to the Freudian model, which depicts physical and psychological disorders as symptoms stemming from repressed childhood experiences. The strict Freudian model demands that the individual be made aware of the relationship between repressed childhood memories and present adult behaviors before the "symptom" will disappear.

To illustrate the difference in approach, consider a hypothetical male patient with a dreaded fear of women. To a Freudian, this fear might be interpreted as symptomatic of an unresolved Oedipus complex (desire to possess his mother sexually) that occurred during the phallic stage (4th year) of psychosexual development. Possibly the patient's fear did have its beginning at this time in childhood. In fact, he might even have fantasized possessing his mother in this fashion and as a result experienced guilt. He may even show physiological reactions associated with anxiety in the presence of females that remind him of his mother. The original experience may have also initiated a behavior pattern that involved avoidance of females into adulthood. The original experience, however, is likely to be defunct as the motivating force for his adult behavior. There is no need to probe his unconscious in the hope of finding the original impulse. Even dragging him back through childhood and making him admit to the original impulse will not provide him with the social skills necessary for approaching females. By simply focusing on the environmental stimuli (attractive females), however, it becomes possible to provide him with the skills necessary to alter his inappropriate psychobiological responses to these stimuli.

A New Look at Conscious and Unconscious Functioning

We have reached a stage of theoretical development where we can no longer automatically attribute psychological and physiological disorders to repressed impulses and childhood conflicts. Even in cases in which extensive psychoanalysis manages to identify and purge some childhood ideation from the patient, we cannot assume that the disorder in question will disappear. We need to revise our thinking about unconscious mental processes. Patients and physicians alike believe that thought processes outside of awareness are the basis of many medical complaints. This is true even though these same individuals may vehemently reject a Freudian explanation of these thought processes. Consider the following letter that I received from a severe migraine headache sufferer:

> I have had migraine headaches for over five years . . . during this period I have received a number of neurological tests to rule out tumors, blockages, etc. All of the tests were negative and I was told that nothing was wrong with me physically. I have also seen a number of psychiatrists, who have all told me that I had come to the wrong place and that they could do nothing to help me.

This patient began to feel that there must be something wrong with her mentally. She had no idea of what it might be other than "bad nerves." This is a common story that characterizes the plight of thousands of individuals.

In recent years a new neurophysiological model of consciousness has emerged that might eventually explain how emotional thoughts outside of awareness influence our attitudes, behavior, and physiology. The model comes from the studies of split-brain patients by Sperry and his colleagues at the California Institute of Technology. The brain consists of two hemispheres that are connected by a bundle of nerve fibers called the *corpus callosum*. Several patients who have had their corpus callosums severed surgically in order to control epilepsy were studied extensively. The result of this operation has been described as follows:

> The most remarkable effect of sectioning the cerebral commissures, continues to be the apparent lack of change with respect to ordinary behavior. [They] . . . exhibit no gross alterations of personality, intellect or overt behavior two years after operation. Individual mannerisms, conversation and bearing, temperament, strength, vigor, and coordination are all largely intact and seem much as before surgery.
>
> Despite this outward appearance of general normality in ordinary behavior . . . specific tests indicate functional disengagement of the right and left hemispheres with respect to nearly all cognitive and other psychic activities. Learning and memory are found to proceed quite independently in each separated hemisphere. Each hemisphere seems to have its own conscious sphere for sensation, perception, ideation, and other mental activities and the whole inner realm of gnostic experience of the one is cut off from the corresponding experience of the other hemisphere—with only a few exceptions as outlined below. (Sperry, Gazzaniga, & Bogen, 1969, p. 275)

The corpus callosum contains some 200 million nerve fibers and it is therefore amazing that these patients did not suffer psychologically after such extensive neurological damage.

On the basis of extensive observations of these patients, Sperry and others have proposed that each hemisphere might engage in specialized kinds of cognitive knowing. Language functions, such as speech and writing, for example, are mediated predominantly by the left hemisphere in most people. Therefore, the disconnected right hemisphere cannot express itself verbally. In addition, the neural pathways from one side of the body and one-half of the visual field cross over and connect only with the opposite side of the brain. Sensations arising from the right side of the visual field are projected to the right hemisphere. Sensations arising from the left side of the visual field are projected to the left hemisphere (Figure 1-4).

Patients with the corpus callosum sectioned can describe, verbally, objects presented to the right visual field but cannot give correct verbal responses when the information is presented to the left visual field. This indicates that speech is controlled primarily by the left hemisphere. The "mute" right hemisphere knows the correct response that is required, for it can, upon request, select with the left hand the correct object. For example, when a picture of a spoon was presented to the right hemisphere and the subject was asked to iden-

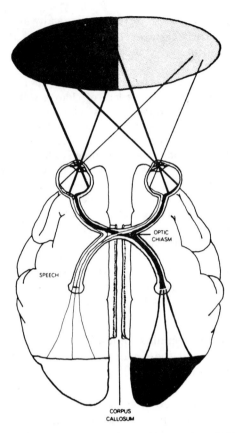

tify the object, he responded not at all or with haphazard guesses
("can opener"). Apparently, the verbal guesses were coming from the
left hemisphere, which had no visual access to the object. If, however,
the patient were asked to feel around with his left hand and locate an
object that matched the picture, he could do so.

   The two disconnected hemispheres are capable of communicating with each other, through a form of *cross-cuing*. Gazzaniga (1967)
describes this intriguing observation as follows:

> We had a case of such cross-cuing during a series of tests of whether the
> right hemisphere could respond verbally to simple red or green stimuli.

At first, after either a red or green light was flashed to the right hemisphere, the patient would guess the color at a chance level, as might be expected if the speech mechanism is solely represented in the left hemisphere. After a few trials, however, the score improved whenever the examiner allowed a second guess.

We soon caught on to the strategy the patient used. If a red light was flashed and the patient by chance guessed red, he would stick with that answer. If the flashed light was red and the patient by chance guessed green, he would frown, shake his head and then say, "Oh no, I meant red." What was happening was that the right hemisphere saw the red light and heard the left hemisphere make the guess "green." Knowing that the answer was wrong, the right hemisphere precipitated a frown and a shake of the head, which in turn cued in the left hemisphere to the fact that the answer was wrong and that it had better correct itself! (p. 170)

Much more is meant by different kinds of hemisphere knowing than is implied by the above examples. The left hemisphere is especially suited for analytical knowing. It is proficient at solving problems that involve taking things apart conceptually and dealing with the parts in isolation. Language facilitates this kind of thinking because it allows us to label the parts. The left hemisphere is also characterized by linear kinds of problem solving. Thus it is adept at solving problems that follow a syllogistic logic (if A is greater than B and B is greater than C, then A is greater than C). Our educational systems, technology, and standard of living depend extensively on highly developed linear and analytic cognitive styles. For many, all that is important to consciousness is contained in this kind of knowing. Apparently, however, the right hemisphere mediates a kind of knowing that has been largely ignored in our culture. It too "knows," but not in the analytical fashion that is characteristic of the left hemisphere. Rather, it uses a nonverbal mode of representation and relies more on sensory information (sight, sound, touch). The right hemisphere is also better equipped than the left hemisphere at grasping part-whole relations. The functioning of the right hemisphere may be the basis of the existential mystical knowing that is characteristic of Eastern religions (Ornstein, 1972). This kind of knowing is nicely contained in the statement, "When you can describe the way it is, then it's not the way."

Illustrating the differences between the two hemispheres in their capacities for cognitive processes is an experiment that involved presenting split-brain patients with two geometric designs, a cross and a cube, and asking them to reproduce the figures, first with one hand, then with the other. The reproductions for two of the patients are shown in Figure 1-5. The left-hand copy (controlled by the right hemisphere) is good in the sense that the essence of the forms is reproduced. The right-hand copy (controlled by the left hemisphere) contains the elements of the forms, a series of connected right angles for the cross, but the essence or configuration of the form is lost.

Figure 1-6 illustrates that the major difference between the two hemispheres is in the style of processing rather than in the content processed. The left hemisphere treats dance in a dictionary fashion, that is to say, in terms of logical precision and categorization. The right-hemisphere treatment is expressed in forms and images whose boundaries are fuzzy. This example emphasizes that one should not adopt some "simple-minded dichotomania" in viewing specialization within the brain (Galin, 1974b).

What does all this have to do with unconscious mental processes? The nonverbal and nonlinear cognitive style of the right hemisphere may, in fact, be what Freud was referring to in his observations of unconscious thought processes (Galin, 1974b). Unconscious mental activity, according to Freud, operated according to the principles of primary-process thought. Here the image of an object is the same as

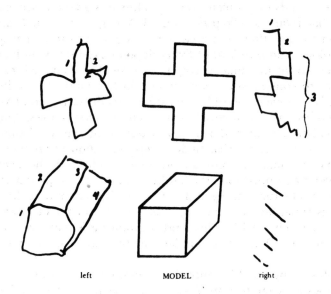

left   MODEL   right

Figure 1-5   Reproduction of cross and cube by left and right hand of split-brain subject (Bogen, 1969). J. E. Bogen, *Bulletin of the Los Angeles Neurological Societies*, 34: 73-105, 1969.

Figure 1-6 "Dance" as viewed by the left and right hemispheres (Galin, 1974b). Photograph by Peter Angelo Simon, © Peter Angelo Simon.

the actual object; reality and fantasy are indistinguishable; and magical thinking takes place. Conscious mental activity referred to secondary-process thought involves rational and logical thought associated with learning, thinking, and remembering.

Several parallels may be drawn between right-hemisphere functioning and primary-process thought:

1. The right hemisphere primarily uses a nonverbal mode of representation, involving images (visual, tactile, kinesthetic, and auditory).

2. The right hemisphere reasons by a nonlinear mode of association rather than by syllogistic logic; its solutions to problems
   are based on multiple converging determinants rather than a
   single causal chain.
3. The right hemisphere is less involved with the perception of
   time and sequence than the left hemisphere.

Observe that the similarities between primary-process thought and
right-hemisphere functioning occur in processes (for example, nonverbal, nonlinear) rather than in content (for example, sexual fantasies).

Schwartz, Davidson, and Maer (1975) used direction of lateral eye
movement to demonstrate the involvement of the right hemisphere in
emotional thought processes. When an individual is asked a reflective
question, he typically, in formulating the answer, shifts his eyes to the
right or to the left. Looking to the right is indicative of left-hemis-
phere involvement, whereas looking to the left is indicative of right-
hemisphere involvement. Schwartz et al. confronted right-handed
subjects with four types of reflective questions:

1. *Verbal-nonemotional.* "What is the primary difference between
   the meanings of the words *recognize* and *remember*?"
2. *Verbal-emotional.* "For you, is anger or hate a stronger emotion?"
3. *Spatial-nonemotional.* "Imagine a rectangle. Draw a line from
   the upper left-hand corner to the lower right hand corner.
   What two figures do you now see?"
4. *Spatial-emotional.* "When you visualize your father's face, what
   emotion first strikes you?"

The greatest number of leftward eye movements occurred while the
subjects were answering the spatial-emotional questions and the
verbal-emotional questions, which provides support for the notion
that emotional processes are largely mediated by the right hemisphere.

There may also be consistent individual differences across people
with respect to preferred or typical eye movements that occur in response to reflective questions. Right-hemisphericity people (left
movers), when compared to left-hemisphericity people (right
movers), have been found to be more emotional, more intuitive, and
more likely to internalize their anxiety. Left movers are also better
able to perceive emotional stimuli presented at speeds preventing

verbal awareness when they are encouraged to think in a holistic and intuitive fashion (Sackeim, Packer, & Gur, 1977).

In the intact person it is possible that the experiences of the right hemisphere can be functionally blocked from awareness to the left hemisphere. In order to illustrate what is meant by *functional blocking,* consider the following description of a film from Sperry's original research with split-brain patients:

> One film segment shows a female patient being tested with a tachistoscope. . . . In the series of neutral geometrical figures being presented at random to the right and left fields, a nude pin-up was included and flashed to the right (nonverbal) hemisphere. The girl blushes and giggles. Sperry asks "What did you see?" She answers. "Nothing, just a flash of light," and giggles again, covering her mouth with her hand. "Why are you laughing then?" asks Sperry, and she laughs again and says, "Oh, Dr. Sperry, you have some machine!" The episode is very suggestive; if one did not know her neurosurgical history, one might see this as a clear example of perceptual defense and think that she was "repressing" the perception of the conflictful sexual material—even her final response (a socially acceptable nonsequitur) was convincing. (Galin, 1974a, p. 573)

The same kind of behavior in the intact person might appear when the experiences of one hemisphere are in conflict with the experiences of the other hemisphere:

> Imagine the effect on a child when his mother presents one message verbally, but quite another with her facial expression and body language; "I am doing it because I love you, dear," say the words, but "I hate you and will destroy you" says the face. Each hemisphere is exposed to the same sensory input, but because of their relative specializations, they each emphasize only one of the messages. The left will attend to the verbal cues because it cannot extract information from the facial gestalt efficiently, the right will attend to the non-verbal cues because it cannot easily understand the words. (1974a, p. 576)

Thus it is possible that mental events in the right hemisphere might be psychologically cut off by the rational left hemisphere.

As shown earlier, conversion reaction disorders are mediated largely by cerebral mechanisms. If the patient's symptoms are restricted to one side of the body and if the right hemisphere is largely involved in the mediation of emotional behavior, then one might expect to find a predominance of conversion reaction patients with left-sided body symptoms. There are isolated accounts in the literature

that support such a hypothesis. As early as 1926 the psychiatrist
Ferenczi observed that many of his patients experienced their conversion reaction symptoms primarily on the left side of the body. Other
investigators (Merskey & Spear, 1967) have observed that lateralized
pain in psychiatric patients is often left-sided.

   One might argue that unilateral conversion reaction symptoms,
when they occur, are more related to the nondominant hemisphere
than the right hemisphere. That is, the possibility exists that left-
handed individuals might experience symptoms on the right side of
the body. A recent study suggests that this is not the case inasmuch as
it was found that conversion reaction symptoms (weakness, paralysis,
sensory loss, numbness) were more prevalent on the left side of the
body for both right-handed and left-handed patients. Although not
all patients experienced their symptoms as restricted to the left side of
the body, the data suggested that the right hemisphere is strongly involved in the mediation of conversion symptoms (Stern, 1977).

Consciousness and Holistic Medicine

The split-brain research has contributed in a major way toward revo-
lutionizing Western thinking regarding consciousness. Intuition, feelings, and holistic experiences have been difficult to study from a rational and analytic perspective. Because of this difficulty, there was a
strong tendency in science to ignore the validity of such concepts. In
psychology we went through an era with behaviorism in which conscious experiences were ignored or even denied existence simply because the data obtained from experience were not "objective." Now
that it has been suggested one-half of our entire brain may be designed to mediate these experiences, there is new interest in the validity of what we, as experiencing humans, always knew was there.

   The current interest in consciousness has also generated interest
in the possibility that an individual may be able to assume more responsibility for his own health. Prior to this interest, there was a tendency to ignore reports of yogis who could exert profound control
over their physiological systems. At the moment there is a tremendous
amount of research dealing with the potential therapeutic usefulness
of self-control techniques such as biofeedback and meditation. This
research is based on the premise that, if something in the mind can
cause illness and disease, quite possibly similar processes might be capable of reversing illness and disease.

Mind-body research has also caused many people to take a look at some of the dehumanizing tendencies of technological medicine:

> The technological approach to health has reached its peak in coronary intensive-care units, kidney-dialysis centers, and cardiovascular surgery theaters with heart-lung machines, cardiac bypasses, and other miracles of modern science and technology. Too often the patient has been ignored and physiological functions stressed instead. Patients often feel that the monitoring and support machines have, in fact, taken over. When this happens, the result is depersonalized and dehumanized health care. Investigators are finding that in some situations people do not respond physically because the human element has not been considered. A new look has to be taken at the human being's reality in these situations. (Lee & Petrocelli, 1974, p. 14)

The rush toward the technological treatment of patients reflects the Westerner's inability to be in touch with consciousness. Physicians and patients alike have been unable to communicate with each other from their experience of themselves and from their experience of the other person. They recommend that medicine become more holistic, more based on treating patients with physical skills, psychological skills, and concern for making the patients become more fully functioning.

2

Brain-Behavior Relationships: Emotions, Rhythms, and Sleep

The understanding of emotion is critical to the health sciences because a great many individuals seek medical assistance for emotional problems. Moreover, emotional variables are considered to be major causes of many physical disorders. The emphasis in this chapter is on the peripheral and central nervous system mechanisms that are known to mediate emotional behavior and the extent to which these mechanisms are sufficient to account for the emotional behavior. The widespread use by the public of psychoactive drugs to control their emotions reflects, at least implicitly, a belief that specific physiochemical disturbances are the basis of their problems. A less frequent, but more dramatic, illustration of this belief is the use of psychosurgery to treat severe emotional disturbances. Again, it is assumed that the brain mechanism being altered is specific in function or controls the emotional disturbance afflicting the patient. But, is this the case? Do specific brain structures control specific emotional behaviors? This is an important question, for the answer will influence theories and treatment procedures for disorders in which emotions play a major role.

Autonomic Nervous System

Peripheral changes that occur during emotional experiences are mediated in large part by the *visceral*, or *autonomic*, *nervous system*. This system innervates the internal organs, glands, smooth muscles, heart and lungs. There are two divisions of the autonomic nervous system, the sympathetic and the parasympathetic, with each division originating from different sections of the brain stem and spinal cord.

In the sympathetic division, the nerve fibers originate in the middle part of the spinal cord, in the segments between the neck and the lower spine. These nerves run to a vertical chain of ganglia (collections of nerve cells that lie outside the central nervous system) that exists on each side of the spinal cord. Fibers that enter the ganglia are called "preganglionic" and those that leave are called "post-ganglionic." In the sympathetic nervous system, every preganglionic fiber connects to several ganglion cells, which means that there is much intercommunication between sympathetic fibers. In fact, the name *sympathetic*, meaning "in sympathy," conveys the observation that this system tends to work as a unit, with all or most of its functions becoming active when stimulated. When we are threatened or angry, or when we are engaging in strenuous exercise, the sympathetic nervous system prepares the body for action by increasing heart rate, causing the liver to release sugar for the muscles, stimulating the release of adrenaline, and inhibiting the digestive processes so that blood can be diverted to the periphery.

The fibers in the parasympathetic division originate above and below the sympathetic nerve fibers. Unlike the sympathetic nervous system, the parasympathetic nervous system has preganglionic fibers that are long and that run right up to the target organ before forming a junction. Because there is little opportunity for interconnection among these fibers, the parasympathetic system tends to function much more discretely. Basically, the parasympathetic system carries out bodily functions that conserve and protect bodily resources such as digestion and the elimination of wastes.

The notion that different emotions have unique autonomic counterparts seems more than reasonable, especially inasmuch as we experience emotions as feeling different from one another. Many of these feelings seem to arise from the autonomic nervous system:

> We speak of the "pallor of fear" and of growing "purple with rage," two quite different vascular responses in the face, and both different still from the "blush of shame." Stagefright gives us "butterflies in our stomachs," but the stench of a dead animal "turns our stomachs" in revulsion and neither is quite the same as feeling our stomachs "tied in knots" when looking down a dizzying stairwell. We skip with joy, and are bowed with grief, and grim with determination. (Sternbach, 1966, p. 80)

The matter is not so simple, however; during strenuous exercise, we also flush, sweat, and experience increased heart rate, and yet we do not necessarily feel emotional.

James-Lange Theory of Emotion

The James-Lange theory of emotion represents one of the earliest theoretical efforts to relate peripheral bodily changes to emotions. We all tend to view bodily changes that occur during an emotional state as being caused by the emotion. In 1890, however, William James caused an uproar among psychologists and physiologists by proposing that this is not the case, and that, in actual fact, the physiological changes precede the emotional experience. A Danish physiologist named Carl Lange proposed a similar explanation of emotion, and the position is now referred to as the James-Lange theory. To quote James,

> We have a scheme perfectly capable of representing the process of the emotions. An object falls on a sense-organ, affects a cortical part, and is apperceived [perceived below awareness] by the appropriate cortical center; or else the latter, excited inwardly, gives rise to an idea of the same object. Quick as a flash, the reflex currents pass through their pre-ordained channels, alter the condition of muscle, skin and viscus; and these alterations, perceived like the original object, in as many portions of the cortex, combine with it in consciousness and transform it from an object simply apprehended into an object emotionally-felt. (James, 1890, p. 474)

There are times when the James-Lange position seems to make intuitive sense. For example, if you have ever been startled by a noise, it seems the autonomic responses (tremors, flushing) occur before you have time to appraise the stimulus as threatening or nonthreatening. In any case, let us examine some of the academic furor that the theory created.

The major criticisms of the James-Lange theory came from Walter Cannon (1929/1970) a physiologist who argued that:

1. Total separation of the autonomic nervous system from the central nervous system does not alter emotional behavior.
2. Internal organs are relatively insensitive structures.

3. Autonomic nervous system responses are too slow to account for the instantaneous nature of emotional experience.
4. Artificial induction of autonomic responses that are characteristic of strong emotion does not produce the emotions.
5. Autonomic responses are basically the same across different emotional states.

Three of these criticisms are here dealt with in detail.

Criticism 1: Separation of the viscera does not alter emotional behavior. James offered the following possibility for a demonstration of support for his position:

> A positive proof of the theory would . . . be given if we could find a subject absolutely anesthetic inside and out, but not paralytic, so that emotion-inspiring objects might evoke the usual bodily expressions from him, but who, on being consulted, should say that no subjective emotional affection was felt. Such a man would be like one who, because he eats, appears to bystanders to be hungry, but who afterwards confesses that he had no appetite at all. (p. 455)

In short, he was saying that support for his theory might come from examining a patient who as a result of some injury no longer had afferent feedback from the autonomic nervous system structures to the central nervous system. James thought that someone with a damaged spine in the neck region would meet this requirement because it was believed that the autonomic system, at least in terms of the sympathetic division, is controlled primarily from fibers entering the middle part of the spinal cord. Dana (1921) described a patient who had a broken neck at the third and fourth cervical level. She was a complete quadriplegic and had very few muscles at her command. Her parasympathetic system was functioning, but her sympathetic was not. Dana reported that she was still capable of showing emotions of grief, joy, displeasure, and affection. A more recent study (Hohmann, 1966) of male patients with spinal cord lesions was supportive of the James-Lange theory. These patients showed considerable decreases in experienced feelings of anger, fear, and sexual excitement. Lader and Tyrer (1975) discussed in the context of the James-Lange theory a genetic disorder that has been called "familial dysautonomia." The syndrome occurs predominantly in Jewish children and is characterized by widespread disorders of the autonomic nervous system including decreased lacrimation, abnormal swallowing, lability of blood pressure, and instability of temperature control. Although the children have emotional problems, Lader and Tyrer suggest that these might be more the result of parental concerns over the disorder than of the autonomic nervous system disorder per se. We still do not know to what extent autonomic nervous activity determines emotional feeling.

Criticism 4: Drug-induced physiological changes do not produce emotions. Because the sympathetic nervous system is definitely involved in emotional behavior, many investigators have attempted to elicit emotion by injecting subjects with drugs that mimic the activity of naturally occurring substances in the body. Maranon (cited in Lader & Tyrer, 1975) reported a study in which 210 patients were injected with epinephrine and then asked to report their feelings. Of the subjects, 71% reported physical symptoms with no emotional overtones; 29% responded with what Maranon labeled as "cold" or "as if" emotions ("I feel as if I were awaiting a great happiness," "as if moved," "as if going to weep," and "as if I had a great fright"). Apparently drug-induced peripheral changes are not sufficient for emotional experience.

Criticism 5: Autonomic responses are the same across different emotions. The James-Lange theory of emotion implied that the quality of each emotion is determined by the pattern of physiological changes that occur due to the emotion-eliciting stimulus. That is, the pattern of physiological changes occurring during anger should be different than those occurring during fear. Cannon (1929/1970) did not believe this to be true, and in fact, he believed that the peripheral changes were basically the same across all emotions—all changes reflecting a massive discharge of the sympathetic nervous system:

> The visceral changes wrought by sympathetic stimulation may be listed as follows: acceleration of the heart, contraction of arterioles, dilation of bronchioles, increase of blood sugar, inhibition of activity of the digestive glands, inhibition of gastro-intestinal peristalsis, sweating, discharge of adrenin, widening of the pupils and erection of hairs. These changes are seen in great excitement under any circumstances. (p. 351)

What is the evidence for specific physiological correlates of emotional stress? One of the first studies to demonstrate physiological differentiation was that of Wolf and Wolff (1947). They performed extensive observations of a patient with a gastric fistula, a device that permitted direct access to the digestive processes. They observed different gastrointestinal responses that were dependent on the emotional state of the patient. For example, acid output and gastric motility decreased when the patient was anxious. The same measures showed an increase in activity when the patient exhibited feelings of anger and resentment.

There have been isolated attempts to induce emotional states in the laboratory. In 1953, Albert Ax performed what has since become a classic study on the psychophysiology of fear and anger. The subjects were told that the study was concerned with physiological differences between hypertensives and normotensives and that their only task was to relax on a bed and listen to music.

> The fear stimulus consisted of a gradually increasing intermittent shock stimulus to the little finger which never reached an intensity sufficient to cause pain. When the subject reported the sensation, the experimenter expressed surprise, checked the wiring, pressed a key which caused sparks to jump near the subject, then exclaimed with alarm that this was a dangerous high-voltage short circuit. The experimenter created an atmosphere of alarm and confusion. After five minutes from the time the subject reported the shock, the experimenter removed the shock wire, assuring the subject that all danger was past, that the short circuit had been found and repaired. (1953, p. 435)

The anger stimulus consisted of an experimenter who verbally and physically abused the subject. (It is unlikely, for ethical reasons, that this experiment will ever be repeated!) Some physiological specificity was observed to occur across the experimental manipulations. For example, increases in average diastolic blood pressure, decreases in heart rate, and increase in muscle potentials were greater for anger than for fear. These average differences were in general not sufficient, however, to be useful in predicting whether a particular subject was expressing fear or anger.

Sodium Lactate Theory of Anxiety Neurosis

The sodium lactate theory of anxiety neurosis (Pitts & McClure, 1967) is a more recent clinical extension of the James-Lange theory. The theory proposes that serum lactate, a metabolite of lactic acid that is formed in the muscles during activity, is causally related to the clinical syndrome of anxiety neurosis.

> Anxiety neurosis is a chronic familial illness characterized by feelings of tenseness and apprehension, breathlessness and shortness of breath,

palpitation, nervousness, irritability, chest pain and chest discomfort, easy tiring, dizziness, numbness and tingling of the skin, trembling and faintness—and by acute anxiety attacks: abrupt spells of intense fear of impending doom that come on without any apparently appropriate stimulus. The attacks are associated with symptoms of smothering and palpitation and often result in a fear of heart attack, cancer, insanity or some other grave disease. The condition most often arises between the ages of 15 and 35; the symptoms persist with fluctuating intensity for many years without in any way reducing longevity or increasing susceptibility to other diseases. The symptoms are frightening and the fatigue is intense, and so the anxiety neurotic quickly seeks medical attention.

Physical examination revals no abnormality; laboratory tests are usually normal. The physician is faced with treating an individual who has many subjective physical complaints and great fear of serious illness but who gives no evidence of such illness. . . . Most physicians either send these patients away after telling them there is nothing wrong or prescribe a sedative, and then forget the whole matter or blame the patient by labeling him a "crock"—medical slang for a neurotic complainer. (Pitts, 1969, p. 69)

A rise in blood lactate is a normal result of exercise. Pitts had observed that the rise with exercise is excessive in anxiety neurotics, and he then wondered what would happen if lactate was injected directly into anxiety neurotics. Would it precipitate an attack of acute anxiety? To test the hypothesis, Pitts and McClure (1967) administered sodium lactate or an inactive substance (glucose in saline) to a group of normals and to a group of anxiety neurotics. When infused with sodium lactate, both the anxiety neurotics and the controls experienced bodily and subjective symptoms of anxiety, but the symptoms were more numerous and intense in the clinical patients. Of the anxiety neurotics, 94% (13/14) experienced "full-blown" anxiety attacks, whereas these occurred in only 20% of the controls. To the anxiety neurotics the attacks were not experienced as artificial, but as similar to some of their worst experiences with anxiety. They reported symptoms such as: "heart pounding, mouth dry, vision blurred, dizzy, headache, and all just like my sick spells, having palpitations, hard to focus my eyes and things are blurred." None of the control subjects experienced such severe symptoms. Pitts (1969) believes, on the basis of this evidence, that high concentrations of lactate may be precipitating clinical attacks of anxiety in susceptible patients. Possibly the excess lactate is the result of an overproduction of epinephrine.

One difficulty with the theory is that normal individuals can exercise strenuously and thereby increase their lactate to "critical" levels and not experience anxiety. The same individuals, if given lactate through infusion, will, however, experience some of the symptoms associated with anxiety neurosis. This means that there must be determinants of the psychological state of anxiety other than simply elevated serum lactate (Ackerman & Sachar, 1974). In addition, not all people suffering from anxiety neurosis have abnormally high blood-lactate concentrations (Grosz & Farmer, 1969).

Another difficulty with the theory is that it is unknown whether patients are susceptible to the effects of lactate because they are anxiety neurotics or whether they are anxiety neurotics because of their susceptibility to lactate. In any case it is evident that the proposed lactate theory must by be modified to take into account cognitive variables involving a variety of higher order intellectual processes. Terms such as *perception, imagery, retention, recall, problem solving*, and *thinking* refer to aspects of cognition. In broader terms yet, *beliefs, attitudes, self-concept*, and *values* represent processes that are largely controlled by cognitive variables. The inclusion of cognitive variables in the analysis of emotions has implications for all forms of disorders and their treatment. To appreciate the importance of cognitive variables in chronic anxiety, one can consider another study in which anxiety neurotic patients were infused with lactate and did *not* experience anxiety. Why? According to the patients, it was because they felt psychologically safe in the presence of the physician. It is likely that cognitive variables are important in the origin of the diversity of symptoms associated with anxiety neurosis as well. Unlike patients with phobias, these patients have difficulty identifying a precipitating stimulus; yet at one time there may have been some set of stimuli that did elicit discrete anxiety attacks. For example, they may have been uncomfortable in certain social situations. Once the autonomic changes occurred, however, they may have shifted their attention from the social events to the autonomic changes and acquired fears that they are suffering a heart attack, for example. This cognitive fear reaction would then intensify the physiological reaction and thereby diversify the severity of the symptomatology.

Cognitive-label Theory of Emotion

Stanley Schachter (1970), a social psychologist, believes that the peripheral physiological changes that occur during different emotions are basically the same. Like Cannon, he maintains that, regardless of the emotion experienced, the physiological outcome is the same: a generalized activation of the autonomic nervous system. According to Schachter's theory, autonomic activation determines only the intensity of the emotion, whereas the content is determined totally by cognitive factors. He often illustrates his theoretical model by asking the reader to imagine a hypothetical individual that has unknowingly received an injection of a drug that mimics the effects of the sympathetic nervous system. According to Schachter, the individual would become aware of the physiological effects of the injection: palpitation, tremor, face flushing, and other symptoms associated with the discharge of the sympathetic nervous system. The individual, however, would be unaware of the source of these sensations. This state of uncertainty would lead to the activation of cognitive evaluative needs because the individual would feel a sense of urgency to understand and label these feelings. Furthermore, he would label his feelings in terms of his knowledge of the immediate situation:

> Should he at the time be with a beautiful woman he might decide that he was wildly in love or sexually excited. Should he be at a gay party, he might, by comparing himself to others, decide that he was extremely happy and euphoric. Should he be arguing with his wife, he might explode in fury and hatred. (Schachter & Singer, 1962, p. 381)

This line of thought led Schachter and Singer (1962) to the following propositions:

> (1) Given a state of physiological arousal for which an individual has no immediate explanation, he will "label" this state and describe his feelings in terms of the cognitions available to him. To the extent that cognitive factors are potent determiners of emotional states, it could be anticipated that precisely the same state of physiological arousal could be called "joy" or "fury" or "jealousy" or any of a great diversity of emotional labels, depending on the cognitive aspects of the situation.
> (2) Given a state of physiological arousal for which an individual has a completely appropriate explanation (e.g., "I feel this way because I have just received an injection of adrenalin"), no evaluation needs will arise and the individual is unlikely to label his feelings in terms of the alternate cognitions available.
> (3) Given the same cognitive circumstances, the individual will react emotionally or describe his feelings as emotions only to the extent that he experiences a state of physiological arousal. (p. 381)

These propositions were tested in an experiment that was described to subjects as a study of the effects of a vitamin compound on vision. Subjects received an injection and then were sent to a waiting room, supposedly to wait for the drug to take effect. In actuality, the subjects received either an injection of placebo or epinephrine (adrenaline). The experimenters also differentially manipulated the evaluative needs of the subjects that were to receive epinephrine. One group (Epi-informed) was informed precisely of the autonomic effects of the drug (flushing, tremor, heart pounding). A second group (Epi-Ignorant) was told that there would be no side effects. A third group (Epi-Misinformed) was falsely told that the side effects would be numbness, itching, and headache. The latter group was included to control for the appropriateness of the explanation factor. Unlike the Epi-Informed group, the Epi-Misinformed group should still experience a need to label the drug-induced physiological changes inasmuch as the explanation given was inappropriate. It was predicted that these latter subjects and the Epi-Ignorant subjects would search their immediate situation for appropriate explanations of what they were feeling.

In the waiting room, each subject found another student, ostensibly waiting like him for the drug to take effect. For half the subjects, he behaved in a euphoric manner, making paper airplanes, shooting paper wads, and twirling a hula hoop. For the remaining subjects, the stooge exhibited anger with a questionnaire that asked personal and insulting questions such as: "With how many men (other than your father) has your mother had extramarital relationships? 4 and under _____; 5–9 _____; 10 and over _____." Finally, the stooge ripped up the questionnaire and stormed out of the room. During these manipulations, the subject's emotional behavior was rated by observers through a one-way mirror. Subjects also filled out self-report questionnaires on their emotional state.

The objective measures indicated that under both the euphoria and anger conditions the greatest emotional changes ocurred with the Epi-Ignorant subjects and the Epi-Misinformed subjects. That is, the subjects with no explanation or a false explanation for their drug-induced symptoms experienced the greatest "evaluative need" to interpret their feelings in terms of environmental cues.

Although Schachter's basic model of emotions might prove to be incorrect, his research has generated exciting interest in the complex interactions that occur between situational variables, cognitions, and physiological states. That is to say, even though different emotions are likely to be more than simply attaching a label to a common physiological condition, the complete explanation of emotional behavior will have to incorporate environmental and cognitive variables as well.

A more convincing example of the power of environmental cues on basic physiology comes from Schachter's (1970) extension of this model to the most basic of all motives: hunger. At the biological level, food deprivation is known to lead to a number of peripheral physiological changes. For example, there is a definite change in levels of blood constituents such as glucose. Insulin injections will lower glucose levels and induce a state known as hypoglycemia. After insulin injections, humans will often report sensations of stomach contractions and feelings of hunger.

Regardless of the physiological mechanism associated with hunger, Schachter still believes that the "unmistakable" cues that we associate with hunger are capable of being actually under powerful environmental control. He feels this is especially the case for obese people. Such a notion has always been the basis for psychoanalytic explanations of obesity. Intrapsychic variables that have been proposed for obesity range from eating to cope with anxiety to eating to undergo pregnancy symbolically.

The psychoanalyst Hilda Bruch (1961) stated that obese patients literally do not know when they are physiologically hungry. She has suggested that these patients, during childhood, might not have been taught proper discriminations between some of the basic drives such as hunger and the emotions such as anxiety, fear, and anger. A study by Stunkard (1959) is often cited as support for this hypothesis. The study involved examining the correlations between self-reports of hunger and stomach contractions in both obese and normal-weight subjects. Each subject was instructed to come to the laboratory with an empty stomach. He then swallowed a gastric balloon that recorded gastric motility. For a period of 4 hours, the subject was asked to respond yes or no to the question, Are you hungry? The results showed that for the period under study both obese and normal subjects manifested the same degree of gastric motility. Also when the stomach was not contracting, the reports of the two groups were approximately the same. When the stomach contractions were present, however, normal subjects gave self-reports of hunger 71% of the time, whereas obese subjects reported being hungry only 47.6% of the time. Schachter takes this discrepancy to mean that normals and obese individuals may not be referring to the same bodily state when they use the term *hunger*.

Furthermore, Schachter proposed that, if the internal state associated with hunger was directly manipulated, then normals would experience hunger while obese subjects might not. To test this hypothesis, he performed an experiment in which bodily state was manipulated by having some subjects tested on full stomachs and other subjects tested on empty stomachs.

> Our experiment was conducted under the guise of a study of taste. A subject came to the laboratory in midafternoon or evening. He had been called the previous evening and asked not to eat the meal (lunch or dinner) preceding his appointment at the laboratory. It was explained that all subjects had been asked not to eat a meal before coming to the laboratory because "in any scientific experiment it is necessary that the subjects be as similar as possible in all relevant ways. As you probably know from your own experience," the experimenter continued, "an important factor in determining how things taste is what you have recently eaten." The introduction over, the experimenter then proceeded as follows. For the "full stomach" condition he said to the subject, "In order to guarantee that your recent taste experiences are similar to those of other subjects who have taken part in this experiment, we should now like you to eat exactly the same thing they did. Just help yourself to the roast beef sandwiches on the table. Eat as much as you want—till you're full." For the "empty stomach" condition, the subjects, of course, were not fed.
>
> Next, the subject was seated in front of five bowls of crackers and told, "We want you to taste these different kinds of crackers and tell us how they taste to you." The experimenter then gave the subject a long list of rating scales and said, "We want you to judge each cracker on the dimensions (salty, cheesy, garlicky, and so on) listed on this sheet. Taste as many or as few of the crackers of each type as you want in making your judgments; the important thing is that your ratings be as accurate as possible." The subject then proceeded to taste and rate crackers for 15 minutes, under the impression that this was a taste test; meanwhile, we were simply counting the number of crackers he ate. There were, of course, two types of subjects: obese subjects (from 14 percent to 75 percent overweight) and normal subjects (from 8 percent underweight to 9 percent overweight). (Schachter, 1970, p. 113)

As hypothesized, the normal subjects ate fewer crackers while full. The obese subjects, however, actually ate more crackers on a full stomach than on an empty stomach. Apparently, obese subjects rely far less on internal cues to regulate their eating behavior. In another experiment, Schachter demonstrated the power of environmental cues by using a trick clock that could be speeded up or slowed down. The obese ate more when they thought it was 6 P.M. than when they thought it was only 5:15 P.M.

Schachter's research does not prove that obesity is solely due to faulty learning, just as the biological research does not prove that hunger is due solely to stomach contractions or some other physiochemical variable. In fact, there is growing evidence that there is a predisposition to obesity. Research has demonstrated that the obese individual actually possesses a greater number of fat cells than the normal weight individual. Dieting does not change the number of fat cells but only their size. The number of fat cells is determined partly through heredity and partly through nourishment in infancy. Pediatricians are now recommending that mothers of infants control their weights and thereby prevent the establishment of an early pattern of oversized fat cells. The important point is that hunger, like many other drives, is the product of an interaction between environmental, cognitive, and biological variables.

Quite frequently medical students, during their training period, experience a variety of physiological and psychological complaints that, taken together, have been termed *medical student's disease*. The syndrome has been estimated to occur in 70% of all medical students (Mechanic, 1974). Mechanic had used Schachter's theory of emotion to explain this phenomenon. The arousal aspect of the theory comes from the general stress that is associated with being a health science student. Fear of failure, course demands, guilt from not studying, and new clinical experiences are all conditions that are capable of eliciting physiological activation in these students. Also because of the nature of the training, these students may begin attending to bodily sensations that previously went unnoticed. At the same time as all this is happening, they are exposed to patients with "similar" problems, to clinical anecdotes, and to textbook information on the meaning of the symptoms. Furthermore, they may even begin the process by learning of a disease and then imagining how the symptoms feel. The outcome of such cognitive activity is that the students may label their own real or imagined bodily changes as being symptomatic of some disease. Usually the symptoms disappear once the students have acquired additional information and experience. Possibly the hypochondriacal patient is one who initially followed a similar mislabeling process of bodily sensations but who never gained sufficient information to disconfirm these beliefs.

Biological Rhythms

A number of popular books have appeared that purport to deal with the relationship between emotional behavior and cyclic fluctuations in physiochemistry. The "mood ring" was devised by a clever entrepre-

neur to capitalize on this interest. There has also been a growing
interest among psychologists and biologists in cyclic phenomena.

The majority of physiological systems, including body temperature, heart rate, blood pressure, adrenal hormones, urine excretion,
and amino acids, follow cyclic patterns of activity. The best known of
these cycles are the *circadian rhythms* (circadian: "about a day," from
the Latin *circadies*). For example, internal and external skin temperature vary a degree or two each 24 hours with clocklike regularity.
Rhythms that are significantly less than 24 hours in duration are
called *ultradian* while those that are significantly longer are called
infradian. The rhythmic nature of living systems is often so great
that repeated measurements in one individual give the same range of
values as do single measurements of a group of individuals. Even in
measures of supposedly stable blood chemicals, an individual may, on
one measurement occasion, appear above the normal range, whereas
on another occasion the same individual may fall far below the normal
range. Serum cholesterol, for example, has been observed to range in
value from 100 to 187 in the same individual, in the absence of any
detectable changes in mental and physical health (Mefferd &
Pokorny, 1967). There is approximately a 70% increase and decrease
in the blood levels of certain adrenal hormones from morning to
night (Luce, 1970).

What precisely is the relationship between physiochemical variation and behavior? Certainly there are abundant anecdotal data that
many human behaviors seem to be cyclic in nature. For example,
pregnant women are known to go into labor more frequently during
the night and early morning hours than during afternoon hours.
Young infants and children seem to enjoy rhythms and repetitive activities such as spoon banging and marching. Most people also have a
definite preference for afternoon or morning work, or they may have
emotional difficulties at certain times of the day, week, or month. A
modern clinical syndrome, called "jet fatigue," is believed to be caused
by the desynchronization of body rhythms that occurs with time-zone
changes. The symptoms associated with this syndrome include
headache, burning eyes and blurred vision, gastrointestinal problems,
loss of appetite, shortness of breath, excessive sweating, insomnia, and
occasionally, nightmares (Stroebel, 1975). Many depressed patients
seem to manifest a cyclic nature to their symptomatology. Richter
(1965) described a salesman with a "48-hour clock" who was depressed
and unable to talk to anyone for 24 hours and then became cheerful,
outgoing, and talkative for 24 hours. His moods were so predictable
that he could book his appointments weeks in advance by crossing

from his calendar alternate days. Since ancient times there has been a belief that the onset of mental illness is related to the lunar cycle. The term *lunatic* comes from the Latin *luna*, meaning moon.

Popular writings on the subject matter are far too simplistic because they often promise the reader the impossible ability to predict his emotional crisis in advance. The theory of biorhythms holds that all living persons operate on a 23-day physical cycle, a 28-day sensitivity or emotional cycle, and a 33-day intellectual cycle. The cycles are believed to begin at birth and to continue throughout the individual's life. The first half of each cycle is thought to be an ascendant, favorable, or "plus" period, whereas the second half is thought to be a descendant, unfavorable, or "minus" period. The periods of greatest danger to the individual are said to be when a cycle is shifting from minus to plus or from plus to minus. Motor vehicle, industrial, and aircraft accidents, along with criminal acts of violence, have all been claimed to occur with a greater frequency when those involved were at a critical or low period of their cycles. Studies have repeatedly failed to support the biorhythm theory inasmuch as the events in question seem to occur with equal probability across all points in the hypothetical cycles (Shaffer, Schmidt, Zlotowitz, & Fisher, 1978).

Although rhythmicity in specific physiological and hormonal systems is difficult to relate to specific psychological and behavioral events, we do know that psychological events are capable of altering specific biological rhythms. The disruption of rhythms by means of psychological stress was demonstrated in an interesting study by Stroebel (1975). He required monkeys to solve discrimination tasks while using a lever to avoid noxious stimuli such as loud noises, flashing lights, and mild shocks. The animals quickly learned to avoid these stimuli by keeping one hand on the lever and periodically pressing it. After 2-to-4 weeks in this situation, the experimenters removed the lever and discontinued the aversive stimuli. The monkeys could still see the lever but could not touch it. Even though the aversive stimuli were not present, the monkeys continued to try and get at the lever, which was recessed into the apparatus. Eventually, 12 of the 13 animals developed behavioral and psychosomatic disturbances that included asthmatic breathing, high blood pressure, and gastrointestinal symptoms. All of the animals showed shifts in their temperature rhythms such that the peak occurred earlier or later in the day. At the end of the experiment, the researchers put the "security lever" back within reach of the animals. This produced recovery and spontaneous resynchronization of temperature, along with improved behavior for some of the animals.

Some writers have speculated that compatibility of rhythms may be the basis of good mother-child relationships:

> For instance, compatibility in parent-child relationships might be influenced by the compatibility of the activity rhythms. A mother who needed nine hours of sleep and who was a slow riser might have difficulty coping with a baby who slept only eight hours a night and awakened like a jack-in-the-box, becoming most alert and demanding at a time when she was discoordinated and sleepy. (Luce, 1970, p. 37)

Although no direct tests of this hypothesis exist, there are reported instances of sleep-cycle synchrony in mothers and infants as they were recorded throughout the night in a sleep laboratory. Furthermore, the synchrony was often disrupted on nights when the mother came to the laboratory in a state of emotional upset.

Premenstrual Tension

The menstrual cycle refers to a periodically recurrent series of physical changes occurring primarily in the uterus and ovaries. The length of the menstrual cycle is quite variable, but the average duration is taken to be approximately 28 days. Menstruation per se refers to the sloughing off of the cells of the lining of the uterus and the rupturing of the tiny blood cells supplying this tissue.

Many females report experiencing a variety of negative psychological and physical symptoms at specific times during the menstrual cycle. The belief in the negative symptomatology of this state has been with us for a long time. Circa 50 A.D. Pliny wrote: "On the approach of a woman in this state, new wine will become sour, reeds which are touched by her become sterile, grass withers away, garden plants are parched up, and the fruit will fall from the tree beneath which she sits" (quoted in Moos, 1968, p. 853). The symptoms are most pronounced at about the 22nd day into the cycle, and Frank (1931) coined the term *premenstrual tension* to describe this syndrome. Depression and general irritability are the symptoms that are found to occur with the greatest frequency while other frequently occurring symptoms include headache, fatigue, blurred vision, and intestinal cramps.

The majority of efforts to explain variations in behavior and mood swings during the menstrual cycle have focused on the changing levels of the female sex hormones, estrogen and progesterone. During the menstrual cycle, estrogen peaks about midcycle and again about day 21 of a 28-day cycle. Progesterone begins to be secreted near midcycle and reaches its highest concentration about day 21 to 24, after which it diminishes rapidly. At the time that premenstrual distress is believed to occur, both hormones are falling rapidly.

Studies have found that a high percentage of women who commit suicide or who engage in criminal acts of violence do so during the premenstrual or menstrual phases of the cycle (Dalton, 1961; Mandell & Mandell, 1967). In another study Dalton (1966) found that 54% of the children who were brought to a clinic with minor colds were brought during the 8 premenstrual and menstrual days of the mother, suggesting that the hormonal changes had an exaggerating effect on the mother's anxiety levels.

The Menstrual Distress Questionnaire is often used to quantify the daily physical and psychological changes that occur during the cycle (Moos, 1968). Sexual arousal has been found to increase until about midcycle and then decrease for the remainder of the cycle (Moos, Kopell, Melges, Yalom, Lunde, Clayton, & Hamburg, 1969). Both anxiety and aggression were found to be high during the menstrual phase (days 1 to 4) and then to decrease until midcycle and then to increase again for the remainder of the cycle. Symptoms of depression showed no consistent pattern. In summary, there are definite mood changes during the cycle, but it is difficult to ascertain whether they occur precisely in line with the changing levels of estrogen and progesterone.

What is the behavioral effect of altering the levels of estrogen and progesterone by means of birth control pills? In the early days of oral contraception, the pill contained a high percentage of estrogen. There are several studies that indicate a decrease in the negative symptomatology of women taking the pill. After examining all the data, Bardwick (1971) concluded that high levels of estrogen are correlated with high levels of positive moods; low levels of estrogen and progesterone, with significant negative emotions.

Implicit in all these correlational studies is the belief that the negative emotions when present are caused by the hormonal changes. According to Bardwick: "The personality changes associated with the menstrual cycle occur in spite of individual personality differences and may even be extreme; they are consequences of endocrine and related physical changes" (p. 27). To what extent might cognitive variables be determining the negative behavioral symptoms? Depression, hostility, and anxiety are psychological conditions and by definition must, therefore, involve higher cortical centers. Thus the indivual's past and present attitudes toward menstruation must influence the symptomatology. Even Bardwick, who believes in the biological basis of menstrual symptoms, has stated that "negative feelings towards menstruation and the menstruating woman are expressed in all cultures. The menstruating woman is dirty, taboo and unclean. This feeling is ancient and widespread, and the menstruating woman is likely to internalize it and also to resent it" (p. 49).

There is some evidence that the negative symptomatology associated with menstrual-related changes may reflect stereotypic beliefs about menstruation. Brooks, Ruble, and Clark (1977) cited a study showing that women who thought they were premenstrual reported a higher degree of stereotypically appropriate symptoms than women who thought they were intermenstrual, even though the actual cycle phase of the two groups of women was the same (6-to-7 days before their next period was to begin). In their own study, Brooks et al. found that college women, although reporting negative symptoms (water retention, negative affect, pain) as characteristic of the premenstrual phase, did not necessarily have negative attitudes toward menstruation. Overall, their sample of college women viewed menstruation as bothersome but also as having positive qualities. The view that menstruation is invariably associated with negative qualities has been, in their view, exaggerated and overemphasized in the literature.

A psychologist (name withheld) once presented a cognitive-label explanation of premenstrual tension to his wife and received the angry response, "It is not all in my head" (she was not asked the day of her cycle). I too would agree that it is not all in her head, but remember the basic premise of the theory is that emotion is the result of complex interactions between physiochemical (in this case hormonal) changes and cognitive variables. Hormonal changes during the menstrual cycle are likely to increase the female's susceptibility to negative psychological experiences rather than to cause such experiences. Even with animals there is evidence that there is a circadian susceptibility effect to the acquisition of conditioned fear responses. Stroebel (1975) found that the acquisition of a conditioned emotional response in rats was highly correlated with the circadian rhythm of adrenal steroids. The emotional response was at its greatest when the adrenal steroid rhythm was also at its peak. In addition, normal women tested during the premenstrual phase had a greater susceptibility to acquiring a conditioned galvanic skin response to a loud noise than during another point in the cycle. Women that were neurotic showed even a stronger tendency to respond in this fashion (Asso & Beech, 1975).

Stating that hormonal changes present during the menstrual

cycle increase susceptibility to negative emotions is vastly different from saying that the hormonal changes cause the negative emotions. Why? Because susceptibility, unlike causality, means that the outcome is not inevitable but depends on many factors such as the person's beliefs, attitudes, and current situation. In an issue of *Time*, psychologist Randi Koeske (1976) advised women to learn to identify premenstrual physical changes as irrelevant to emotion. For example, some women add several pounds of fluid because of hormone changes. If so, says Koeske, "Say, 'Water retention makes my tear ducts feel full,' not 'I am depressed and about to cry.'" In order to modify any negative feelings and beliefs toward menstruation, a feminist writer proposed that mothers have parties to celebrate their daughters' first menstruation.

Nightly Rhythm—Sleep

Modern sleep and dream research has established the strikingly rhythmic nature of sleep. As an individual passes from wakefulness to sleep, there is a gradual slowing of the EEG. The waking EEG is replaced by a low-amplitude mixed-frequency pattern that is referred to as Stage 1 sleep. After 5 to 10 minutes of Stage 1 sleep, bursts of waves in the frequency range of 12 to 14 hertz (cycles per second) appear along with higher amplitude waves. The bursts are referred to as sleep spindles, and the overall pattern is called Stage 2 sleep. If the sleep continues, high-amplitude, low-frequency *delta waves* appear, which signify the onset of Stage 3 sleep. When the delta activity increases and dominates the tracing (over 50%), the subject has entered Stage 4 sleep. It is extremely difficult to awaken a subject during Stage 4 sleep (Rechtschaffen, 1973).

Rapid eye movement (REM) activity usually appears beginning with the second hour of sleep. The presence of REM is taken as a sign that the subject is dreaming. These REM periods last from a few minutes to a half hour and reappear at about 90-minute intervals during sleep. On the average, there are about four REM periods a night, comprising altogether about one-fourth of total sleep.

At first it was believed that dreaming only occurred during REM periods. For example, Dement and Kleitman (1957) found that 80% of awakenings from REM sleep produced dream recall whereas 7% of awakenings from non-REM (NREM) sleep produced dream recall. Later studies, however, found a much higher incidence of dreaming to occur in NREM periods (Rechtschaffen, 1973). One explanation for these data is that NREM dreams differ qualitatively from REM dreams in that REM dreams are "more dreamy" than NREM dreams. To illustrate the difference, consider the following two dream reports from the same subject, one obtained after a REM period and the other obtained after an NREM period:

> *NREM report*: "I had been dreaming about getting ready to take some type of exam. It had been a very short dream. That's just about all that it contained. I don't think I was worried about them."
> *REM report*: "I was dreaming about exams. In the early part of the dream I was dreaming I had just finished taking an exam, and it was a very sunny day outside. I was walking with a boy who's in some of my classes with me. There was a sort of a, a break, and someone mentioned a grade they had gotten in a social science exam. And I asked them if the social science marks had come in. They said yes. I didn't get it, because I had been away for a day." (Rechtschaffen, 1973, p. 160)

This example is intended to demonstrate that NREM dreams are less emotional, more like thinking, less vivid, less visual, and similar to daydream activity.

Current views on dream function tend to emphasize the adaptive nature of dreaming. That is, dreaming represents a psychological process, much like the process underlying daydreaming, for solving problems. In this sense the psychological processes underlying dreaming are not different from the processes underlying normal conscious thought. During the dream, however, the individual is not constrained by the laws of rational behavior that guide our thinking during the waking state. During a dream, the individual is free to use magical solutions, fantasy, symbols, without worrying how others will react. The following example illustrates this position:

> Suppose that a student is concerned and anxious about a pending examination and that this concern is related to a group of conflicting feelings about his overall adequacy. He goes to sleep after a night of anxious studying with these conflicts aroused. His dreams that night represent the current situation but also regress into (other) memory systems . . . allowing the presentation of other, related conflict situations and their resolutions. For example, he might dream of playing with a sibling to whom he felt inferior as a child but whom he eventually bested by withdrawing from active games into intellectual pursuits with accompanying fantasies of his superiority, rationalizations about the greater value of intellectual work over cloddish athletics, and so on. In effect, the present conflict is made potentially solvable, just as the similar situation was in the past. (Breger, 1969, p. 218)

Some investigators believe that a period just prior to the onset of sleep, called the *twilight state* (Budzynski, 1976), is often associated with intense imagery, inspiring thoughts, and creativity. This period is characterized physiologically by a slowing of the brain-wave patterns and the appearance of slow-rolling eye movements. Many famous individuals from the fields of science, music, literature, and art have credited the imagery produced during the twilight state for acts of creativity. For example, a dream is credited with leading to the discovery of the benzene molecule (C_6H_6). The discoverer, Friedrich August Kekule, had a dream in which he saw six snakes biting each other's tails and whirling around in a circle. Upon awakening, he interpreted the six snakes as a hexagon and suddenly realized that he had discovered the structure of benzene. For these individuals, innovative solutions to problems became possible once their thought processes were released from the disciplined control characteristic of the waking state.

Having a solution to a problem present itself during the twilight period or during a dream is not a guarantee that the individual will recognize the solution upon awakening. In a classroom demonstration, students were asked to work on a problem 15 minutes prior to sleep and to record dream content the next morning. In one problem the students were asked to figure out the word that represents the following sequence: H, I, J, K, L, M, N, O. The solution is water or "H to O." One student who solved the problem incorrectly with the word *alphabet* reported several dreams that had water in them (ocean, swimming, raining) but upon awakening was not aware of the relevance of these elements to the solution. Perhaps only individuals who are extremely perceptive and who are emotionally and intellectually committed to solving the problem at hand will recognize solutions that are presented in symbolic fashion during dreams. For example, the Nobel Prize winner, Albert Szent-Györgyi, stated, "My work is not finished when I leave my work bench in the afternoon. I go on thinking about my problems all the time, and my brain must continue to think about them when I sleep, because I wake up, sometimes in the middle of the night with answers to questions that have been puzzling me" (Dement, 1972, p. 98).

> We cannot eliminate the possibility that all of us are presented solutions to our problems quite regularly in our dreams. Perhaps only the most perceptive dreamers possess the ability to recognize a solution that is presented in a disguised or symbolic fashion. Most of us, most of the time, are like the student who failed to recognize the word "water" as

the solution to his problem even though he was deluged by water in his dreams! One can easily imagine Kekule shrugging as he awakened from the dream of the six circling snakes: "What nonsense! I must forget about snakes and concentrate on chemistry." (Dement, 1972, p. 101)

Night Terrors and Nightmares

One of the most frightening experiences to undergo or witness is the night terror. The night terror often begins with a sudden loud piercing scream or series of screams of blood-curdling, animal-like intensity indicating uncontrolled panic. There may be excessive profanity accompanied by cries for help as in the following:

> (Sharp PIERCING SCREAM) . . . "I'M DYING . . . I'M DYING . . . I'M
> D-Y-I-N-G! ! . . . I'M D-Y-I-N-G! ! . . . H-E-L-P! ! ! ! H-E-E-E-E-L-P!!
> GOD ALMIGHTY! ! . . . GOD ALMIGHTY-Y-Y! ! . . . H-E-E-L-P! !
> . . . H-E-E-L-P!! . . HEY YOU FUCK!!! . . . HELP ME-E!! . . .
> H-E-L-P!! H-E-E-L-P!! . . . H-E-E-E-E-L-P!! (Fisher, Kahn, Edwards, &
> Davis, 1973, p. 81)

The night terror is also associated with extreme degrees of autonomic and motor activity; heart rate may increase to 170 beats per minute within a few seconds. Such dramatic increases in heart rate are seldom achieved in any other state, including violent exercise and orgasm. Psychologically, the individual appears to be out of contact with the environment, delusional, hallucinating, or all three. Fisher et al. reported that many of their subjects claimed that they also engaged in complex motor behaviors during an episode. Some subjects have injured themselves or engaged in violent acts, such as striking a spouse, slashing a picture, or smashing through a door. The duration of an episode is quite brief (1-to-3 minutes) and there is often a rapid return to normal sleep with complete amnesia for the event. Recall of the event is much better if the individual is questioned immediately after spontaneous awakening from the attack. Common themes reported by subjects during attacks include fear of aggression from others, choking, falling, and dying (Fisher, Kahn, Edwards, Davis & Fine, 1973).

Night terrors are quite rare in the general population and occur more frequently in children. The night terror is not the same state as a nightmare, which involves far less autonomic and motor disturbance. In addition, sleep and dream researchers have determined that nightmares and night terrors are associated with different points in the dream cycle. Nightmares are typically associated with REM sleep, whereas night terrors are associated with NREM sleep. In fact, it has been established that night terrors usually occur just as the individual is coming out of slow-wave (Stage 3 or 4) sleep. At the point of an attack, the EEG pattern resembles that occurring in the awake state. The major differences between night terrors and nightmares are summarized in Table 2-1.

Table 2-1   Characteristics of the Nightmare and the Night Terror

	Nightmare	*Night Terror*
EEG characteristics	occurs during REM sleep, at no particular time of the night	occurs in Stage 4 sleep, primarily during the first NREM period of the night
Physiological changes	mild increase in autonomic activity	very rapid and intense autonomic activation
Motility	less movement	great activity, often associated with sleepwalking
Verbalizations	may be present, but subdued	almost always present at onset; may include screaming
Mental content	elaborate, vivid, longer duration	single, overwhelming feeling or memory; violently aggressive, terrifying content
Mental state if awakened	lucid very quickly, clear memory of dream	confused, disoriented, unresponsive to the environment, amnesic

Adapted from Keith, Paul R. Night Terrors: A review of the psychology, neurophysiology, and therapy. *Journal of the American Academy of Child Psychiatry*, 1976, *14*, 477-489.

What happens during slow-wave sleep to trigger the night terror? Broughton (1968) proposed that the stimulus might be mental, physical, or both. Following Freudian theory, he suggested that during Stage 4 sleep superego barriers are lowered permitting the surfacing of repressed emotional conflicts. Another possibility is that these individuals suffer from disorders of autonomic arousal that become manifest during Stage 4 sleep. In some subjects it is possible to precipitate an attack simply by sounding an external buzzer. The autonomic nervous system of these individuals may have developed a hypersensitivity to virtually any stimulus. The complete explanation of the night terror is likely to involve both mental and physiological variables. The mental content associated with the night terror is often directly related to previous traumatic experiences. For example, one subject who had repeated attacks involving themes of choking also had previously undergone surgery in the neck region. Stimuli in the immediate environment also enter the content of the night terror. Some laboratory subjects report themes involving choking on electrodes or being attacked by members of the sleep lab. The content of night terrors is apparently heavily influenced by thought processes that occur during the waking state.

Continuity of content across the waking and sleeping states is also evident in less intense emotional dreams (Webb & Cartwright, 1978). Children are known to experience emotional dreams that reflect daytime emotional difficulties. Adult men are known to experience a high percentage of emotional dreams involving other men, whereas adult women experience emotional dreams involving both sexes with equal frequency. Apparently, daytime emotional problems in men are caused primarily by other men, whereas women have to contend with both sexes.

One's characteristic style of daydreaming is also known to influence the content of dreams. Singer (1975) identified three types or styles of daydreaming that characterize individuals during the waking state. The "Guilty" style involves a waking fantasy that is dominated by fear of failure, hostility, resentment, and ambition. The "Anxious-Distractable" style is characterized by anxious and worrisome fantasies. The third style, "Positive-Vivid," characterizes the "happy daydreamer." These individuals use fantasy in a positive fashion, as a means of enhancing their freedom, flexibility, and nonconformity. Individuals who score high on the two negative daydreaming styles report a higher incidence of nightmares, insomnia, and childhood sleep disturbances than individuals who score on the Positive-Vivid daydreaming style (Starker & Hasenfeld, 1976). These observations suggest that sleep disturbances are a manifestation of an individual's broader fantasy style. For example, Starker and Hasenfeld described the relationship between daydreaming style and insomnia as follows:

> Picture yourself lying in bed at day's end and beset by visions of guilty deeds, anticipated failures, burning ambitions, and/or hostile fantasies. Perhaps some lucky person can escape temporarily through rapid sleep onset, but the data indicate that the more likely response is to lie awake, tossing and turning, unable to "turn off" long enough to relax and sleep. The more often one experiences such waking fantasy, the more likely one will suffer the misery of insomnia. Should one tend toward the Positive-Vivid daydream pattern, on the other hand, the situation changes drastically. Your vivid, positive fantasies are especially absorbing in the absence of competing environmental stimuli, their pleasant nature helps you to relax deeply and quickly, and you drift off easily. (p. 397)

Because daytime fantasy influences sleep disturbances, it may be possible to treat such disturbances by modifying the daytime fantasy style of the individual. Several studies have already been reported indicating that it is possible to eliminate recurring nightmares by training patients to cope with images associated with the nightmare during the waking state. For example, Shorkey and Himle (1974) successfully treated a patient who had a recurring nightmare, associated with insomnia, that he was being persecuted and abused by the devil. For this individual, the devil appeared in his dreams as a snake. The therapists trained the patient to handle a live snake while maintaining a state of deep muscle relaxation. After eight sessions, the patient found that he was able to hold the snake without experiencing anxiety. The patient also reported a complete disappearance of the nightmare and insomnia.

Central Mechanisms of Emotion

The relationship between emotions and physiology has been examined up to this point primarily with respect to peripheral physiological indexes. The issue is even more complex when one attempts to identify specific relationships between emotions and central nervous system structures. Specific structures within the brain that control sensory and motor behaviors have been identified. For example, researchers have demonstrated with single-cell recording techniques that cells from the visual cortex are highly specialized in function. They have shown that some cells respond only to orientation of a visual stimulus, whereas others will respond only to movement. Thus a horizontal stimulus might cause a specific cell to fire, whereas a vertical stimulus will cause another cell to fire. The issue to examine now is whether the same degree of specificity exists between central nervous system structures and complex emotional behavior.

Limbic System

Emotional behavior is to a great extent controlled by brain structures that are collectively referred to as the *limbic system*. The general region of the brain that includes the limbic system is shown in Figure 2-1. The term *limbic system* comes from the Latin word *limbus*, which means "border," and the system itself refers to structures that outline the inner surface of both cerebral hemispheres. Three structures within the limbic system that are heavily involved in emotional behavior are the thalamus, the hypothalamus, and the amygdala. Each of these structures is formed from clusters of nuclei or cells that have a certain degree of specialized functioning. The thalamus con-

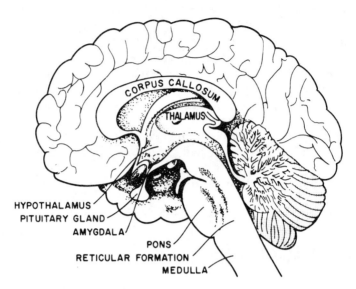

Figure 2-1   Midline view of the brain depicting structures that comprise the limbic system.

tains nuclei that receive sensory impulses from the spinal cord and the brainstem. Heat, cold, warmth, touch, and pain impulses are registered within thalamic nuclei. The hypothalamus, the area underlying the thalamus, is more concerned with emotional behavior as well as with states of wakefulness and sleep. Hypothalamic nuclei exert subcortical control over a number of autonomic nervous system functions, including blood pressure, heart rate, respiration, gastrointestinal activity, and fat and carbohydrate metabolism. Hormonal activity, especially from the pituitary gland, is also mediated by the hypothalamus. The amygdala is an almond-shaped nucleus that lies behind the temporal lobe of the cortex. This structure is known to be involved in aggressive and violent behavior.

The limbic brain, in terms of evolution, is a very old structure. It is believed to have originated some 400 million years ago at a time when reptiles dominated the earth. A major function of the limbic system in all living organisms is to control fight or flight responses. In humans, however, limbic structures are under extensive neocortical control. Thus, although we possess an innate mechanism for fight-flight reactions, where and when this mechanism is used is largely, if not totally, determined by social and psychological variables.

Triune Brain

Paul MacLean (1967) proposed that the human brain, as a result of evolution, consists of three brains in one, or what he calls for short, the *triune brain*. He labeled the three substructures the "reptilian," the "paleomammalian," and the "neomammalian" brains (Figure 2-2). The reptilian brain is the oldest brain structure and consists of systems in the upper spinal cord, brainstem, and parts of the midbrain. MacLean considers the reptilian brain to be responsible for stereotyped behaviors based on "ancestral learning and ancestral memories," behaviors that are now generally referred to as "species-specific." The concept of species-specific behavior has generally replaced the term *instinct* in order to signify that all behaviors are under some degree of environmental control. Migratory behavior of birds is an example of a species-specific behavior. There is considerable debate as to what behaviors in the human might be species-specific. Some of the simple reflexes exhibited by human infants might be cited as examples: Newborn infants will exhibit a grasping reflex as well as a walking reflex. At the adult level, there are very few behaviors that are exhibited by all members of the species. Eibl-

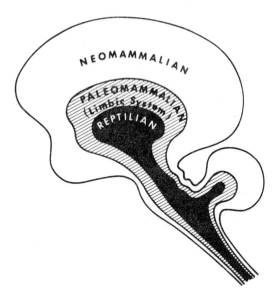

Figure 2-2 A schematic illustrating the triune brain (MacLean, 1967). Copyright © 1967 by The Williams & Wilkins Co., Baltimore. Reprinted by permission of the publisher.

Eibesfeldt (1970) hypothesized that emotional expression such as cries of pain or signs of grief are universal and therefore species-specific. A few years ago, Desmond Morris (1967), in his best seller *The Naked Ape*, suggested that certain female characteristics (lips, breasts, buttocks) act as key stimuli for releasing species-specific male sexual behavior. The matter is not so simple, however, because there are large cultural differences in what physical characteristics are deemed attractive.

The major difficulty faced by the investigator who is attempting to establish human species-specific behavior is that the humans, largely because of their highly developed cortex, are the most flexible and malleable of all living creatures. In fact, many social scientists believe that human behavior is totally determined by the culture in which it occurs (a concept known as "cultural relativism"). At the same time, however, the culture had to come from somewhere. Thus, some investigators continue to examine the possibility that hidden somewhere in the human brain there are mechanisms that mediate certain innate preferences for specific symbols, aesthetics, tastes, shapes, and rhythms. For example, some ethologists believe that the rounded head and relatively large brain case of young humans and animals may serve as a key stimulus for "cuteness."

The second structure, the paleomammalian brain, refers to the limbic system, while the third, the neomammalian brain, refers to the cortex. MacLean believes that each of the three divisions has "its own special kind of intelligence, its own memory, its own sense of time and space, and its own motor and other functions." In some respects it sounds very similar to the Freudian concepts id, ego, and superego. Freud did believe that one day science would identify the physiological basis for some of his ideas about the functioning of the human mind.

Pleasure Centers

In 1954, Olds and Milner demonstrated that electrical stimulation of certain regions of the limbic system seemed to produce rewarding effects. That is, the animals would engage in behaviors such as lever pressing in order to increase the occurrence of brain stimulation. Stimulation of areas within the hypothalamus seemed to elicit the most rewarding effects, inasmuch as some rats with electrodes at this site would stimulate their brains more than 2,000 times per hour for 24 consecutive hours. Other regions of the limbic system were found to be associated with unpleasant sensations (Delgado, Roberts, & Miller, 1954). Hungry animals, for example, were found to avoid food in the presence of such stimulation. These animals would even learn a new response to avoid such stimulation.

This early brain-stimulation research caused a great deal of excitement because researchers felt that they had discovered pleasure and punishment centers within the brain. The excitement was quickly tempered, however, by the discovery that brain stimulation of a specific region did not invariably produce the same behavior. For example, stimulation of a specific site within the brain might elicit drinking behavior from a rat placed in the presence of water. If the rat was now left overnight in the cage with no opportunity to drink and periodically stimulated throughout the night, he might in the morning, with the resumption of brain stimulation, begin to drink or begin to chew with equal probability. The point is that the behavior that is elicited depends, not only on the region of the brain stimulation, but also on the environmental situation in which the stimulation occurred (Valenstein, 1973).

The persistent belief in the existence of one-to-one brain–behavior relationships is partly traceable to the widely publicized research of Wilder Penfield (Penfield & Roberts, 1966), who claimed that stimulation of specific sites within the temporal lobe often evoked memories of long-forgotten experiences. Many of the patients used by Penfield failed, however, to experience detailed and complete memories following brain stimulation. The majority of hallucinations were incomplete and fragmented. Also, when vivid hallucinations are elicited by brain stimulation, the hallucinations are often more related to the patient's immediate situation than to previous experiences. For example, one patient who received brain stimulation while simultaneously being interviewed reported the intrusion into awareness of the word *kerchief*. Just prior to the stimulation, the patient had told the interviewer, "I'm all wet—I mean I'm sweating—warm." During a later portion of the interview, the patient became very warm and began to perspire and requested a handkerchief. Apparently the immediate situation was more instrumental in determining the content of the hallucination than previous memories were. Finally, the repeated stimulation of the same brain site does not produce the same hallucination or visual experiences. In fact a different hallucination usually results with each subsequent stimulation (Valenstein, 1973).

Surgical Control of Emotion

Numerous experiments with animals have demonstrated that emotional behavior can be drastically altered by surgically interrupting pathways within the nervous system. Some 40 years ago, Kluver and Bucy reported the outcome of several experiments that involved removal of the amygdalae in monkeys. The behavioral outcome has been called the Kluver-Bucy syndrome and has been described as follows:

> In the laboratory, most of the operated animals seemed to become less aggressive, and friendlier toward their human handlers . . . . But, when the animals rejoined their old troop in the wild, a very different picture began to emerge. Although they had exhibited increased friendliness toward their human captors, they appeared confused and fearful among their former friends and relations. When other troop members approached in a neutral and nonthreatening way, the amygdalotomized animals would usually cower or flee. Conversely, when a dominant member of the troop made a threatening gesture, an altered animal, which would otherwise have adopted a submissive posture, would instead display an unseemly degree of insubordination; it would attempt to attack the dominant animal, and thereby invite a predictable and often terrible beating. All in all, the amygdalotomized monkeys were incapable of coping with the complexities of social life in their normal environment. This incapacity caused them to become social isolates. Eventually they all died, either from starvation or from attack by predators. The results of these animal experiments suggested that no single part of the limbic system is concerned with only a single aspect of emotional behavior. (Chorover, 1974, p. 63)

Thus, although emotional behavior in general was altered, the precise nature of the emotional change was unpredictable. Apparently environmental cues still had a powerful effect on whether the animal exhibited tame, submissive behavior or violent, aggressive behavior.

The importance of taking the environment into account when attempting to predict the effects of tissue removal on aggressive behavior is clearly evident in the following study (Pribram, 1976). Eight preadolescent male monkeys were kept together until they had formed a clear social-dominance hierarchy (Figure 2-3). Psychosurgery was then performed on the most dominant monkey and he quickly fell to the bottom of the hierarchy (Figure 2-4). The same outcome occurred when psychosurgery was performed on the next successor to the throne (Figure 2-5). When the procedure was repeated for the third time, however, this particular monkey actually became

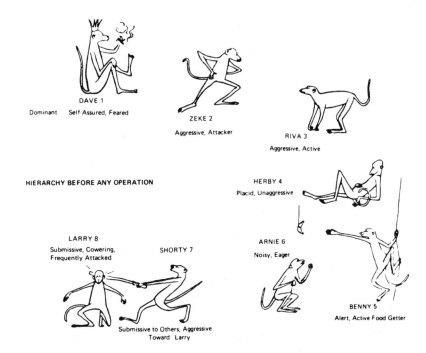

DAVE 1
Dominant   Self-Assured, Feared

ZEKE 2
Aggressive, Attacker

RIVA 3
Aggressive, Active

HIERARCHY BEFORE ANY OPERATION

HERBY 4
Placid, Unaggressive

LARRY 8
Submissive, Cowering,
Frequently Attacked

SHORTY 7

ARNIE 6
Noisy, Eager

Submissive to Others, Aggressive
Toward Larry

BENNY 5
Alert, Active Food Getter

Figure 2-3   Dominance hierarchy of a colony of eight preadolescent male rhesus monkeys before any surgical intervention (Pribram, 1976). Copyright © 1976 by Plenum Press. Reprinted by permission of the publisher.

more aggressive and dominant (Figure 2-6). In the first two cases, the second monkey in the resulting hierarchy was aggressive; in the third case, the second monkey (Herby) was a kind of social recluse and posed no real threat to the dominant monkey. Pribram concluded that it was "unlikely that some fundamental mechanism for aggression had been excised; rather some brain process sensitive to the social environment seems to have been tapped" (p. 63).

The surgical control of behavior disorders in humans, called "psychosurgery," began in 1935 when a Portuguese neuropsychiatrist, Egas Moniz, began performing frontal lobe ablations in psychiatric patients. Moniz had recently heard of animal experiments in which frontal lobe ablations produced major reductions in the emotional behaviors of monkeys and chimpanzees. He reasoned that a similar operation might produce a "calming effect" in psychiatric patients with severe emotional disturbances. In 1936 psychosurgery was in-

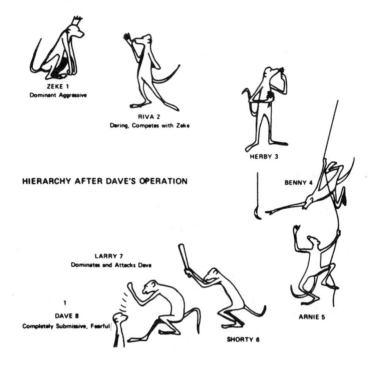

ZEKE 1
Dominant Aggressive

RIVA 2
Daring, Competes with Zeke

HERBY 3

HIERARCHY AFTER DAVE'S OPERATION   BENNY 4

LARRY 7
Dominates and Attacks Dave

1
DAVE 8
Completely Submissive, Fearful   ARNIE 5

SHORTY 6

Figure 2-4   Dominance hierarchy after bilateral amygdalectomy had been
              performed on Dave; note his drop to the bottom of the hierarchy
              (Pribram, 1976). Copyright © 1976 by Plenum Press. Reprinted
              by permission of the publisher.

troduced into North America by Freeman and Watts. These two individuals are credited with performing over 3,500 lobotomies between
1936 and 1955. With the development of psychoactive drugs in the
1950s, the psychiatric community began to lose interest in psychosurgery as a means of controlling emotional disturbances. The technique
is still in limited use in many countries, however.

Modern-day psychosurgery bears no resemblance to the operations that were performed during the 1930s and 1940s. No longer are
operations performed by the insertion and twirling or "swishing" of a
crude instrument into nonspecific regions of the brain. Modern
neurosurgeons use a vast array of highly sophisticated instrumenta-
tion for pinpointing specific targets within the brain. Taken together
these techniques are referred to as *stereotactic surgery*. With the aid
of three-dimensional anatomical maps (called "stereotactic atlases")

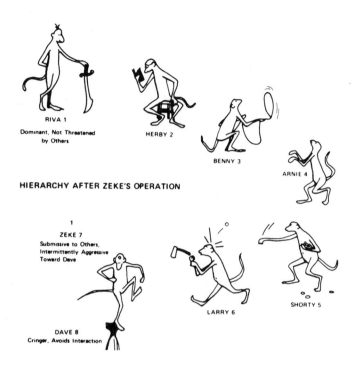

Figure 2-5 Dominance hierarchy after bilateral amygdalectomies on both Dave and Zeke (Pribram, 1976). Copyright © 1976 by Plenum Press. Reprinted by permission of the publisher.

and other electronic devices (brain scanner, X ray, EEG), the surgeon is able to locate structures within the limbic system with a high degree of precision. Very small electrodes can then be inserted into the localized brain region. These electrodes can be used to record electrical activity of the brain in the region of the tip or they can be used to stimulate the brain tissue in the region of the electrode tip. Furthermore, by increasing the strength of the current passed through the electrode, the surgeon is able to destroy tissue only in the region of the electrode tip. Stereotactic techniques have provided surgeons with access to limbic structures that are deep within the brain. Consequently, the majority of surgical interventions are now performed on limbic structures rather than on cortical structures. Some of the sites within the limbic system that represent favorite targets for neurosurgeons are shown in Figure 2-7.

The high degree of precision associated with stereotactic surgery

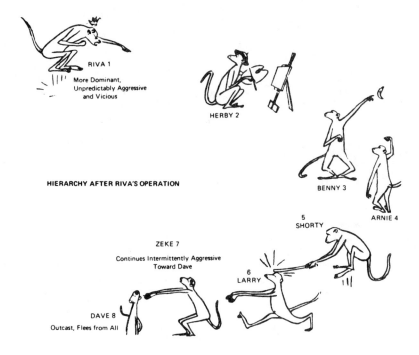

RIVA 1
More Dominant,
Unpredictably Aggressive
and Vicious

HERBY 2

HIERARCHY AFTER RIVA'S OPERATION

BENNY 3

5
SHORTY   ARNIE 4

ZEKE 7

Continues Intermittently Aggressive
Toward Dave
                                        6
                                      LARRY

DAVE 8
Outcast, Flees from All

Figure 2-6   Final social hierarchy after Dave, Zeke, and Riva have all had
                bilateral amygdalectomies. Note that Riva fails to fall in the
                hierarchy (Pribram, 1976). Copyright © 1976 by Plenum Press.
                Reprinted by permission of the publisher.

has effectively disproved critical claims that psychosurgery results
in extensive brain damage. The theoretical issue that is seldom discussed, however, by either the proponents or critics of psychosurgery
is whether the specific targets identified for destruction control the
patient's behavior disorder. What kinds of patient disorders have
been treated with psychosurgery? The National Commission for the
Protection of Human Subjects of Biomedical and Behavioral Research recently examined all aspects of psychosurgery. One of the
contributors to the final report, E. S. Valenstein (1977), found considerable agreement among psychiatrists and neurosurgeons as to the
kinds of patient most likely to be helped by psychosurgery. Patients
with thought disorders are not considered to be good candidates. The
best candidates are considered to be patients with intense and persistent emotional disturbances. These patients are often so possessed by

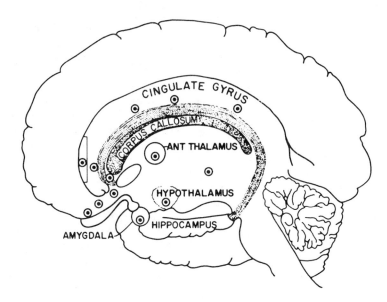

Figure 2-7   Brain Targets (◉) of psychosurgical procedures (Valenstein, 1977).

fears that they will not leave their homes. Some patients spend all their time and energy engaging in repetitive and ritualistic behaviors. Others are disturbed by severe depression. Diagnostically, these patients are "severely depressed, anxious, and obsessive-compulsive neurotics." Valenstein believes the following case study is representative of patients who are considered by neurosurgeons to be good candidates for psychosurgery:

> Case 1: Severe intractable obsessional neurosis: J. G., Aged 34, female. Referred for treatment of an intractable obsessive-compulsive disorder. Her symptoms began when she was 23, after an unwanted pregnancy had forced her into an unhappy marriage. A year later, when the baby developed asthma, her feelings of guilt deepened and from that time her symptoms were of such severity that she was unable to cope with even the simplest tasks of everyday life. Her day was totally occupied with checking and rechecking actions such as washing, dressing and household tasks. She had, for example, to wash her face in a special order—starting with the left side, nose, right side, forehead—up to thirteen times. A similar elaborate system was involved in her bathing, which took her over an hour each day. After washing clothes she had to

squeeze them a certain way, repeating the proceedings twenty-two times, the bottom of the bowl was then examined, checking the maker's mark numerous times to make sure the bowl was empty. Cleaning her teeth was a major task, taking over half an hour. Making a bed, with checking at each stage that the sheets and blankets were exactly symmetrical, might take over half an hour.

Household chores such as washing-up or polishing a table were completely impossible for her, as they took so long and caused her such distress. Her husband and mother were, therefore, forced into running her home and, on medical advice, her two children were at boarding school. The patient felt extreme guilt at her disruption of the family's existence and, at times, felt very depressed and that life was not worth living. Between 1962 and 1970 she was admitted to Severalls Hospital seven times, and received a variety of treatments including ECT, MAOI drugs, tricyclics, major and minor tranquilizers and psychotherapy. During 1968 and 1969 she was admitted on two occasions to the Royal Waterloo Hospital and had a total of five courses of modified narcosis, combined with ECT and antidepressants. After each admission she obtained symptomatic relief for about 2–4 weeks and then relapsed. (p. 39)

Does psychosurgery "work" and if so how does it work? Members of the commission were initially quite skeptical of finding any therapeutic value to psychosurgery. They were surprised to learn that a number of patients had improved following this form of treatment. Some of the more impressive successes occurred in patients with severe emotional disorders that had previously proved resistant to conventional forms of treatment (chemotherapy, psychotherapy, electric shock). The operation did not destroy their intelligence or make them incapable of experiencing feelings. Other patients, however, showed little change or no improvement in their condition. In short, some patients were found to improve following psychosurgery and other patients were found not to improve.

Precisely how psychosurgery achieves its therapeutic effects with some patients is unknown. The effect is not simply due to the patient's expectancy of relief. Valenstein reviewed two reports in which the surgeons performed a "mock operation" with several patients. A skin incision was made followed by drilling of the necessary holes in the skull. None of these patients experienced relief until the actual stereotactic surgery was performed at a later date. The limbic structures designated for destruction obviously contribute to the disorder. One hypothesis is that stable and pathological structural changes have developed in patients suffering from emotional disturbances. These structural changes result in an inability of the patient to maintain emotional behaviors within normal limits. Surgical lesions are believed to lower this excessive activity to normal levels. The hypothesized structural changes have yet to be identified at the neurophysiological level.

The structural change hypothesis is a reasonable model for an emotional disorder in which the sole complaint is affective disturbance. Some individuals do suffer from uncontrollable feelings of panic, anxiety, depression, or guilt in the absence of an apparent psychological or environmental cause. These individuals believe that their interpersonal functioning would improve dramatically if the negative feelings could be brought under control. In such instances, surgical alteration of the limbic system might result in a significant reduction of their affective distress. On the other hand, if the emotional disorder is related to a complex belief system, the effects of surgical intervention would be extremely unpredictable. Limbic structures may mediate the affective properties of a disorder, but such structures do not mediate the cognitive properties of a disorder. To illustrate, one patient with an intense fear of germs and dirt reported, following psychosurgery, that her fear of germs and dirt was still there but this fear no longer bothered her as much. Although the affective component of the disorder was reduced, the cognitive component remained.

Chorover (1974) provided a case study to illustrate what may happen when cognitive variables are not considered relevant in deciding whether or not to perform psychosurgery. The patient in question suffered from epilepticlike bouts of violent rage. The attacks of rage were not spontaneous but rather seemed to be intricately related to a paranoid belief system. The patient believed himself to be persecuted by co-workers, friends, and family members. He was firmly convinced that his wife no longer loved him and that she was "carrying on with a neighbor." The relationship between the uncontrolled attacks of aggression and the paranoid ideations was ignored. Psychosurgery was performed on the patient's amygdala. What was the outcome? According to Chorover, the patient became extremely psychotic and could no longer cope with any aspect of living. He was eventually placed in a psychiatric ward because of hallucinatory and delusional behaviors. One of his "delusions" was that people were trying to control him by means of microwaves through electrodes placed in his brain.

The complex interactions that take place between environmental cognitive and emotional variables make it difficult to advocate the use of psychosurgery under any circumstances (other than the presence of physical damage to the brain). The precision of modern-day surgery does not obviate the fact that complex human disorders are not under the sole control of specific mechanisms within the brain. This fact may explain why psychosurgery may lead to improvement in the short run but to a gradual deterioration in the long run. In this regard the commission reported several instances of patients that received multiple operations for recurring symptoms.

Failure to deal with the cognitive and environmental bases for the disorder, combined with the plasticity of the human brain, would account for the reappearance of symptoms. There are cases in the clinical literature of patients who, after suffering severe brain damage, eventually recovered lost bodily functions. Because brain cells do not regenerate, the undamaged part of the brain must eventually perform the functions. Goleman (1976b) gave an example of a young girl who had her entire right hemisphere removed as a means of controlling epileptic seizures. Because each half of the brain controls the opposite side of the body, this patient should have experienced considerable difficulty in bodily control. This was not the case, inasmuch as the majority of her senses on the left side of the body were operating within normal limits. She also had no problems with cognitive functions that are believed to depend primarily on right-hemisphere functioning, such as coordinating movement and sight and recognizing nonverbal sounds such as music. Medically speaking, if a neat one-to-one relationship existed between behavior and brain function, this patient should not have been able to function as she did. Apparently, the remaining brain structures were able to pick up and perform the functions that were previously performed by her right hemisphere.

If a patient suffering from uncontrollable violence also has a firmly entrenched paranoid and delusional belief system behind this violence, one might expect that other, undamaged portions of the brain would restore the complete bizarre behavior pattern in time. In short, other brain cells could pick up the functions that were previously controlled by the surgically removed tissue. Roy John (1972) has developed a "statistical configuration" theory of brain function to account for such a possibility. According to this theory, brain functions are distributed throughout most regions of the brain, with some regions contributing more than others to any specific function. In one experiment John implanted 34 electrodes in different parts of the brain of a cat. He then observed the electrical rhythms from different parts of the brain as the cat watched a flashing light. Brain rhythms to this simple stimulus only appeared in a specific region of the brain, that part associated with the visual system. When, however, the light became a signal to perform a task such as jumping a hurdle, rhythmic activity began to appear throughout the brain. According to John, it is not the location of brain cells that determines memory but, rather, the rhythm of firing of an overall pattern of cells. When we learn something new, small groups of cells do not form new connections. Rather, cells in many parts of the brain learn a new rhythm of firing that corresponds to the new learning. Thus, the memory of what is learned is not to be found in any specific brain region but, rather, in its unique cell-firing rhythm. This theory, if correct, would make the behavioral outcome of psychosurgery extremely unpredictable.

It is recommended that alternatives to brain surgery be found for controlling emotional disorders—even in cases in which traditional forms of treatment involving psychotherapy and chemotherapy have failed. Psychosurgery is often described as the "treatment of last resort," but psychotherapy and chemotherapy should not be viewed as the only alternatives to psychosurgery. Several investigators have used behavior therapy successfully to treat patient disorders very similar in nature to patient disorders considered to be appropriate candidates for psychosurgery. Two of the patients treated with behavioral techniques have been described as follows:

> Patient 4, aged 38, feared contamination by germs, resulting in washing and cleaning rituals. Her child was restrained in one room which was kept "germ free." Doors were opened with feet to avoid contaminating her hands (20 years duration).
>
> Patient 5, aged 22, had pervasive checking rituals (10 years duration) which occurred 50–100 times each day, especially when he had doubts about the tidiness of his room, contents of a letter, etc. Each check was associated with a distinctive motor movement. His doubts and checks made him excessively slow and finally led to his unemployment. (Valenstein, 1977, p. 85)

The researchers who have used behavioral techniques claim to have achieved a very high success rate. Even in instances in which behavior therapy fails, there is a need to find alternatives to psychosurgery. Emotional disorders involve the entire person and are not likely to be brought under control with the destruction of a few brain cells.

3

Stress and Illness

As stated in the opening chapter, technological medicine is based on the premise that disease is the outcome of specific agents or bodily malfunctions. Illness is viewed as a thing in itself that is unrelated to the patient's environment and lifestyle. The biomedical model of illness, on which technological medicine is based, is not sufficient, however, for understanding the majority of current health problems that afflict individuals in our culture. Individuals do not "catch" disorders such as hypertension, migraine headache, or coronary heart disease. Instead, these disorders develop over a life-span and are therefore much more open to the direct influences of psychological variables (Wadsworth, 1974). Acute illnesses, such as those caused by communicable diseases, appear very rapidly and treatment is specific and immediate. The patient's social environment and lifestyle have no opportunity to have any serious influence on the course of the illness. Chronic illness is a far different matter, however, because the disease has a slow onset. Heart disease might first appear in the form of chest pains that appear and disappear over a time span. Now the individual's psychology and his reaction to the developing symptoms are likely to influence the very course of the disorder. The situation is much more multifaceted or psychobiological with chronic illness than it is with acute illness.

Psychological stress is considered to be the principal cause of disorders that defy explanation at the biochemical level. This chapter is an examination of what is known of the relationship between stress and medical disorders. A model for understanding the interaction of psychological stress with physiological variables is presented along with a model for understanding the psychological processes that influence the magnitude of stress reactions. The latter model is important for understanding patient stress reactions to hospital-related stimuli. Finally, the relationship between specific lifestyles and illness—a topic that is becoming extremely important to the field of preventive medicine—is examined.

Diathesis-Stress Model of Illness

The argument that psychosocial variables play an important role in illness does not rule out the significance of biochemical variables for understanding illness. The problem facing all health-related research is to explain how these different variables interact in the disease process. A conceptual framework for understanding the complex interactions that occur between environmental, psychological, and physiological variables is illustrated in Figure 3-1. At a physiological level it is assumed that the individual possesses a predisposition to develop a specific disorder, whether it be headache, ulcers, or hypertension. Given the physiological predisposition and given that the appropriate psychosocial stimuli are present, the individual will then manifest a variety of psychological and physiological reactions. These reactions, if prolonged, may act as major precursors of disease or as causes of disease. As shown in Figure 3-1, the sequence is not necessarily a one-way process but, rather, a system in which the variables are continually interacting. This interactionist model is called *the diathesis-* (meaning "predisposition") *stress* model of illness.

Viewing disease from this perspective has a number of implications for understanding illness and patient care. The model indicates that biochemical vulnerability, although necessary, is not sufficient to explain disease onset. Whether or not a disease becomes manifest depends on a complex of other variables that include psychological and social factors. Thus psychophysiological reactions of life and life changes interact with biochemical factors to alter susceptibility and thereby influence the time of onset, the severity, and the course of a disease (Engel, 1977). Even broad cultural variables need to be considered, for it has been demonstrated that higher rates of illness occur among peoples exposed to conflicts between their cultural backgrounds and the demands of the social situation in which they are living and working (Cassel, 1964). These same variables also influence when patients view themselves as sick and whether or not they are willing to enter a health care system to become a patient. The model also has implications for treatment, for it suggests that more than a biochemical abnormality may have to be corrected before the patient

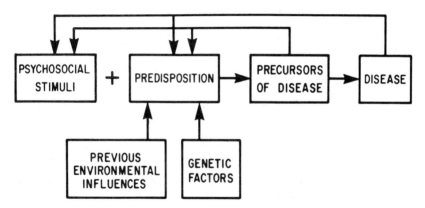

Figure 3-1 Schematic of the diathesis-stress model of illness. (From Levi, 1974. In Gunderson, E. K., & R. H. Rahe (Eds.), *Life Stress and Illness,* 1974). Courtesy of Charles C Thomas, Publisher, Springfield, Illinois.

becomes well. Understanding the full range of variables involved is clearly a difficult but necessary task facing every health professional:

> The psychobiological unity of man requires that the physician accept the responsibility to evaluate whatever problems the patient presents and recommend a course of action, including referral to other helping professions. Hence the physician's basic professional knowledge and skills must span the social, psychological, and biological, for his decisions and actions on the patient's behalf involve all three. (Engel, 1977, p. 133)

How Normal Is Abnormal?

An understanding of individual differences in vulnerability or susceptibility to disorders begins with an appreciation of the tremendous variation that exists at the anatomical level across individuals. Many people believe that underlying anatomy is pretty much the same from one person to the next. Although we all manifest considerable differences in physical appearance, from foot size to head size, few people believe that much larger individual differences might exist in the structures within our bodies.

In this context, physicians are often asked by patients, "Is my heart rate normal?" or "Is my blood pressure normal?" The term *normal* is a statistical concept, and it implies that the property in question follows the normal curve in the larger population. Heart rate, for example, is assumed to be normal at approximately 72 beats per minute. This is taken to mean that the majority of people in the population have a heart rate near this value. As the rate deviates increasingly from 72 beats per minute, it is assumed to occur less and less frequently in the population and therefore to be more and more abnormal.

In actual fact, there are very little data as to whether physiological systems are distributed normally in the population. R. J. Williams (1967), a biochemist, entitled one of his books *You Are Extraordinary* to emphasize his belief that many properties may not, in fact, be normally distributed in the population. In the book he provides fascinating examples in support of his thesis that each of us is unique with respect to anatomy, biochemistry, and physiology. One of his examples, presented in Figure 3-2, shows a "textbook" stomach followed by the shapes of stomachs taken from "normal" individuals. Some of the illustrations do not even look like stomachs. He presents similar observations for a number of biochemical and physiological systems. People with no known stomach ailment were shown to exhibit varia-

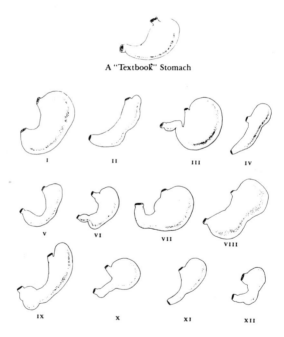

Figure 3-2   Drawings of 12 real stomachs in contrast to the drawing of a "textbook" stomach (Williams, 1967). Williams, R.J. *You are extraordinary*. New York: Random House, 1967.

tion in gastric-juice pepsin levels of 0 to 4,300 units. Normal hearts were observed to beat more than twice as fast as others and some pumping capacities to be at least three times as great as others.

After reading this book, I began to wonder how any two people, unless they are fortuitously physiochemically compatible, are able to live together for any period of time. Possibly a greater appreciation of these differences might make us all more tolerant of those who do not behave as we feel they should. In this context, I have frequently been the brunt of criticism for the rapidity with which I devour food. I usually counter this criticism by stating that my esophagus may simply be very large. At a more serious level, Williams's observations provide a basis for assuming that there must be tremendous variation at the anatomical level in terms of susceptibility to disorders. Additional support for this argument has been provided from studies dealing with individual differences in physiological reactivity to stress-eliciting stimuli.

Physiological Response Specificity

In the previous chapter, it was stated that the sympathetic nervous system tends to respond en masse. However, even though the autonomic nervous system does respond to stress as a whole in the sense that all structures seem to be activated, it does not necessarily respond as a whole in the sense that all structures show the same degree of activation. In fact, individuals tend to exhibit maximal activation to stressful stimulation in one particular physiological response modality. In addition, some individuals show the same maximal activation in the same modality (for example, heart rate or blood pressure) across different stimuli. Lacey (1959) was the first researcher to explore systematically individual differences in patterns of sympathetic nervous system responses. Lacey called this phenomenon *individual response specificity*.

In healthy individuals, response specificity for a particular physiological variable might be predictive of a disorder associated with that variable if a problem should develop. Malmo, Shagass, and Davis (1950), in fact, formulated the related principle of *symptom specificity*, which states that for individuals with a bodily symptom the physiological mechanism underlying the symptom is specifically responsive to activation by stressful stimuli. Malmo and Shagass (1949) examined the responses to stress stimuli of psychiatric patients with a history of cardiovascular complaints and of psychiatric patients with a history of head and neck pains. In support of the principle of symptom specificity, they found that heart rate, heart-rate variability, and respiratory-variability scores were all reliably greater for the group of patients with a history of cardiovascular complaints, whereas muscle-potential scores were greater for patients with a history of head and neck pains.

It must be emphasized that the stability of response specificity is difficult to establish. Some individuals exhibit very little consistent responsiveness to different stimuli or even to the same stimuli across time. At the other extreme, however, are some individuals who seem to have very rigid systems because they produce the same pattern in situation after situation. Possibly individuals who exhibit little variation in their patterns might be the same individuals who develop a psychophysiological disorder. Let us now examine the diathesis-stress model with respect to a specific disorder: chronic headache. This disorder, because of its cyclic nature, lends itself well to this kind of analysis. It is important, however, to recognize that a similar analysis can be applied to many other disorders, even those associated with definite structural damage.

Chronic Headache

Chronic headache is probably the most common health complaint of individuals living in western societies. This statement does not include the instances of headache that are infrequent and controllable with mild analgesics and rest. Rather it refers to extremely debilitating headaches that can require the hospitalization of the afflicted individual. Some individuals experience these attacks on a daily basis over periods of many years. The exact incidence of chronic headache in the population is unknown but is assumed to involve 10% to 15% of the population. Most statistical studies have also found that a preponderance of sufferers are females (Bakal, 1975).

Headaches are usually classified into one of three broad categories: *organic*, *migraine*, and *muscle contraction*. The vast majority of headaches are not due to an organic pathology and are classed as migraine or muscle contraction. Migraine headache is characterized by a throbbing pain that usually begins on one side of the head. The pain is experienced in the temporal region. The headache attack is often preceded by an *aura*, or warning symptoms. These symptoms are sensory in nature and may include dizziness and partial blindness. Nausea, vomiting, or both are additional symptoms that occur during the prodromal, or preheadache, phase. Muscle contraction headache, on the other hand, is experienced as dull pressurelike pain located in the region of the forehead, the neck, or both and the back of the head. Chronic headache sufferers are usually familiar with both classes of symptoms (Bakal & Kaganov, 1977).

Migraine vulnerability, in particular, is assumed to have a hereditary basis. Goodell, Lewontin, and Wolff (1954) found 84% of migraine patients had at least one relative with migraine. Lennox (1960) reported data on five identical (monozygotic) twin pairs with migraine, and in each pair both twins were affected. Refsum (1968) reported several European studies that found concordance rates ranging from 60% to 100% for identical twins and 10% to 40% for fraternal (dizygotic) twins. Not all studies have found a high familial incidence of migraine (Waters, 1971), but the majority of such studies are supportive of an inherited predisposition for migraine. The possibility of an inherited predisposition for muscle contraction headache has not been examined.

The physiological mechanisms underlying migraine and muscle contraction headache are assumed to be different (Dalessio, 1972). Muscle contraction headache is believed to arise from the sustained contraction of skeletal muscles about the face, scalp, neck, and shoulders. The pain associated with migraine headache, on the other hand, is believed to result from vasodilatation of intracranial (inside the skull) and extracranial (outside the skull) arteries. One of the large extracranial vessels involved in migraine is the superficial temporal artery. During the preheadache phase it is assumed that this artery is in a state of vasoconstriction, which then changes to an exaggerated vasodilatation that causes the throbbing head pain.

What actually precipitates the headache attacks in these individuals? Only a small minority of headache sufferers are able to identify specific physical stimuli (foodstuffs, alcohol, noise, weather changes, hormonal changes) that are capable of eliciting an attack. Wine and chocolate are often implicated and both are known to contain tyramine, which is a vasodilator substance. In one of the few studies available, Moffett, Swash, and Scott (1974) identified 25 migrainous individuals, all of whom initially stated that their headaches could be precipitated by the consumption of chocolate. Subjects were told that they would be required to eat two different kinds of chocolate, but in actuality one of the samples was made from a noncocoa substance that tasted like chocolate. Only a small percentage of the subjects reported experiencing headache following ingestion of the chocolate, and this percentage was not different from that reported for the noncocoa substance. This study suggests that foodstuffs are not likely to account for a significant proportion of headache attacks. Furthermore the avoidance of such stimuli seldom leads to a significant reduction in the frequency of attacks in chronic headache sufferers. Physical stimuli are not the major problem for these individuals.

In line with the diathesis-stress model, the primary cause of headache is assumed to be psychological stress. Anger, frustration, anxiety, and personal difficulties are frequently listed as the major causes of chronic headache. Yet there are many patients who experience attacks independently of any specific stressful stimulus. Some patients report attacks on awakening or when they are about to have a good time. Other patients experience no headaches during their regular workweek but are totally incapacitated on weekends or during vacations. One investigator observed that, although 68% of a patient group recognized that psychological stressors could play a part as the precipitating factor, 32% denied this possibility. Moreover, all of the patients believed that many of the attacks occurred spontaneously with no apparent cause (Dalsgaard-Nielsen, 1965).

Until very recently, there was a pervasive belief that a personality type was characteristic of migrainous individuals. Migraine patients have been described as perfectionistic, achievement oriented, over-controlled, obsessional, inflexible, and highly intelligent. The latter trait may explain why in some circles migraine is a "status disorder." Because of lack of supporting evidence, the belief in the migrainous personality is quickly vanishing (Pearce, 1977).

The depiction of the causes of headache as obscure is intentional, for exactly the same problem characterizes patients suffering from other disorders. It has been observed that many instances of hypertension, asthma, epilepsy, and stomach dysfunctions cannot be linked to a precipitating stressful stimulus (Luborsky, Docherty, & Penick, 1973). Consequently, many medical researchers believe that psychosocial stimuli, when present, are of secondary importance, the primary cause being some dysfunction in one or more central nervous system regulatory mechanisms. For example, Sicuteri (1976) hypothesized that the migraine disorder stems from a derangement of the mechanism controlling the production and release of brain amines. The absence of obvious personality and emotional variables does not, however, rule out the possibility that more subtle psychobiological variables maintain the disorder.

One possibility is that headaches (as well as other disorders) acquire a degree of autonomy from the emotional condition of the individual. It is known that autonomic responses, once conditioned, are extremely resistant to extinction. In a classic experiment Liddell (1934) demonstrated the persistence of conditioned autonomic responses within the framework of classical conditioning. His experiment involved conditioning sheep to flex a leg to the sound of a bell. The response was established by pairing the bell with an electric shock to the leg. The sheep quickly acquired the flexion response. The sheep also manifested autonomic nervous system responses to the bell that included increased rate and irregularity of the heart cycle. With the discontinuation of shock, the sheep eventually stopped making the flexion motor response to the bell, but surprisingly, the autonomic responses continued.

Gantt (1966) coined the term *schizokinesis* to describe the dissociation that occurred between the motor and autonomic response systems of these animals. That is, even though the stimulus was having no effect on the motor system at the end of the experiment, it was still capable of eliciting an autonomic response. These observations may prove to have some relevance for psychophysiological disorders, especially in our efforts to explain autonomic and skeletal changes outside awareness:

> The fact that conditional reflexes are so difficult to eradicate, once formed, makes the individual a museum of antiquities as he grows older. . . . He is encumbered with many reactions no longer useful or even . . . detrimental to life. This is especially true for the cardiovascular function, and it is these conditional reflexes that are most enduring. A person may be reacting to some old injury or situation which no longer exists, and he is usually unconscious of what it is that is causing an increase in heart rate or blood pressure. The result may be chronic hypertension. This may be the explanation of many cardiac deaths. (Gantt, 1966, p. 62)

Chronic headache and other disorders may owe their maintenance, at least in part, to some form of dissociation between psychological and physiological systems. In the case of headache, there may have been a stormy psychological period during the individual's developmental history. At that time the individual's physiological system may have become conditioned to stressful stimuli. With increasing maturation, the individual may have come to redefine these stressful events, such that similar events are no longer viewed as disturbing. Adolescent crises, for example, are often viewed retrospectively as being minor, if not humorous, in nature. What may not change, however, is a physiological susceptibility to headache. Moreover, the headaches may have initially been muscle contraction in nature but with repeated attacks have come to include vascular systems along with autonomic disturbances that mediate nausea and vomiting. There is some evidence that headaches in children increase in severity with increasing age (Bakal, in press).

I have a case study that illustrates how a muscular disorder may come to operate independently of specific stressful stimuli. The patient, a 50-year-old female, came to our laboratory complaining of a facial twitch or tic that had plagued her for a period of 27 years. She complained of an inability to enter any social situation without the muscles that controlled the left side of her face beginning to twitch in a spasmodic fashion. The afflicted portion of her face became quite grotesque during an attack, and almost any social activity (shopping, golfing, attending a movie) was capable of precipitating one. She did not manifest any pathological personality traits nor did she complain of feelings such as anxiety or inadequacy. At the sensory level she was aware of feelings of "numbness" from the afflicted side of her face. We recorded the muscle activity, with an electromyogram (EMG), from the left and right sides of her face. The tracings were obtained during a period when the disorder was not present. Although visual inspection of her face during this period revealed no immediate differences between the two sides, the EMG activity from the afflicted side of her face was far greater than the EMG activity from the nonafflicted side. This represents a good illustration of a psychophysiological condition that is not adequately captured with traditional psychosomatic terminology.

A similar condition has been identified in chronic migraine and muscle contraction headache sufferers (Bakal & Kaganov, 1977). Both classes of headache sufferers have been found to manifest, in the symptom-free conditions, greater muscle activity from the head region than individuals free of headache. Figure 3-3 shows illustrative recordings of the differences in frontalis (forehead) EMG levels observed across the three groups. The recordings were obtained while the subjects simply relaxed on a bed. Such activity may be a correlate of a predisposition for headache that operates largely outside of the patient's awareness. (In Chapter 7 there is an examination of the extent to which it is possible to train patients to become aware of this activity and to reduce its presence.)

General Adaptation Syndrome

Any discussion of stress must include the theoretical model developed by Hans Selye (1956, 1974). His lifework on stress came about, like many important discoveries, quite accidentally. He was attempting to

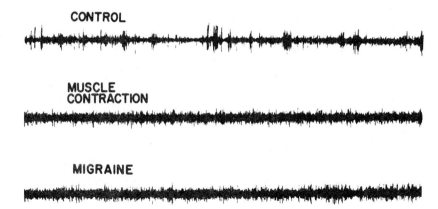

CONTROL

MUSCLE
CONTRACTION

MIGRAINE

Figure 3-3 Frontalis EMG activity in headache patients and control subject; recordings obtained during a headache-free period (Bakal & Kaganov, 1977). Copyright © 1977 by the American Association for the Study of Headache. Reprinted by permission of the publisher.

isolate a new sex hormone by injecting ovary extracts into rats. To Selye's surprise, the rats showed a physiological response pattern that was hardly characteristic of any known or unknown sex hormone. First, there was secretion of corticoid hormones from the adrenal cortex, which is the outer part of the adrenal gland. A second change that occurred was a shrinking of the thymus and the lymph nodes. The lymph nodes are little nodules in the groin, under the armpits, along the neck, and in various other parts of the body. These nodules contain the lymphocytes, which are white blood cells. The thymus is a huge lymphatic organ just in front of the heart in the chest. A final response that was characteristic of some animals was ulceration in the lining of the stomach. In a series of later experiments, Selye discovered that the more impure he made the extracts, the more this general bodily reaction occurred. He eventually theorized that this general reaction of the body, which he called the *general adaptation syndrome*, occurred to all forms of physical stress. That is, in addition to localized changes produced by specific damage such as a cut or a burn or an infection, the general adaptation syndrome was superimposed on the specific changes. According to Selye, the general adaptation syndrome is what is common to all patients who are sick regardless of their particular illness. The general adaptation syndrome is a response that the body manifests to all illnesses.

The physiological pathway underlying the general adaptation syndrome has been called the *pituitary-adrenal axis.* The pituitary gland consists of two major subdivisions or lobes: the adenohypophysis, or anterior lobe, and the neurohypophysis, or posterior lobe. The pituitary gland is under the control of hormones, the hypothalamus, and the autonomic nervous system. The anterior portion of the pituitary gland secretes several hormones called *trophic homones* because their function is to stimulate other glands to secrete their own hormones. ACTH is the pituitary hormone that completes the pituitary-adrenal axis by stimulating the adrenal cortex to secrete cortical steroids.

Through a series of experiments, Selye demonstrated that the general adaptation syndrome occurs in three distinct phases: the alarm reaction, the stage of resistance, and the stage of exhaustion. At each stage the organism undergoes a change in susceptibility to additional stress:

1. *Alarm reaction.* This initial stage is sometimes called the emergency reaction because it is during this stage that the organism's physiological changes reflect the initial reaction to the stress-providing stimulus. During the alarm reaction, the anterior pituitary gland secretes ACTH, which then activates the adrenal cortex to secrete additional hormones. During the alarm reaction the hormone output from the adrenal cortex is high.

2. *Stage of resistance.* If the stress-producing stimulus continues, the alarm reaction is followed by a stage of resistance. During this period the physiological changes that occurred during the first stage cease.

3. *Stage of exhaustion.* If exposure to the injurious stressor is prolonged further, the organism eventually reaches a state in which it can no longer respond either with an alarm reaction or with resistance. The anterior pituitary and the adrenal cortex lose their capacity to secrete hormones, and the organism can no longer adapt to the stress. Exhaustion and even death are the outcome.

How did Selye establish that this triphasic response exists in organisms? In one experiment he placed rats in a room at near-freezing temperatures. At the end of 48 hours, one group of animals was sacrificed, and they all manifested changes characteristic of the alarm reaction. After the 48 hours, a second group was taken from the cold chamber and placed, along with another group taken from a normal-temperature environment, in a still colder chamber. The rats that had the initial experience with the cold were even less than normally resistant to the colder temperatures, which suggests that an organism is more susceptible to stress if that stress is applied during a period in which it is already in the alarm reaction. After several weeks another group was taken from the initial cold room, and they were found to be able to tolerate more cold than the control animals, which suggested to Selye that organisms can tolerate considerably more stress during the stage of resistance. Eventually, however, these animals entered the stage of exhaustion and could not even withstand the initial cold room temperatures. It is as though their reserves had been depleted and their bodily mechanisms simply gave out.

Concept of Adaptation Energy

The observation that some animals entered a stage of exhaustion and finally died intrigued Selye. He eventually postulated that all living organisms possess a finite amount of adaptation energy for combating stress:

> People can get used to a number of things (cold, heavy muscular work, worries), which at first had a very alarming effect; yet, upon prolonged exposure, sooner or later all resistance breaks down and exhaustion sets in. . . .
> It is as though, at birth, each individual inherited a certain amount of adaptation energy, the magnitude of which is determined by his genetic background, his parents. He can draw upon this capital thriftily for a long but monotonously uneventful existence, or he can spend it lavishly in the course of a stressful, intense, but perhaps more colorful and exciting life. (Selye, 1956, p. 66)

The concept of adaptation energy has been loosely applied to psychophysiological disorders. The basic argument is that individuals are not born with these disorders, but with years and years of repeated arousal of the defense alarm system, the end result may be the appearance of irreversible disturbances such as hypertension or heart failure.

Nature of Psychological Stress

The majority of stressors used by Selye in his extensive research were laboratory-controlled physical stimuli such as cold or electric shock. The situation with respect to humans, however, is exceedingly more complex. Now the stress is psychological in nature and virtually impossible to define in discrete physical terms. Stress cannot be defined exclusively by situations because the capacity of any situation to produce stress reactions depends on the characteristics of individuals. In short, job security may be stressful to one individual and not to the next. Whether any stimulus is stressful or not then depends ultimately on an individual's perception of an event. A workable definition of stress within this context has been provided by Cofer and Appley (1964): "the state of an organism where his general well-being is threatened, and where no readily available response exists for the reduction of the threat" (p. 451).

R. S. Lazarus (1975a) proposed that the key stimuli in Selye's experiments might not have been physical stress (heat, cold, shock) per se but, rather, the animals' perception that they were in trouble. Unless the animal perceives the stimulus as dangerous, the general adaptation syndrome will not occur:

> An animal that is unconscious can sustain bodily harm without the psychoendocrine mechanisms of the general adaptation syndrome becoming active. Data from Symington, Currie, Curran, and Davidson (1955), for example, suggest that unconsciousness and anesthesia eliminate the adrenal effects of psychological stress. It was observed that patients who were dying from injury or disease showed a normal adrenal cortical condition as assessed during autopsy as long as they have remained unconscious during the period of the fatal condition. In contrast, patients who were conscious during the periods of the fatal disease process and died, did show adrenal cortical changes. (p. 555)

Other evidence points to the importance of psychological, rather than physical, factors in assessing an organism's reaction to stressful stimulation. Emotional stimuli are extremely potent natural stimuli for eliciting pituitary–adrenal cortical responses.

> In fasting, for example, little or no corticosteroid change occurs in monkeys, if fruit-flavored nonnutritive cellulose fiber, i.e., placebo food, is given in place of similarly flavored and shaped food pellets, in order to minimize discomfort from emptiness of the gastrointestinal tract and to avoid the psychosocial stimuli associated with sudden deprivation of routine food dispensation by the animal caretaker. (Mason, 1975, p. 24).

A historical paradox of stress research is that 20 years ago, physiologists, in their studies of the physiological effects of heat, shock, and trauma, maintained that psychological variables were not important. Now the shoe is on the other foot, for the investigator of physical stressors must be very careful to rule out the possibility that any observed changes might have been due to the animal's psychological reaction to the situation.

Because the majority of events that are stressful to humans are psychological, R. S. Lazarus (1966, 1975a, 1975b) developed a model of stress in which the basic theme is that a stress reaction follows only when an individual "appraises" his current situation as stressful. In one of his early studies, Lazarus and his colleagues (Speisman, Lazarus, Mordkoff, & Davison, 1964) exposed subjects to a film that depicted some very crude genital operations carried out as part of male initiation rites in a primitive Australian tribe. The authors reasoned that, if the threat and physiological stress reactions depended on the appraisal of threat, and if the beliefs produced by the stimulus events could be altered, the psychophysiological stress reactions would be reduced.

> Three different sound tracks for the silent film were constructed, reflecting different ways of interpreting or thinking about the events portrayed in the film. One sound track was called "trauma" because it emphasized the harmful features—for example, the pain, the mutilation of the body, and the danger of disease that might befall the victims of the operation. A second was called "denial" because its theme was mainly that the operation did not produce harm. Pain and danger of disease were denied, and the adolescent boys were even characterized as looking forward happily to the whole procedure which established them as accepted members of the tribe. The third sound track was called "intellectualization." The perspective offered was that of the detached attitude of the anthropologist who looks with interest at strange customs and describes these without emotional involvement. (Lazarus, R. S., 1966, p. 46)

The researchers found that the physiological-stress response to the film was significantly lower for the defense-oriented (denial and intellectualization) sound tracks. The subjects were thus able to short-circuit the physiological effects that would normally occur to such a stimulus.

In another study (Lazarus, R. S., Opton, Nomikos, & Rankin, 1965) subjects were exposed to presentations of a film showing woodmill accidents in which the fingers of an operator are lacerated, another cuts off his middle finger, and a bystander is killed after a plank of wood is driven through his midsection. Half the subjects were provided with a denial orientation (the events were not really happening and the blood was simply a liquid being squeezed by the actors). The other half of the subjects were given an intellectualization framework (the events were described as real, but the emphasis was placed on the educational value of the film with respect to safety). A control group was given no special instructions. As with the previous study, the denial and intellectualization frameworks were effective in reducing the degree of physiological arousal to the film that occurred.

The important outcome of such studies is not that the appraisal of threat can be influenced but that such appraisals underlie the actual experience of threat. Stress reactions, then, reflect, to a large extent, the success or failure of coping mechanisms. The cognitive model of stress is presented schematically in Figure 3-4. The stress reaction begins when the individual perceives some important motive or value being threatened. To quote Lazarus, "the appraisal of threat is not a simple perception of the elements of the situation, but a judgment, an inference in which the data are assimilated to a constellation of ideas and expectations." The same stimulus event will be perceived as threatening by some individuals and not by other individuals. Given that the stimulus event is perceived as threatening, an individual then engages in secondary appraisal. Now coping mechanisms are activated that determine the nature of the final response outcome. The difference between primary and secondary appraisal is that the former is concerned mainly with an evaluation of the situation while the latter is concerned with an evaluation of consequences of actions taken to minimize the threat. With primary appraisal the issue is "How much am I in danger from this situation?"; whereas with the secondary appraisal, the issue is "How much am I in danger from anything I do about the threat or to what extent will any particular action relieve the danger?" Primary and secondary appraisal are not necessarily sequential, although the latter depends on the former.

The inclusion of secondary appraisal in theoretical models of stress is essential because from primary appraisal alone one cannot understand the vast array of possible outcomes associated with the perception of an event as stressful. In some individuals secondary appraisal may lead to anger, whereas in other individuals the outcome may be sadness or grief or depression. Secondary appraisal is also intricately related to the coping strategies used by an individual. Emotional responses represent a form of coping, indicating again the importance of appraisal at all levels of stress reactions.

Coping or self-regulation mechanisms are classified into two categories: *direct action* and *palliative*. In direct-action coping an individual tries to alter his behavioral interactions with the environment by demolishing, avoiding, or fleeing the threatening person or event. In addition, an individual may take action to meet the threat. Study-

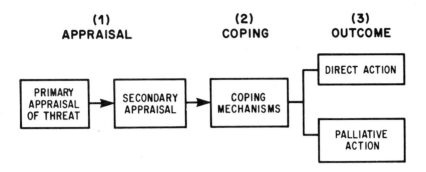

Figure 3-4 A schematic representation of Lazarus's cognitive model of stress.

ing and rehearsal represent good examples of direct-action behavior for a student who is facing a threatening examination; these behaviors may lead to a sense of mastery of the stress before it is faced.

Palliative coping results when direct action is too costly or difficult. Here potential stress reactions are reduced by altering the internal environment through the use of tranquilizers, defense mechanisms, or alcohol, or through engaging in behavior such as relaxation training, meditation, and hypnosis. Palliative forms of coping are directed at reducing the affective (feeling), motor, and physiological disturbances that are distressing an individual. These disturbances may represent the basic problem or, if reduced, may permit an individual to deal with the problem at the direct-action level.

A popular belief is that individuals working in stressful environments and who do not show any overt signs of stress must be seething on the inside. Doctors, nurses, and police are often admired by the public for maintaining a "front" of calmness in situations that would for the average citizen be extremely stressful. However, professionals that are continually exposed to death, mutilated bodies, and other human misery might, in fact, not be hiding their emotions; instead they may no longer be responding at the psychological or physiological level to such events. These individuals have defused the threatening aspects of such situations by cognitive reappraisal techniques. R. S. Lazarus (1975a) provided a relevant example to illustrate this possibility:

> Moreover, by successfully distancing themselves from the emotional features of an autopsy, the medical students observed by Lief and Fox (1963) not only behaved unemotionally, but in all likelihood, if the ap-

propriate measurements had been made, would have been shown to react with little or no affect and without the bodily disturbances that are an integral part of stress emotion. Lief and Fox (1963) conducted extensive interviews with medical students witnessing for the first time a medical autopsy. Most such students, who are probably self-selected to a high degree, achieve detachment from the experience, though there are some failures too. Certain features of the procedure itself and of the institutionalized behavior of the participants, probably evolved out of the wisdom of long professional experience, providing great help to the student in the process of achieving detachment. During the autopsy, for example, the room is immaculate and brightly lit, and the task is approached with seriousness, skill, and a professional air facilitating a clinical and impersonal attitude toward death. Certain parts of the body are kept covered, particularly the face and genitalia; and the hands, which are so strongly connected with human, personal qualities, are usually not dissected. Once the vital organs are removed, the body is taken from the room, bringing the autopsy down to isolated tissues that are more easily depersonalized. Students avoid talking about the autopsy; and when they do, the discussion is impersonal and stylized. Finally, whereas in laboratory dissection humor appears to be a widespread and effective emotional control device, it is absent in the autopsy room, perhaps because the death has been too recent and joking would appear too insensitive. One senses here the process of struggling to achieve a proper balance between feeling things and looking at them objectively, in short, an effort to regulate a common and expected emotional reaction in which detachment or distancing is the mode of coping. We also recognize that some individuals in medicine and nursing overdo the coping strategy of detachment or dehumanization and appear to their patients as cold and indifferent. (p. 557)

We apparently have much more control over our emotional behavior than we realize. Psychological processes involving denial and detachment are capable of changing the basic emotion itself. The proper expression of grief is a good example of the role of self-regulatory mechanisms in emotional behavior:

The person is expected to experience and display grief appropriately, that is, in the proper degree, in the appropriate circumstances, and in the appropriate form. In our society, for example, if the person shows too much grief, he will be criticized. He should not express criticism of or anger toward the deceased, and if there is some bitterness or self-pity, this is acceptable to an extent, but it should not be extended too long. In Japan, the person learns to cover up his grief with strangers or casual acquaintances lest it produce distress in the other person and shame to the griever. This leads to the anomaly of someone from another culture seeing a person who has just experienced the death of a loved one, but who on the surface seems to treat the whole thing very lightly. On the other hand, in our own culture if the person gives too little evidence of grief he is also subject to social criticism and is likely to be accused of being cold or indifferent. Thus, the person may experience the cruel dilemma of struggling within himself to control and work through his grief, while being pressured by others to do just the opposite as though in a charade. He must walk a tightrope between the alternative courses. (Lazarus, R. S., 1975b, p. 51)

Lazarus believes that the positive emotions are also under a high degree of cognitive control. He objects to phrases such as "smitten by love" because they imply that the feeling is beyond the individual's control. The cognitive model suggests that feelings of love are much more deliberate in nature. That is, if one's positive feelings toward another are not initially reciprocated, then it is not likely that one will "fall in love" with that person.

Psychological Stress and Surgery

Surgery can be a most terrifying experience. Many clinicians believe that the psychological state, that is, the appraisal mechanisms of an individual undergoing surgery, may affect the success of the operation both in terms of recovery and in terms of postsurgical symptoms. The course of recovery includes physical healing as well as complaints of pain, use of tranquilizers and pain medication, and willingness to practice physical rehabilitation (Cohen & Larzarus, 1973).

Irving Janis (1958) found that a moderate amount of fear expressed prior to surgery facilitates postsurgical recovery. Patients who showed extreme fear reactions or who showed little or no fear before the surgery coped less well during the recovery period. Patients who showed the least preoperative anticipatory fear were presumably employing denial defenses. After surgery the denial group exhibited considerable anger and disappointment, and they actively resisted efforts to promote their recovery. Janis hypothesized that the group who showed moderate fear used their fear constructively to engage in a cognitive process that he labeled *work of worrying*. These patients used their fear to prepare themselves for the discomforts and frustrations that they were to experience later. Janis believes that the absence of cognitive preparation in the form of work of worrying characterizes patients who fail to cope adequately with surgery. Because the patient has failed to cognitively rehearse the outcome, he may be overwhelmed when the danger materializes.

Cohen and Lazarus (1973) studied the coping processes and their differential effects on surgical outcome in 71 patients. They divided their patients into two basic categories: those who relied primarily on denial coping mechanisms and those who relied primarily on vigilance coping mechanisms. Denial and vigilance represent defensive strategies for coping at the secondary appraisal stage. The principal coping strategy used by a patient was inferred from an interview. Patients who indicated a reluctance to seek out information about their condition, the impending surgery, and postsurgical symptoms were considered to be using denial coping mechanisms ("All I know is that I have a hernia. . . . I just took it for granted . . . it doesn't disturb me one bit and I have no thoughts about it"). Vigilance mechanisms reflected patients who actively sought out, in an exaggerated fashion, information about their medical condition and who were extremely ready to discuss thoughts about the operation ("I have all the facts; my will is prepared; it is major surgery; it's a body opening; you're put out; you could be put out too deep; your heart could quit"). The comments used by the vigilance patients suggest that although they were seeking out information, they were not doing so in a totally rational and realistic fashion. They appeared to be whistling in the dark or engaging in a neurotic form of worrying. A middle group that exhibited neither a dominance of avoidance nor vigilance coping strategies was included for comparisons. The patients that used a vigilant mode of coping showed the poorest recovery on three of the four recovery variables: number of days in the hospital, frequency of minor complications, and negative psychological reactions. The patients that used avoidant coping strategies actually did the best in terms of these measures. To some extent this latter finding contradicts the observation of Janis inasmuch as he found that those who used denial defenses actually had the worst postsurgical recovery rates. In this study, the use of denial defense mechanisms seemed to facilitate the patients' recovery. Apparently, no simple relationship exists between coping styles and surgical outcome.

Burstein and Meichenbaum (1974) examined the work of worrying process in 20 children between 4 and 9 years of age who were about to undergo surgery. The researchers used two measures of denial. The first was derived from their play behavior, prior to surgery, with hospital-related and nonhospital-related toys. The second measure was a defensiveness questionnaire that measures a tendency to deny common weaknesses (for example, "I never worry about what people think of me; I always tell the truth; I like everyone I know"). The results showed that the highly defensive children tended not to play with the hospital-related toys prior to surgery and also manifested the greatest postsurgical distress. Illustrative comments made by the two classes of children are:

Work of worriers	Deniers
Q. What do you remember about going to the hospital?	
A bath, going to the operating room, going to the playroom, going in the stretcher to the operating room, going to the hospital with my mother, making in the cup near the nurses room, nurse giving me needle. She took me to the weighing room. That little ice thing on my neck.	I got nice food; I got my tonsils out; I got a good bed; that's all. I went to sleep, started playing with a truck from the other room. A girl came in and we played with the teddy bear. I went back to bed again.
Q. Suppose that a friend of yours was going to have to go to the hospital for the same thing you went for. What would you tell him (her)?	
You should know everything before. It calms you down, doesn't make me scared. If you expect them then you don't get scared, like the nurse coming to give a blood test.	It's better that you don't have to know everthing because they will make you so afraid, you wouldn't want to go.
Well, when you first get in and your mom leaves, you might be a bit scared, but then when you meet somebody it's not as scary.	I wouldn't tell him what happens about the big needle because he'll be so frightened. The only thing I'd say was the needles didn't hurted and when they take blood it doesn't hurt.
I would tell her that her throat would be sore after she came up from the operation. That when she got a needle it would hurt a lot. They are nice nurses and doctors there.	You'll like it. That it'll be lots of fun and you'll get drinks.

Psychological Preparation of the Surgery Patient

Given that the coping processes characteristic of a patient influence his response to surgery, how might the patient be prepared
psychologically for surgery? All patients are generally given an explanation of their impending surgery, the assumption being that the explanation will serve to reduce the patients' fears and concerns. An
early study by Egbert, Battit, Turndorf, and Beecher (1963) is often
cited to support this assumption. Egbert et al. found that patients who
were given detailed information about impending surgery required
less morphine and were discharged earlier than a group that was denied such information. Recent research indicates, however, that the
issue is far more complex than is often recognized. Studies have
shown that the effectiveness of communication before surgery depends on a host of factors that include the style of the communication
and the coping mechanisms in use by the patient receiving the communication.

Andrew (1970) examined the effects of providing or not providing surgical patients with information as a function of their preferred
coping styles. Patients were classified as using primarily vigilant, denial, or vigilant-denial coping strategies. The vigilant-denial group
showed the fastest recovery, whereas the vigilant group was not affected by the information. The subjects using denial coping strategies
actually required more medication when given information. For these
individuals, the presentation of information succeeded only in dis-
rupting their defenses. A similar finding has been reported by
Williams, Jones, Workhoven, and Williams (1975). They manipulated
the kind of preoperative visit given to patients. One kind of visit,
called "cursory," was only of sufficient duration to provide the patient
with a brief explanation of the forthcoming procedures. Another
kind of visit was called "supportive" because the patient was encouraged to seek all the information that he wished. Both cursory and
supportive interviews were successful in decreasing the levels of anxiety in highly anxious patients. In low-anxious patients, however, the
supportive interview had no effect on anxiety levels, whereas the cursory interview actually increased anxiety levels. These data suggest
that staff communications may not always be effective or may even be
disruptive for patients that are prone to using denial coping
strategies.

We need more information on the relationship between patient
coping styles and hospital programs designed to alleviate concerns
about surgery. The time at which the hospital communication is de-

livered might also be a critical variable. De Long (1970) found that patients prone to using denial mechanisms were disrupted if specific and detailed information was given 24 hours prior to the surgery. On the other hand, patients who began to deal cognitively with the impending surgery immediately upon being informed of the need for surgery by their physician benefited from this kind of communication. The patient prone to using denial effectively blocked all thoughts related to surgery, so that the communication overwhelmed their defenses. In this context, Fenz (1975) observed that experienced parachutists also show maximal anxiety reactions much earlier in the jump sequence than novice parachutists. Experienced jumpers use the anxiety early to prepare themselves for the event. Thus by the time they are standing at the open door their anxiety is on the decrease. Novices, on the other hand, continue to show increasing anxiety, even when into the jump (a perfectly reasonable reaction). The point being made is that presurgery information programs might be more effective if presented early to the patient.

Life Stress and Illness

It is clear that environmental events cannot be defined as "stressors" a priori because an event is stressful only insofar as an individual perceives it as such. There is a further difficulty in establishing the etiological significance of stress with respect to physical disorders. Human concerns, fears, hostilities, and other negative emotions do not occur in a discrete fashion and, therefore, are not easily identifiable. That is, someone who harbors strong feelings of resentment and hostility may have acquired these feelings and an accompanying lifestyle as a reaction to environmental events many years prior to the appearance of a physical disorder. It, therefore, becomes difficult to demonstrate that environmental events, emotions, and lifestyle have anything to do with the "sudden" appearance of a disorder such as coronary heart disease. Such information is crucial, however, to demonstrate that stress does indeed precipitate disease.

There have been a few attempts to quantify events in social environments that might be generally perceived as stressful by large segments of the society. A scale has been constructed that assesses life stress in terms of life changes or what are called *life change units* (Rahe, 1975). Each life change, such as marriage or promotion, according to theory, requires some form of adaptation, and this in itself is stressful. Too much adaptation might trigger a physical illness in an already vulnerable individual. This line of thinking is very close to Selye's (1956) concept that organisms have a finite capacity for tolerating stress and if this is exceeded, the organism will break down.

Life change units (LCUs) are measured by the Social Readjustment Rating Questionnaire (Table 3-1). The scale items were initially presented to a large number of subjects who were instructed to rate them for the degree of necessary adjustment required. The event relative to which each item was rated was marriage, which was assigned an arbitrary value of 100 points. For example, when a subject evaluated a life change unit, such as a change in residence, he was to ask himself: "Is a change in residence more, less, or perhaps equal to the amount and duration of life change and readjustment inherent in marriage?" The death of a spouse was viewed as the most stressful act of all life changes; vacation and Christmas were examples of events that were perceived as minimally stressful.

Table 3-1   Life Change Units
Measured by the Social Readjustment Rating Scale

Life Change Events	Values
Family:	
Death of spouse	100
Divorce	73
Marital Separation	65
Death of close family member	63
Marriage	50
Marital reconciliation	45
Major change in health of family	44
Pregnancy	40
Addition of new family member	39
Major change in arguments with wife	35
Son or daughter leaving home	29
In-law troubles	29
Wife starting or ending work	26
Major change in family get-togethers	15
Personal:	
Detention in jail	63
Major personal injury or illness	53
Sexual difficulties	39
Death of a close friend	37
Outstanding personal achievement	28
Start or end of formal schooling	26
Major change in living conditions	25

In one study, a large number of navy personnel were required to complete LCU scores for a period of 4 years prior to the testing. They were also asked to recall their illness experience during the same period. The 4-year period was divided into eight 6-month intervals. Whenever an illness was reported during the 4-year period, the 6-month interval in which it occurred was labeled the illness period. LCU totals were examined for all illness periods along with the LCU totals for the two 6-month intervals immediately prior to their illness period. The LCU total was highest for the illness period (174 LCUs). In the 6-month interval prior to the illness period, the subsequently ill subjects reported an average LCU total of 125 units, and in the 6 months prior to that, an average of 100 LCUs. Do these data prove that life changes precipitate illness? Not conclusively, because the study was retrospective in nature. That is, the subjects were asked to *recall* both their frequency of life changes and illnesses. Thus, it might

Major revision of personal habits	24
Changing to a new school	20
Change in residence	20
Major change in recreation	19
Major change in church activities	19
Major change in sleeping habits	16
Major change in eating habits	15
Vacation	13
Christmas	12
Minor violations of the law	11
Work:	
Being fired from work	47
Retirement from work	45
Major business adjustment	39
Changing to different line of work	36
Major change in work responsibilities	29
Trouble with boss	23
Major change in working conditions	20
Financial:	
Major change in financial state	38
Mortgage or loan over $10,000	31
Mortgage foreclosure	30
Mortgage or loan less than $10,000	17

Source: Rahe, R. H. Life changes and near-future illness reports. In L. Levi (ed.) *Emotions: Their Parameters and Measurement.* New York: Raven Press, 1975. Copyright © 1975 by Raven Press, Publishers, New York. Reprinted by permission of the publisher.

be that the subjects reporting the greatest number of illnesses, because of a general dissatisfaction, might have had a greater tendency to recall negative life changes than did relatively healthy subjects.

Some prospective evidence on the relationship between life change units and illness has also been reported (Rahe, 1975). In one study, LCU scores were obtained from navy personnel *prior* to their departure on a 6-month voyage. Thus it was possible to tabulate medical disorders as they occurred during the voyage. The investigators found a linear relationship between illness rate and LCU totals. The higher the LCU scores prior to the voyage, the greater the number of reported illnesses during the voyage. One should keep in mind that these data are still not demonstrable proof that life change leads to illness. The majority of illnesses reported were minor in nature involving gastrointestinal, musculoskeletal, genetourinary, and dermal complaints. The men with the greater LCU scores prior to the voyage might simply have been more predisposed, again because of a general dissatisfaction, to report to sick bay with such minor complaints. These studies are suggestive of a relationship between life stress and illness, but one must be cautious in assuming that a cause-effect relationship has been demonstrated.

How many LCUs might a subject experience and still remain healthy? According to Rahe (1975), subjects that reported 150 or less LCUs a year also reported being in good health for the succeeding year. If the yearly LCU values range between 150 and 300 LCUs, an illness was reported during the following year in approximately half the subjects. The probability of an illness rose to 70% if the LCU scores exceeded 300 units. Examine briefly the case history of an individual who scored above the 300 units:

> The subject, a Negro male, joined the U.S. Navy in 1941 at the age of 20 years. He was stationed aboard ship in Pearl Harbor when the Japanese attacked. He was transferred to another ship which was torpedoed and sunk. In 1943 he went to sick call for tension headaches; a few months later he had a circumcision. The following year he experienced two more changes of duty station and received a promotion to Steward, First Class. Late that year his tension symptoms returned and he also contracted mumps. At the end of the war he married; subsequently he developed low back pain symptoms. In 1947, at 26 years of age, he experienced a dramatic clustering of life changes. He was transferred, his first child was born, he re-enlisted, he received two further transfers, and his wife became pregnant again. The following year he contracted gonorrhea, developed tonsillitis, and injured his wrist and knee. From 1951 through 1955 the subject's life changes were at a minimum. The

only illnesses recorded over that period were two minor ones in 1955. In 1958, when the subject was 37 years old, he experienced a calamitous number of life changes. His wife developed a depressive illness while he was on a cruise. He returned home to find out she had moved out with all of his household effects, including $5,000.00 from their savings account. He located her in another city, living with another man. He was unable to recover any of his belongings. One week after returning to ship, while working in the galley, he received a severe electrical shock and almost died. His recovery was delayed by the development of aphonia [loss of voice] which was thought to be on the basis of a conversion reaction. He gained a divorce and took charge of his two children. Subsequently, however, he entered into a chronic neurotic depressive reaction for which he received discharge and disability. Around this time his tension symptoms, headaches, and gastric distress returned. (p. 517)

A variation of the life change questionnaire has been developed that is specific to the hospital situation. Volicer, Isenberg, and Burns (1977) have devised the Hospital Stress Rating Scale to assess the degree of stress associated with different aspects of hospitalization. The questionnaire was devised by having a large number of medical and surgical patients rate a number of hospital-related events in terms of perceived stressfulness. As shown in Table 3-2, the events rated as most stressful were not, as one might think, always related to the physical situation (sleeping in a room with strangers, using a bedpan, staying in bed all day). Some of the most stressful events involved failures of communication, such as not being told the nature of the diagnosis, having questions ignored, not knowing the results or reasons for treatment, and perceiving the staff as using difficult words and being in a continual hurry. These problems are easy to solve by improving communication between the health professional and the patient.

Life Stress and Perceived Control

The Social Readjustment Rating Questionnaire does not distinguish between life changes that are positive and life changes that are negative. Both marriage and death, for example, are viewed as two events that simply require so much adaptation and are, therefore, stressful. As shown in terms of R. S. Lazarus's model, any system of stress must take into account the coping mechanisms at an individual's grasp. One powerful coping variable that has been examined extensively is the

Table 3-2   Hospital Stress Factors

Factor	Stress-scale Events	Assigned Rank	Mean Rank Score
1. Unfamiliarity of surroundings	Having strangers sleep in the same room with you	01	13.9
	Having to sleep in a strange bed	03	15.9
	Having strange machines around	05	16.8
	Being awakened in the night by the nurse	06	16.9
	Being aware of unusual smells around you	11	19.4
	Being in a room that is too cold or too hot	16	21.7
	Having to eat cold or tasteless food	21	23.2
	Being cared for by an unfamiliar doctor	23	23.4
2. Loss of independence	Having to eat at different times than you usually do	02	15.4
	Having to wear a hospital gown	04	16.0
	Having to be assisted with bathing	07	17.0
	Not being able to get newspapers, radio or TV when you want them	08	17.7
	Having a roommate who has too many visitors	09	18.1
	Having to stay in bed or the same room all day	10	19.1
	Having to be assisted with a bedpan	13	21.5
	Not having your call light answered	35	27.3
	Being fed through tubes	39	29.2
	Thinking you may lose your sight	49	40.6
3. Separation from spouse	Worrying about your spouse being away from you	20	22.7
	Missing your spouse	38	28.4
4. Financial problems	Thinking about losing income because of your illness	27	25.9
	Not having enough insurance to pay for your hospitalization	36	27.4
5. Isolation from other people	Having a roommate who is seriously ill or cannot talk with you	12	21.2
	Having a roommate who is unfriendly	14	21.6
	Not having friends visit you	15	21.7
	Not being able to call family or friends on the phone	22	23.3

	Having the staff be in too much of a hurry	26	24.5
	Thinking you might lose your hearing	45	34.5
6. Lack of information	Thinking you might have pain because of surgery or test procedures	19	22.4
	Not knowing when to expect things will be done to you	25	24.2
	Having nurses or doctors talk too fast or use words you can't understand	29	26.4
	Not having your questions answered by the staff	37	27.6
	Not knowing the results or reasons for your treatments	41	31.9
	Not knowing for sure what illnesses you have	43	34.0
	Not being told what your diagnosis is	44	34.1
7. Threat of severe illness	Thinking your appearance might be changed after your hospitalization	17	22.1
	Being put in the hospital because of an accident	24	26.9
	Knowing you have to have an operation	32	26.9
	Having a sudden hospitalization you weren't planning to have	34	27.2
	Knowing you have a serious illness	46	34.6
	Thinking you might lose a kidney or some other organ	47	35.6
	Thinking you might have cancer	48	39.2
8. Separation from family	Being in the hospital during holidays or special family occasions	18	22.3
	Not having family visit you	31	26.5
	Being hospitalized far away from home	33	27.1
9. Problems with medications	Having medications cause you discomfort	28	26.0
	Feeling you are getting dependent on medications	30	26.4
	Not getting relief from pain medications	40	31.2
	Not getting pain medication when you need it	42	32.4

Source: Volicer, B. J., Isenberg, M. A., and Burns, M. W. Medical-surgical differences in hospital stress factors. *Journal of Human Stress*, 1977, *3*, 7. Reprinted from *Journal of Human Stress*, vol. 3, no. 2, June, 1977, p. 7.

perceived control an organism believes that it has over a stressful stimulus.

For years it was believed that organisms in control of situations were much more susceptible to the effects of stress than organisms not in control. This notion came directly from the classic "executive monkey" study that was carried out by Brady, Porter, Conrad, and Mason (1958). In this study, pairs of monkeys were placed in an environment in which one of the members (the "executive") had to press a lever in response to the onset of a light if they both were to avoid shock. In this study only the executive monkeys developed the ulcers. This study could not be replicated, and according to Weiss (1972) the results might have been an artifact of the procedure. The monkeys were not initially randomly assigned to the two conditions; rather, the executives were chosen from the group that began to bar press first. These monkeys, according to Weiss, might have been more emotional to begin with.

The general view today is that organisms that do not have control over stressful stimuli are the most susceptible to physical disorders. Evidence for this hypothesis is based mainly on animal experiments. For example, Weiss uses an experimental situation in which one rat can avoid electric shock by touching its nose to a panel. A second rat is given exactly the same shock, but it has no control over it. Both animals receive exactly the same number of shocks, but only one has control over the shock. The animals that have control over the shock develop far fewer ulcers than their helpless partners. Additional experiments have demonstrated that relevant response feedback is also an important variable in determining the degree of ulceration. Thus, if an animal makes a response to avoid a shock and as it does so it hears a tone that serves as a signal that the "correct" response was made, this animal shows less ulceration than animals that simply make the response and avoid the shock but do not receive immediate feedback that the response was the correct one.

Engel (Weiss, 1972) believes that the experimental situation created by Weiss comes very close to what actually occurs in the clinical situation. He believes that the single most important correlate with disease onset is that, before the disease becomes manifest, the patient goes through a period of *giving up*. *Giving up* means that for the moment the person has, or believes he has, no solutions to his dilemma. In a sense, he simply has lost control over the situation. The concept of loss of control has special significance for understanding problems of the aged. Schulz (1976) found more positive feeling expressed by senior citizens who could predict and control visits by an undergraduate student than by senior citizens who could not predict and control similar visits. Gerontology programs should provide the aged with as much control over their lives as is possible. Seligman (1975) has also emphasized the dangers of loss of control in the aged: "The aged are most susceptible to loss of control. . . . We force them to retire at 65, we place them in old age homes. We ignore our grandparents, we shunt them aside—we are a nation that deprives old persons of control over the most meaningful events in their lives. We kill them" (p. 185). To support this strong statement, Seligman referred to an unpublished study by Ferrari. A group of 55 women over 65 years of age that had applied for admission to an old-age home were asked how much freedom of choice they had in moving to the home, how many other possibilities were open to them, and how much pressure their relatives applied to them. Of the 17 women who said that they had no alternative but to move to the home, 8 died after 4 weeks in residence and 16 were dead by 10 weeks. Apparently only 1 person out of the 38 who had an alternative died in the initial period. These deaths were called "unexpected" by the staff. The women who died might have had the strongest feelings of loss of control over their lives.

Coronary-prone Behavior Pattern

Modern civilizations are witnessing a frightening increase in the incidence of coronary heart disease. Not only is heart disease increasing in frequency, it is also afflicting younger and younger individuals. Unless its cause and prevention are isolated, the World Health Organization has predicted that coronary heart disease may result in coming years in the "greatest epidemic mankind has faced" (Jenkins, 1971). Coronary heart disease occurs when the coronary arteries narrow to such an extent that they cannot transport enough blood to supply the muscles of the heart with sufficient oxygen and nourishment. The condition is often experienced as pain emanating from the chest, shoulder, and arm. This state is called *angina pectoris* and occurs at the moment the heart suffers from the shortage of oxygen. If the lack of oxygen is prolonged and part of the heart muscle dies, a condition known as *myocardial infarction* results.

What causes heart disease? High-cholesterol diet, elevated blood pressure, and cigarette smoking are the major physical factors that are known to influence the incidence of coronary heart disease. Cholesterol in particular is believed to lead to a narrowing of the arteries by contributing to the formation of grease-laden plaques within the arteries. Although these factors are major determinants of heart disease, there are many instances of heart disease in which the afflicted individual has normal cholesterol levels, normal blood pressure, and does not smoke. It is seldom mentioned, however, that these physical risk factors are totally absent in nearly 50% of all new cases of coronary heart disease (Russek & Russek, 1976).

In recent years attention has shifted from physical risk factors to psychological risk factors in heart disease. The shift began with the publication of a book by two cardiologists Friedman and Rosenman (1974) entitled *Type A Behavior and Your Heart.* Their thesis was that a specific behavior pattern, called *coronary-prone behavior* or *Type A behavior,* may contribute more to heart disease than all the physical risk factors combined. Actually, physicians have suspected for years that a certain lifestyle might be the basis of many instances of heart disease.

The coronary-prone, or Type A, behavior pattern is described as a lifestyle characterized by extremes of competitiveness, striving for achievement, aggressiveness, haste, impatience, restlessness, hyper-alertness, explosiveness of speech, tenseness of facial musculature, and feelings of being under the pressure of time and under the challenge of responsibility (Jenkins, 1971). The Type A behavior pattern represents a coping style geared toward asserting and maintaining control over potentially uncontrollable situations (Burnam, Pennebaker, & Glass, 1975). Because control over all aspects of the environment is critical for these individuals, they must accelerate the pace at which they live and work in order to maintain this mastery. Thus time urgency becomes an essential part of their psychological makeup. In a simple but clever experiment, Type As and Type Bs were asked to read a technical passage out loud with the instruction to stop after they had estimated 1 minute had elapsed. The hypothesis was that Type As, because of their sense of urgency, would find time to pass very slowly. Indeed, the mean number of seconds that elapsed before signaling was 52.6 for Type As and 75.0 for Type Bs. In addition, Type As, because of their hard-driving ambitious behavior patterns, worked harder and faster than Type Bs at solving simple arithmetic problems in the absence of time deadlines.

Friedman and Rosenman use a clinical interview to determine the presence (Type A) or absence (Type B) of these behaviors in their subjects. Emphasis is placed mainly on the motor characteristics rather than on the content of a subject's responses. The researchers have been criticized for using clinical techniques, as opposed to objective techniques, to classify subjects into Type A or Type B groups. In defense of their approach, however, they maintain that a questionnaire method of assessment is a weaker predictor of coronary heart disease than the interview procedure (Jenkins, Zyzanski, & Rosenman, 1971).

Regardless of the type of behavioral assessment used, a number of studies (reviewed by Jenkins, 1976; Rowland & Sokol, 1977) have demonstrated a relationship between coronary-prone behaviors and heart disease. The most extensive series of observations have been made by Friedman and his colleagues (Rosenman, Friedman, Straus, Wurm, Jenkins, & Messinger, 1966; Rosenman, Friedman, Straus, Jenkins, Zyzanski, & Wurm, 1970; Rosenman, Brand, Jenkins, Friedman, Straus, & Wurm, 1975). Their project, often referred to as the Western Collaborative Group Study, began in 1961 when over 3,000 men between the ages of 39 and 59 and free of heart disease were rated as Type A or Type B. These men were then measured annually on behavior patterns, physical risk factors, and changes in cardiovascular status. The cardiovascular assessment was performed by a technician who had no knowledge of the men's initial behavior-pattern ratings.

After 2½ years, the researchers examined the Type A and Type B groups for the development of heart disease. In the age categories of 39-to-49 years and 50-to-59 years, Type A men had 6.5 and 1.9 times the incidence of coronary disease as Type B men. In a later study of 133 of the initially healthy men, a higher incidence of coronary disease was again found in the Type A men. Twice as many Type A men as Type B men were found in the heart-disease group. The relationship held even after the use of a statistical technique to control for the influence of physical risk factors such as age, heredity, cigarette usage, serum cholesterol levels. Thus the relationship between Type A behavior and heart disease could not be explained away by the argument that Type A men may simply smoke more than Type B men, for example. After 8½ years of the study, 257 men had developed coronary heart disease, and the results showed that the incidence of clinical coronary heart disease was twice as frequent in Type As as in Type Bs. This extensive project represented a convincing demonstration of the involvement of behavior in heart disease and requires that we begin seriously to question the rationale behind value systems that encourage the development of such behavior patterns.

Sex Differences and Heart Disease

In an article entitled "Why Do Women Live Longer than Men," the biologist Ingrid Waldron (1976) pointed out that in 1920 the life expectancy for women was 56 years and for men, 54. Also in 1920, male death rates were no more than 30% higher than female death rates. By 1970 the sex differential for mortality had changed drastically. The life expectancy for females had increased to 75, almost 8 years longer than the life expectancy for males. By 1970 male death rates exceeded female death rates by as much as 180% for the age group 15-to-24 years old and 110% for those 55-to-64 years old.

Coronary heart disease strikes twice as many males as females. Why the difference? One explanation that has been offered to account for the sex difference in coronary rates relates to genetic differences. It is assumed that female sex hormones reduce cholesterol levels in the blood and thereby reduce the risk of heart disease. The evidence for this hypothesis is not conclusive. Another variable that contributes to the sex difference in heart disease is smoking. Cigarette smoking increases the risk of heart disease and more males than females smoke cigarettes. Although smoking contributes to heart disease, nonsmoking males still suffer from more coronary disease than women. Therefore, smoking alone cannot account for the sex-ratio differences.

Waldron proposed that a major factor that might account for the sex differences in heart disease is that more males than females manifest the coronary-prone behavior pattern. She has shown that Type A females, although suffering less heart disease than Type A males, experience more heart disease than both Type B males and Type B females. Males who do not develop the ambitious, time-pressured behavior pattern have as low a risk of coronary heart disease as Type B females.

Historically, the female has not been reinforced, either during childhood or during adult years, for aggressive, competitive behaviors. Aggression in males is typically rewarded with a successful career, whereas aggression in females is often rewarded with the label "frustrated bitch." One might expect, with more and more females seeking careers, that the sex-ratio differences in heart disease will decrease. For example, females employed full-time are more Type A than housewives. As of now, there is no indication that male-female mortality ratios are decreasing. The present data indicate that, for most diseases, the ratios are stable or increasing (Johnson, 1977). Women continue to enjoy lower death rates than men, and the improvement in women's longevity is increasing faster than it is for men. Johnson states that deleterious health effects associated with the changing status of women, if present, will not be visible for some time because chronic diseases take years to develop.

The Future

Is it possible to retrain individuals not to engage in the pattern of behavior characteristic of the Type A personality? Some preliminary data suggest that such a goal is indeed possible. Suinn (1974) has designed a cardiac stress management training program that has two objectives. First, the coronary-prone individual is taught to reduce his exposure to stress-eliciting situations associated with deadlines, rapid-paced activities, and competitive activities. Much of this objective is accomplished without a loss in productivity simply by rescheduling activities. The second objective deals with the anxiety a Type A individual experiences when he initially discontinues habitual activities. The Type A person often experiences intense anxiety after his behaviors are reduced. The anxiety eventually compels the individual to return to his previous lifestyle. To combat the anxiety Suinn trains the individual to use muscle relaxation.

Suinn reported that all of the individuals that have undergone his program have been enthusiastic about the results. Some of the individual comments were: "I've learned since my heart attack to delegate more authority and responsibility to my employees." "I feel that I could accomplish as much or more without the previous stress that I put on myself." "It's easier for me to cope with matters than it was. . . . I don't fly off the handle at every little thing. Through the help of this program the stress has more or less vanished from my picture."

The Stanford Heart Disease Prevention Program is working toward the development of programs that are capable of reducing the risk factors for heart disease in the public at large. In one study the researchers (Farquhar, Wood, Breitrose, Haskell, Meyer, Maccoby, Alexander, Brown, McAlister, Nash, & Stern, 1977) compared the effectiveness of a mass-media campaign (involving television, radio, newspapers, billboards, posters) with face-to-face counseling and instruction. Both forms of intervention led to similar reductions in the coronary risk factors of the subjects and to similar maintenance of these changes at a 2-year follow-up. Efforts are now underway to develop mass-media techniques that will stimulate the public to develop and coordinate their own prevention programs.

Although such programs are encouraging, greater preventive efforts are required at the societal level if the incidence of heart disease is to be reduced substantially. Waldron and Johnston (1976) described the large-scale changes that are required as follows:

> We believe that efforts to change or to avert the Coronary Prone Behavior Pattern will be more successful and beneficial if directed at

teenagers and young adults, rather than at middle-aged cardiac patients whose coronary arteries already have suffered considerable irreversible damage. Many young people appear to adopt the Coronary Prone Behavior Pattern only at times when they are under pressure, especially pressure arising from competition for the limited number of highly rewarding jobs available. . . . Thus, a major cause of the development of the Coronary Prone Behavior Pattern appears to be the scarcity of satisfying jobs and the large differentials in pay and intrinsic rewards for the jobs which are available. This suggests that fewer people would develop this behavior pattern if more institutions were restructured along the lines already accomplished by a variety of businesses, with substantial increases in the sharing of responsibility and profits. This type of restructuring leads to increased satisfaction for most employees and a decrease in hierarchical differentials. Such changes could reduce the competitive pressures which currently contribute to man's excess mortality; they could also open the way for women to obtain the benefits which more and more of them are seeking in jobs, without the excessive pressures and elevated mortality which men currently suffer.

These are but some examples of the types of social and behavioral changes which are suggested by our analysis. Many of these changes will be difficult to achieve; however, the potential benefits include not only decreased mortality but also improvements in the quality of life. (p. 25)

Depression

Virtually everyone has experienced states of depression. In the majority of instances, the symptoms are mild and disappear within a short time. In other instances the symptoms are more persistent, more recurrent, and more debilitating. Eventually the individual may come to view these symptoms as a "disease" and seek medical assistance. Depression may be the most common psychological disorder seen in general practice and outpatient clinics (Beck, 1972). The exact incidence of clinical depression is unknown, but drug-consumption statistics indicate that antidepressant prescriptions are second only to those for tranquilizers. Clinical depression is at least twice as frequent in women as in men (Paykel, 1976).

Although it is difficult to know whether the incidence of depression has increased over the years, there is evidence that the incidence of suicide has increased dramatically during the past 20 years. Unsuccessful attempted suicide has increased fourfold during this period, the greatest frequency occurring among young women. Depression is considered to be the most frequent psychological disorder that precedes suicide.

Because of its prevalence and its association with suicide, depression has been the target of extensive research. This research has been hampered, however, by the lack of a precise definition of depression. Some theorists believe that clinical depression is simply a more intense form of the normal condition of feeling unhappy or "down." Other theorists reject the notion that normal depression and clinical depression differ only in terms of intensity. These theorists believe that clinical depression differs qualitatively from normal depression. Related to the problem of definition is the fact that there is no single comprehensive theory of depression. Different theorists have emphasized the importance of social, environmental, psychological, and biochemical variables in understanding the etiology of depression. Unfortunately, these theories are generally not considered from an integrated perspective. The failure to appreciate the psychobiological nature of depression often leads to confusion as to whether any particular patient instance of depression is caused by biochemical or psychological disturbances. The patients themselves will often vehemently deny that psychological factors are the basis of their depressed condition. In Chapter 3, exactly the same problem was noted with stress-related disorders such as chronic headache. Is one to conclude, as many writers have done, that some forms of depression have a psychological cause whereas other forms of depression have a biochemical cause? Definitely not. The search for either-or causes of depression fails to recognize that subtle psychobiological processes may cause and maintain the disorder. Repeated negative life experiences can produce a vulnerability to depression that operates largely outside of the patient's awareness. If the vulnerability goes unrecognized, attacks of depression will seemingly occur in the absence of provocation, leading to a situation that is puzzling to both the practitioner and the patient.

Symptoms of Depression

Depression is associated with both psychological and physiological symptoms. The most common signs and symptoms of depression are:

1. sad, lonely, apathetic, or irritable mood;
2. an exaggeratedly negative, self-punitive self-concept;
3. disturbed bodily functioning, accompanied by decreased appetite, poor sleep, constipation, and diminished sexual interest;
4. physical complaints of aches, weakness, fatigue;
5. altered activity level with slowing or agitation;
6. impaired thought processes with high distractibility, indecisiveness, disinterestedness, and preoccupation with hopelessness and helplessness. (Becker, 1974)

The emotional feelings of depressed patients center on *dysphoria*, a technical term for feeling badly. Commonly used adjectives to describe this condition are blue, sad, hopeless, and miserable. There is also a loss of interest in many activities, with the loss becoming more widespread as the depression becomes more severe. Loss of interest might begin with activities related to the patient's role, as a professional, student, husband, or wife, and eventually encompass family and friends. Loss of interest usually begins with activities involving responsibility and obligation (Beck, 1967). Thus a student might lose his desire to study and a college professor might lose his desire to prepare lectures. Associated with this loss of motivation is a desire to break away from the monotony of existing duties. Such escapist tendencies are seldom actualized except through daydreaming.

The general dysphoria and loss of interest, if severe, may lead to what has been called "paralysis of the will":

> The patient may have a major problem in mobilizing himself to perform even the most elemental and vital tasks such as eating, elimination, or taking medication to relieve his distress. The essence of the problem appears to be that, although he can define for himself what he should do, he does not experience any internal stimulus to do it. Even when urged, cajoled, or threatened, he does not seem able to arouse any desire to do these things. (Beck, 1967, p. 28)

From this description it is not surprising that severe depressives also show loss of appetite and weight and also a loss of sexual interest. Additional physical symptoms include sleep disturbance and easy fatigability. The term *masked depression* is used to describe patients whose initial complaint is of some physical symptoms but who upon examination admit to being depressed.

Reactive versus Endogenous Depression

In diagnosing depression, a distinction is frequently made between *exogenous* depression and *endogenous* depression. The term *exogenous* (coming from without) *depression* is used to describe depression that results from psychosocial causes, such as a death in the family or the loss of a job. When the onset of a depressive episode is not traceable to a precipitating life experience, it is assumed that the disorder is endogenous (coming from within) and hence biological in origin.

Table 4-1 lists the major symptom differences that are believed to exist between exogenous and endogenous depression (Lewinsohn, Zeiss, Zeiss, & Haller, 1977). The focus of concern for the exogenous depressive is primarily negative interpersonal events, whereas the focus of concern for the endogenous depressive is primarily negative

Table 4-1   Symptoms Associated with Exogenous and
Endogenous Depression (Lewinsohn, Zeiss, Zeiss, & Haller, 1977)

Exogenous	*Endogenous*
1. feelings of bearing troubles	1. feeling helpless and powerless
2. concern for the welfare of family and friends	2. feeling self-lazy
3. feeling at "end of rope"	3. feeling unable to act
4. crediting problems to excessive family and/or job responsibilities	4. "retarded" (slow, feeling tired, worn out, without energy) for no adequate reason
5. precipitating stress	5. insomnia
6. self-pity	6. showing no interest in life

subjective and bodily feelings. Does the presence of different symptoms mean that the cause of each class of depression is unique? Not necessarily, because depression may begin as a reaction to psychosocial events but eventually lead to a condition in which subjective and bodily feelings are the primary focus. Endogenous depression might reflect the outcome of years of nonspecific poor life experiences. A housewife who suddenly becomes clinically depressed might not recognize that she became so largely because she was increasingly ignored by her family. Once in the state of severe depression she may now be too disturbed to recognize (or care about) the precipitating events. Also it is characteristic of some depressed patients to deny strongly that external events could have precipitated their condition or that these events, if they were reversed, could improve their condition. It is not surprising, therefore, that clinicians have a difficult time identifying psychosocial causes for complaints of depression. Environmental and cognitive events probably precede all instances of the depression syndrome, especially in the formative stages. Once the feelings and symptoms of depression become established, the afflicted individual shifts his attention to these same feelings and symptoms and becomes less and less aware of the environmental and cognitive events that precipitated the condition.

Biogenic Amine Theory of Depression

Depressed patients usually are treated with antidepressant medication. This form of treatment assumes that the patient's problem is primarily the result of (or at least controlled by) a biochemical deficiency. Interest in the biochemistry of depression began in the 1950s with reports that 15% to 20% of patients receiving the drug reserpine for controlling hypertension developed symptoms of depression. In 1957 it was discovered that reserpine depletes body cells of specific biogenic amines, namely *norepinephrine* and *serotonin*. Norepinephrine and serotonin are transmitters within the central nervous system that belong to the larger class of biochemicals labeled *catecholamines* and *indoleamines*, respectively. The catecholamine hypothesis of depression states that some, if not all, depressions are associated with an absolute or relative deficiency of catecholamines in the brain (Schildkraut, 1965). One site in particular that is believed to be involved is the hypothalamus, which plays a major role in emotional behaviors. Interestingly, the hypothalamus also contains the highest concentration of norepinephrine-activated nerve cells in the entire brain (Frazer & Stinnett, 1973).

Klein (1974) hypothesized that structural changes within unspecified regions of the hypothalamus may account for the depressed patient's inability to gain pleasure from activities in general:

> It is postulated that if the pleasure mechanism becomes unresponsive, one cannot experience pleasure either from current sensory input or via the method of anticipatory or recollective imagery. The person with a normal pleasure mechanism when thinking of a future pleasurable situation, experiences an anticipatory glow. If the pleasure mechanism is malfunctioning, however, this glow does not occur and the person simply has the cold experience of anticipating a situation that does not evoke any warm affective response.
>
> This specific impairment in the ability to respond pleasurably to anticipation is quite different from the decreased ability to anticipate future positive reinforcement that occurs following a severe disappointment or the belief that the world is a nonrewarding place. Somebody who has suffered an acute dysphoric disappointment reaction can experience pleasure, given the proper input. Although his pessimism would seem quite similar to the pessimism of the [endogenous] patient, they represent two quite different processes. (p. 449)

Are the symptoms of severe depression controlled by the depletion of biogenic amines? One general finding that is emerging from the complex literature dealing with this question is that biogenic amines, in isolation, cannot account for the feelings of depression. Recall from the beginning of this section that the biogenic amine hypothesis originated with the observation that reserpine led in some instances to symptoms of depression. Yet the incidence of reserpine-induced depression has been grossly exaggerated (Mendels & Frazer, 1974). Symptoms of depression occur only in patients that have a previous history of psychiatric disturbance. Thus biogenic amine depletion may not cause depression but instead may induce depression symptoms in susceptible patients. Also, injections of reserpine do not produce depression in normal subjects. A small percentage of the subjects develop what is called "pseudodepression," a reaction characterized by tranquilization and fatigue. None of the subjects becomes suicidal, self-deprecatory, or blue. These observations are very similar to the as-if-afraid reactions of normal subjects after receiving injections of epinephrine to elicit fear and anxiety (see Chapter 2). Once again, it is apparent that any emotion, abnormal or normal, is likely to be an outcome of a complex interaction of cognitive and physiological variables. Reserpine-induced depression, when it occurs, may be due, not to the pharmacological action of reserpine per se, but rather to the psychological meaning attributed by the patient to the drug-produced physiochemical changes. Investigators have used other substances to deplete biogenic amines in normal subjects and have found similar outcomes. Alpha-methyl-para-tyrosine (AMPT) selectively depletes the brain of dopamine and norepinephrine by interfering with the synthesis of these substances. Sjoerdsma, Engelman, and Spector (1965) gave large doses of AMPT to medical students. The most frequently reported symptoms were sedation and fatigue. None of the patients developed a true depression.

Other investigators have reported lower-than-normal levels of biogenic amine metabolites in depressives (van Praag, Korf, & Schut, 1973). Moreover, biogenic amine depletion may occur only in some forms of depression. Asberg, Thoren, and Traskman (1976) found a depletion of the serotonin metabolite 5-hydroxyindoleacetic acid (5-HIAA) in only one subgroup of depressives. Within this subgroup, the levels of 5-HIAA were negatively correlated with the severity of rated depression: the lower the 5-HIAA the more severe the depression. It is unknown whether the depression produced the biochemical changes or the biochemical changes produced the depression.

The biogenic amine hypothesis has increased our understanding of the physiochemical systems contributing to depression. The available evidence suggests, however, that other variables that are psychological in nature determine whether biogenic amine depletion will lead to depression. The notion of a direct one-to-one relationship between a specific chemical event and symptoms of depression is being abandoned (Akiskal & McKinney, 1975). Depression is neither a biological phenomenon nor a psychological phenomenon but, rather, a psychobiological phenomenon.

If a simple relationship between brain amines and depression does not exist, then why are so many patients treated with antidepressive drugs? Some clinicians believe that depression is now largely under chemical control. The majority of antidepressant drugs are believed to exert their effects primarily by increasing the central nervous system levels of circulating amines. One chemical class of antidepressants is the tricyclic compounds, the best known of which is imipramine. This drug is believed to potentiate or enhance the effects of the available norepinephrine. Another class of antidepressants, the monoamine oxidase inhibitors, are believed to work by inhibiting the action of monoamine oxidase, which is an enzyme that breaks down amines. Consequently, the circulating amines circulate longer. With both classes of drugs it is assumed that by increasing circulating levels of norepinephrine, the depression will lift.

Do antidepressants in fact work? Apparently, the overall therapeutic effectiveness of tricyclic andidepressants is greater than that of individual psychotherapy and group therapy (Ban, 1975). For example, an average improvement rate of 65% to 70% has been claimed for imipramine treatment. Morris and Beck (1974), after reviewing a number of drug-outcome studies, concluded that between 60% and 70% of depressed patients treated with antidepressant medication show a significant improvement. It must be emphasized that the benefits of antidepressant medication are restricted to providing patients with short-term relief from the debilitating sensations and feelings of depression. In instances in which the patient has a well-established negative belief system or is functioning in a nonrewarding environment, antidepressant medication is likely to provide little lasting relief.

ECT or EST represents another form of physical treatment for depression. One hypothesis is that ECT increases the level of circulating amines (Baldessarini, 1975). ECT involves placing electrodes on either side of the head at the temples and introducing a strong, brief current. The current induces a convulsive seizure that lasts for a number of seconds. A muscle relaxant is administered prior to the electric shock to minimize the danger of undesirable side effects such as bone fractures and cardiovascular dysfunctions. Although ECT has been condemned by many as a barbaric form of treatment, there is a persistent feeling by those who use the technique that it often produces immediate and dramatic recoveries from severe depression. For years Costello (1976) has maintained that the literature supporting the efficacy of ECT is poorly designed and poorly controlled. If one doubts the importance of controlled research, consider an incident referred to by Costello that took place in a mental hospital in

England. Patients in that hospital had received ECT from a machine that unknown to anyone had not worked in 2 years. No one noticed any change in the success or failure rates during this period. One fact that is known is that many patients relapse following ECT treatment. Thus if the technique does lead to an improvement in the patient's condition, the improvement is transitory. The patient then requires more and more ECT sessions separated by shorter and shorter intervals. Increasing amine circulation, if that is how ECT works, is not a sufficient technique for treating depression.

Given that there may be a deficiency of catecholamines associated with depression, we are still left with the problem of why this is so. Schildkraut and Kety (1967) emphasized this point in their review of the biogenic amine hypothesis of depression:

> It is not likely that changes in the metabolism of the biogenic amines alone will account for the complex phenomena of normal or pathological affect. Whereas the effects of these amines at particular sites in the brain may be of crucial importance in the regulation of affect, any comprehensive formulation of the physiology of affective state will have to include many other concomitant biochemical, physiological, and psychological factors. Although in this review of the relationship of biogenic amines to affective state relatively little has been said concerning the intricate set of environmental and psychological determinants of emotion, the importance of these factors must be stressed.
>
> The normally occurring alterations in affective state induced by environmental events is well known to all, from personal experience. The interactions between such environmental determinants of affect, various physiological factors, and the complexity of psychological determinants, including cognitive factors derived from the individual's remote and immediate past experiences, have received only limited study . . . however . . ., only within such a multifactorial framework may one expect to understand fully the relationship of the biogenic amines to emotional state. (p. 28)

Personal Loss and Separation

An experience variable that has received attention with respect to depression is past and present personal loss. Freud emphasized the importance of loss in depression. By *loss* is meant the disruption of a significant attachment bond, such as the death of or separation from a loved one. Freud observed that both mourning over a personal loss and depression are characterized by symptoms of dejection and loss of interest in the environment. He also observed that self-criticism and guilt are usually only characteristic of depression, and it was this observation that led to his theory of depression. The individual who is mourning will eventually at a conscious level reinvest the psychic energy that was tied to the lost person in another object or person, and by doing so, the individual will gradually come out of the mourning state. The depressive, on the other hand, is not able to reinvest the energy in others. Rather he introjects or incorporates, at an unconscious level, the characteristics of the lost person and now displays love and hate feelings toward himself just as he would if the significant person were still present. Thus hostility and self-hate are now expressed directly at his own ego.

Although Freud's position on separation and loss as leading to inwardly directed aggression is not widely accepted, a number of theorists continue to examine the hypothesis that separation and loss are major participants of depression. Depressivelike behaviors following loss have been observed in both man and animals.

In a naturalistic study, Spitz (1946) studied the behavioral effects of mother-infant separation. Spitz observed 123 infants of unwed mothers in an institutional nursery. There were periods during which the mothers had to be away from their infants for months at a time. Some of these infants developed signs of apathy and passivity that Spitz termed *anaclitic depression*. The anaclitic depression syndrome occurred in 19 of the total number of infants observed. It began with an initial reaction of sadness followed by crying, screaming, and general protesting. As the reaction progressed the infants began to lose interest in all aspects of their environment. Finally, the infants became totally dejected and manifested many symptoms suggestive of severe depression. There was lack of responsiveness to persons in the environment, slowness of movement, loss of appetite, insomnia, withdrawal, and apathy. The final stage of the reaction appeared 4-to-6 weeks after the initial separation. The reaction was reversible inasmuch as the infants improved rapidly with the return of their mothers. No effort was made to assess whether this transitory separation in childhood had any influence in terms of susceptibility to depression in adulthood.

Separation and loss produce a similar syndrome in some species of lower organisms, suggesting that the behaviors observed by Spitz are innately determined. Kaufman and Rosenblum (1967) examined in four infant pigtail monkeys the effects of separation from their natural mothers. Prior to the separation, the infant monkeys were housed with their mother, father, and another adult female. The immediate reaction to the separation was loud screams, agitation, and general erratic behaviors. These behaviors lasted for 24-to-36 hours during which time the infants did not sleep.

The pattern of reaction then changed dramatically for three of the four infant monkeys. These monkeys ceased the majority of their behaviors and sat huddled in a ball. Their facial muscles sagged creating the appearance of dejection and sadness. Their movements became slow; responses to social invitation ceased; and play behavior stopped. Interestingly, eating behavior was not disrupted. This reaction persisted for 5-to-6 days and then began to lift. The recovery began with the resumption of an upright posture followed by renewed interest and exploration of the environment. By the 4th week of separation, their behaviors were approaching those of preseparation. Later when they were returned to their mothers there was an increase in the strength of the mother-infant relationship.

In primates the effect of separation is often species-specific and influenced by a host of environmental and developmental variables (Becker, 1977). It is possible, however, that a common physiochemical mechanism is the basis of human depression and primate "depression." No studies known to me have attempted to alleviate primate depression with ECT.

The possibility that adult depressives have acquired a susceptibility to depression because of personal loss or separation that occurred during childhood has been examined. Some studies have found a small association between early parental death and depression, whereas other studies have found no association between early loss and depression (Akiskal & McKinney, 1975). Brown, Harris, and Copeland (1977) found that the loss of a mother, but not a father, before the age of 11 was associated with increased vulnerability to depression in females. Moreover, the relationship was strongest for female depressives who were severely disturbed (retarded in movement, thought, and emotion). Of patients having a past loss by death of mother, 82% were severely disturbed. Brown et al. hypothesized that, during the early years of development, the mother is the primary source of the support and appreciation necessary for adequate development of a girl's self-esteem. The absence of this support may act as a vulnerability factor with the way the female deals with loss in adulthood. Other vulnerability factors for females identified by the researchers were: presence at home of three or more children aged less than 14; lack of a confiding relationship with a husband; and lack of full- or part-time employment.

Paykel (1976) examined the loss hypothesis in terms of the more immediate situation of depressives. He initially set out to determine if life changes occurred more frequently in depressives than nondepressives. He compared the life change scores (discussed in Chapter 3) of 185 depressed patients with the similar responses of a nonpatient control group. To minimize patient distortions, the data were collected, not when the patients were depressed, but several weeks later, when clinical improvement had taken place. Depressives were asked to indicate the frequency of life changes experienced for the period 6 months prior to the onset of the depressive symptoms. For the controls the same information was obtained for the period 6 months prior to data collection.

Overall, the depressives experienced more life changes than the controls. The depressives reported 1.69 events from the list per person as opposed to .59 for the controls. The greatest differences occurred with the following events: (a) increase in arguments with spouse, (b) marital separation, (c) start of a new type of work, (d) death of an immediate family member, (e) departure of a family member from home, (f) serious personal illness, and (g) change in work conditions.

Paykel then classified the events into a category that signified loss, as defined by a departure (such as death, divorce, separation) of a person from the patient's social field. These events were called *exits*. A secondary category of events, called *entrances*, was defined as the entrance (such as marriage or birth of a child) of a person into the patient's social field. Exits were reported far more frequently by depressives than by normals. The frequency of occurrence of entrances was similar across both groups. These data indicate the importance of searching for life changes in patients complaining of depression.

Learned Helplessness

Martin Seligman (1974, 1975) proposed an animal analogue of depression that might prove to be useful in isolating some of the cognitive and environmental precipitants of depression. His animal model is based on the concept of *learned helplessness*.

Seligman has demonstrated in dogs the debilitating effects of learned helplessness. The experimental technique consisted of a conditioned avoidance procedure. The dog was placed in a two-chamber device, called a *shuttlebox*, and required to jump the partition with the onset of a warning signal. A warning stimulus was presented followed by painful electric shock. If the dog made the appropriate response of jumping the barrier, it was able to avoid the electric shock. Under normal conditions dogs have no difficulty quickly learning this response.

> When an experimentally naive dog receives escape-avoidance training in a shuttlebox, the following behavior typically occurs: at the onset of the first traumatic electric shock, the dog runs frantically about, defecating, urinating, and howling, until it accidentally scrambles over the barrier and so escapes the shock. On the next trial, the dog, running and howling, crosses the barrier more quickly than on the preceding trial. This pattern continues until the dog learns to avoid shock altogether. (1974, p. 85)

What would happen in this situation to a dog that had previously been conditioned into a state of helplessness? Would this animal, Seligman wondered, learn the avoidance response as rapidly as the dogs that were not pretreated. To answer this question, Seligman exposed one group of dogs to a series of unavoidable shocks prior to the conditioned avoidance trials. Each of these dogs was strapped into a hammock and given a series of unsignaled, inescapable shocks. Then, 24 hours later, the dog was given signaled escape training in the shuttlebox.

> Such a dog's first reactions to shock in the shuttlebox are much the same as those of a naive dog. In dramatic contrast to a naive dog, however, a typical dog which has experienced uncontrollable shocks before avoidance training soon stops running and howling and sits or lies, quietly whining, until shock terminates. The dog does not cross the barrier and escape from shock. Rather it seems to give up and passively accepts the shock. On succeeding trials, the dog continues to fail to make escape movements and takes as much shock as the experimenter chooses to give. (1974, p. 85)

The debilitating effects of helplessness in animals have been known for some time. In 1957 Richter demonstrated that a condition of helplessness could produce sudden death in rats. He observed this phenomenon while comparing the stress reactions of wild and domestic rats. As the experimental stressor, he placed the rats individually in a tank of water from which there was no escape. He simply recorded the length of time the rats struggled to swim before drowning. He observed that a wild rat would usually swim for about 60 hours in a large tank of water before it drowned. A few rats, however, died within minutes after being dropped in the water.

Why did some rats drown so quickly after being placed in the tank? A partial answer to this question came when Richter discovered that he could manipulate the condition. If he gripped the rats in his hand until they stopped struggling before he placed them in the water, they would often dive suddenly to the bottom and drown. Richter hypothesized that restraining the rats and then confining them to the inescapable water tank abolished hope. He found additional support for his theory when he was able to prevent sudden death by teaching the rats that their situation was not hopeless. To do this he held the rats briefly and then let them go and then immersed them into the water and took them out again. These animals seemed to gain hope from this experience and swam much longer (before drowning).

What does learned helplessness in animals have to do with human depression? According to Seligman, there are a number of similarities between the two conditions. Both conditions are associated with behavioral passivity. His dogs would make no effort to make any response that might terminate the shock, a condition that he believes is analogous to the depressive's *paralysis of will*. Seligman also believes that both helpless dogs and depressed humans have learned that responding and reinforcement are independent. Even if the dogs were shown how to escape the shock, they resisted doing so. Initially the dogs had to be dragged from one side of the shuttlebox to the other side. Seligman feels that this condition is the basis of the depressive's complaints of feeling helpless, hopeless, and powerless:

> The depressed patient has learned or believes that he cannot control those elements of his life that relieve suffering or bring him gratification. In short, he believes he is helpless. Consider a few of the common precipitating events. What is the meaning of job failure or incompetence at school? Frequently, it means that all of a person's efforts have been in vain, his responses have failed to bring about the gratification he desired, and he cannot find responses that control reinforcement. When an individual is rejected by someone he loves, he can no longer control his significant source of gratification and support. When a parent or lover dies, the bereaved is in a situation in which he is powerless to produce or influence love from the dead person. Physical disease and growing old are helplessness situations par excellence. In these conditions, the person finds his own response ineffective and is often thrown into the care of others. (1974, p. 98)

There are other similarities between learned helplessness and depression. Both states dissipate with the passage of time. Dogs make little effort to escape if tested within 24 hours after the experience with inescapable shock. When intervals longer than 48 hours separate the sessions, the dogs respond in a normal fashion. Depression also dissipates in time; for many individuals, attacks of depression seem to follow a time course of days, weeks, or months. Norepinephrine depletion is another symptom that Seligman claims is common to both learned helplessness and depression.

The key to treating and preventing depression from the helplessness perspective is to teach the patient that responding and reinforcement are not independent. That is, the depressive must be taught that responding will produce the reinforcement that he desires. To illustrate, Seligman (Seligman, Klein, & Miller, 1976) described a treatment program called *antidepression milieu therapy.* The goal of this program in treating depressives is to induce anger, which Seligman believes is a powerful response for controlling one's environment.

> The Anti-Depressive (AD) program involves the attitude of "Kind-Firmness" (KF): patients are dealt with in a kind but firm manner, and patients are required to complete menial and monotonous tasks assigned to them without receiving any positive social reinforcement. Aggressive responses are encouraged and reinforced. When the patient emits depressed behavior, he is placed in the "sanding room" where he engages in such tasks as sanding a small block of wood, counting tiny seashells, and mopping floors. These activities are supervised by nursing assistants who forbid the patient to talk and continually point out all imperfections in the patient's work. Within a few hours, the patient typically becomes overtly hostile and "blows up." The patient is then allowed out of the room, and the staff responds to his aggressiveness with acceptance. (1976, p. 184)

This form of treatment has been found to be effective in reducing feelings of depression, passivity, and dependency (Taulbee & Wright, 1971). Whether or not it is learned helplessness that is being alleviated, however, is unknown. For example, anger may not be creating a "sense of control." Instead, it may simply be a response, like humor, that is incompatible with depression.

A number of concerns have been raised with respect to the learned helplessness model of depression. The behavioral passivity and lack of responding observed in the dogs may only bear a superficial resemblance to the human condition of depression. The depiction of depression as the more or less inevitable outcome of loss of control over some environmental event ignores the complex coping mechanisms available to humans (Rippere, 1977). Thus, some humans might react with depression to perceived loss of control, but others might not. The learned helplessness model does not specify the variables that will determine which kind of reaction will occur. Many of us, for example, hold beliefs that outcomes are independent of responses—at least for some situations. Some students, for example, believe that an essay grade is independent of their effort (not, it is to be hoped, a valid belief). In such cases, depression is not likely to result if the individual has an otherwise generally positive view of the self and the world (Blaney, 1977).

Another criticism is that depressives may generally not view their problem as originating from the loss of control over their environment. Rather than feeling helpless, depressives seem to be excessively concerned with personal responsibility for events that they view are within their immediate control. Guilt and self-criticism are characteristics common to depressed patients (Costello, 1978).

> The depressive's perseverating self-blame and self-criticism appear to be related to his egocentric notions of causality and his penchant for criticizing himself for his alleged deficiencies. He is particularly prone to ascribe adverse occurrences to some deficiency in himself, and then to rebuke himself for having this alleged defect. In the more severe cases, the patient may blame himself for happenings that are in no way connected with him, and abuse himself in a savage manner. (Beck, 1972, p. 24)

Calhoun, Cheney, and Dawes (1974) found that depressed women were more likely than others to attribute their periods of depression to causes within their personal control. Blaney concluded that "depressive individuals'. . . appear to be characterized by a great sense of responsibility and control regarding the outcomes in which they are involved, and this is the opposite of what the helplessness notion appears to predict" (p. 213). At this point, learned helplessness cannot be viewed as the main cause of all depressions but only as one of many possible cognitive-environmental determinants.

Faulty Cognitions

A major characteristic of depressed patients is their exaggerated negative self-concept. Cognitive themes involving low self-regard, self-criticism, self-blame, overwhelming problems, and suicidal wishes are common to depressives. The cognitions are distorted or unrealistic in that a patient tends to exaggerate his faults and problems. From this perspective, depression is more a cognitive disorder than an emotional disorder (Beck, 1967, 1972, 1976). The idiosyncratic nature of the depressive's reasoning processes often leads to behaviors that on the surface appear to be quite bizzare:

> A scientist, shortly after assuming the presidency of a prestigious scientific group, gradually became morose and confided to a friend that he had an overwhelming urge to leave his career and become a hobo.
> A devoted mother who had always felt strong love for her children started to neglect them and formulated a serious plan to destroy them and then herself.
> An epicurean who relished eating beyond all other satisfactions developed an aversion for food and stopped eating.
> A wealthy businessman publicly proclaimed his guilt over a few minor misdemeanors of some decades before, put on a beggar's clothes and begged for food.
> A woman, on hearing of the sudden death of a close friend, smiled for the first time in several weeks. (Beck, 1976, p. 3)

Beck gives a description of how faulty cognitions may initiate a chain reaction leading to clinical depression. Assume that a wife deserts her husband. The impact of the desertion will depend on the nature of the cognitions the husband has about his wife. The cognitions might consist of a series of positive associations that range from the realistic ("she is important to me") to the unrealistic ("I enjoy life only because of her"). The more absolute these positive associations, the greater will be the sense of loss. Thus, if the positive associations are exaggerated in nature, he might now begin to formulate exaggerated negative statements with respect to his self ("I am nothing without her;" "I can't go on without her").

A further outcome of the reaction might be that the husband begins to question his own self-worth ("If only I had been a better husband"). As the reaction develops, the husband's self-doubts expand into negative generalizations about himself, his world, and his future. The husband, now better described as the depressed patient, stops all activities that previously gave him pleasure. Life becomes meaningless, and he may begin to contemplate suicide. Physiological symptoms involving sleep disturbance and loss of appetite further aggravate the condition.

It is apparent from this example that Beck believes depressives engage in thinking that involves considerable distortion of reality. In his terms, depressives feel as they do because they commit certain errors of reasoning. From an examination of his interview data with depressed patients, he found that depressives tend to distort their daily interactions in the direction of self-blame, low self-esteem, and pessimism toward the suggestion of change. The depressive, for Beck, is constantly creating false problems and false conclusions. One of his patients, for example, reacted to his wife's tardiness in meeting him with the thought, "She might have died on the way." Such cognitions predispose the patient to see any positive event as potentially negative. This negative style is evident in the following passage provided by one of my students:

> I experienced a period of total hopelessness unlike any state I have known. In my mind, I felt that I had lost whatever chance I may have had for happiness. I felt defeated and was frightened of the future . . . I used apathy as a defense against this fear . . . It became an effort to relate to anything and to anyone . . . Good things that happen just don't count . . . Everything is either bad or neutral . . . I have a constant feeling that my brain is fogged . . . I am always tired . . . I must constantly fight against both these thoughts and the fatigue . . . .

Depressives have been shown to selectively screen input in a fashion that would perpetuate a negative outlook (Blaney, 1977). They have been found to recall material of negatively toned content more easily than material of positively toned content. Depressives have also been found, when given the choice of examining information positive or negative about themselves, to spend more time with the negative information than do controls. One study found that mild depression could be induced in undergraduate women by presenting false feedback and indicating that they were immature and uncreative (Ludwig, 1975). This study illustrates that manipulating a person's self-esteem can result in depression.

In treating depressives, Beck (1976) attempts to restructure their illogical thinking patterns. One goal in the procedure is to direct the depressive toward his use of *maladaptive ideation*. *Maladaptive ideation* refers to thinking that "interferes with the ability to cope with life experiences, unnecessarily disrupts internal harmony, and produces inappropriate or excessive emotional reactions that are painful." Beck believes that the thoughts of depressives are too absolute, too extreme, and too highly personalized. For example, a man suffering from depression following the death of his wife was possessed with extreme ideas such as "It's all my fault that she died."

Maladaptive thoughts often operate in an automatic fashion in that the individual is not aware of the presence of depressive ideations. Beck uses a technique called "filling in the blank" to bring these ideations to the patient's full awareness. Developing this awareness is achieved through practicing an A, B, C analysis of the problem. The activating stimulus is A, and C is the excessive, inappropriate response. B is the blank in the patient's mind that, when filled in, acts as a bridge between A and C. To illustrate, a patient may feel depressed in the presence of certain other individuals and not know why. The other individuals are represented by A; the depression by C; and the missing link may be a host of negative cognitions with the basic theme "people don't like me." By developing an awareness of these cognitions, it becomes possible to develop strategies with the patient for altering the nature of the cognitions. The simple act of becoming aware of their presence can be therapeutic because this awareness allows the patient to distance himself from the thoughts and to look at the thoughts in an objective fashion.

The goal of cognitive therapy is to modify the rules that currently govern the patient's behavior. Some of the rules used extensively by depressives are:

1. In order to be happy, I have to be successful in whatever I undertake.
2. To be happy, I must be accepted by all people at all times.
3. If I make a mistake, it means that I'm inept.
4. If somebody disagrees with me, it means he doesn't like me.

Beck breaks down a depressive's problem into several components and then goes to work on each of the components. For example, a complaint of depression can be analyzed at three levels: (a) the abnormal symptoms involving fatigue, crying, and suicidal threats; (b) the underlying motivational disturbances, such as the wish to escape from life; and (c) the illogical beliefs maintaining the depression, such as the belief that striving toward a goal is futile. Effective treatment involves effecting change at all three levels.

Very little information exists with respect to the demonstrated effectiveness of cognitive therapy in alleviating depression. Beck describes a study of his own that compared drug therapy (imipramine) with cognitive therapy. Initially the chemotherapy group and the cognitive therapy group showed similar improvements in their condition. At a 6-month follow-up, however, the improvement for the group treated with cognitive therapy was better than that of the drug-treated patients. Another study (Weissman, Klerman, Paykel, Prusoff, & Hanson, 1974) found cognitive therapy in combination with chemotherapy to be more effective in improving social adjustment in depressives than chemotherapy in isolation.

Existential Neurosis

For Beck, the majority of depressives have a distorted view of reality. Many individuals who experience depression view their perception of reality as quite accurate, however. A syndrome that comes to mind in this context is existential neurosis. The syndrome was especially pervasive in college students a few years ago.

> The cognitive component of the existential neurosis is meaninglessness, or chronic inability to believe the truth, importance, usefulness, or interest value of any of the things one is engaged in or can imagine doing. The most characteristic features of affective tone are blandness and boredom, punctuated by periods of depression which become less frequent as the disorder is prolonged. As to the realm of action, activity level may be low to moderate, but more important than the amount of activity is the introspective and objectively observable fact that activities are not chosen. There is little selectivity, it being immaterial to the person what if any activities he pursues. If there is any selectivity shown, it is in the direction of ensuring minimal expenditure of effort and decision making. (Maddi, 1967, p. 313)

These symptoms are very similar to those observed in depression.

The key to the origin of the syndrome is the manner in which an individual defines himself. A susceptible person is one who defines himself solely in terms of social roles and biological needs. Life then consists of seeking the means for gratifying a few biological needs and also of fulfilling obligations that are associated with particular social roles. Thus, such a person might define himself as a doctor, a nurse, a teacher, or a student. The behaviors of the person are then bound by materialistic expectations and social roles. Such a person would tend to worry about things such as whether he is considered by others to be conscientious or whether he is viewed as a nice person. These individuals are prone to develop an existential syndrome.

What are the conditions that will produce the syndrome? A major cause is any stress that forces the person to see the shallowness of his own self-definition. Economic recession, for example, may make the person's major social role useless to the larger society. We saw this happen in universities when far too many students were entering the labor market and suddenly could not find employment. The acquired social role provided by the university was suddenly perceived as worthless in a monetary sense.

A second and more subtle precipitant of existential neurosis is repeated confrontation by others on one's values. If we are repeatedly told that our values and goals are meaningless, then we might through introspection eventually reach the same conclusion. Such a phenomenon occurred on a mass scale when student radicals attacked the structures and values of society, including war, the work ethic, and motherhood. As a result, many people found it impossible to find a meaningful self-definition because they could no longer define themselves in terms of the roles that were traditionally associated with these activities. For many individuals, the confusion continues.

How does one acquire a self-concept that is immune to this kind of disorder? According to Maddi, the individual must learn to effectively utilize the psychological processes of symbolization, imagination, and judgment. The proper use of these processes allows the individual to lead a gratifying existence regardless of the particular role that he is currently engaged in. The individual sees a role for what it is and can quickly obtain satisfaction through other pursuits. Thus the individual is able to transcend whatever current role he may be in danger of losing. Social upheaval, for such a person, might lead to periods of intense creativity rather than periods of depression.

Low Rate of Reinforcement

The discussion of depression to this point has focused on processes, both physiological and psychological, within the individual. It may be that these processes and the associated symptoms of depression are under a degree of control by variables outside the individual—by people and events in the depressive's immediate environment. Long-term negative interpersonal interactions are a likely precipitant of many depressions seen in medical practice. For example, a married woman who is continually criticized by her spouse might someday suddenly awaken in a state of severe depression. The husband might view her problem as being medical in nature and rush her off to a physician to be "fixed."

Lewinsohn (1974) proposed that a low rate of reinforcement from the environment can contribute to depression. Lewinsohn maintains that the amount of reinforcement received by an individual is a function of three factors: the number of activities and events that are potentially reinforcing for him, the number of reinforcers provided

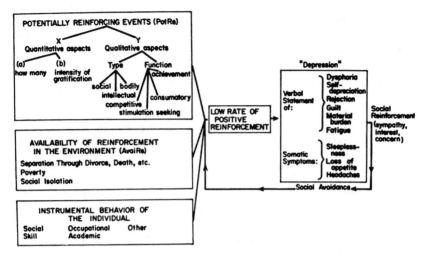

Figure 4-1   Schematic representation of Lewinsohn's (1974) model of depression. Reproduced by permission of the Hemisphere Publishing Corporation.

by the environment, and the extent to which he possesses the skills necessary to elicit reinforcement for himself from the environment. A schematic of Lewinsohn's model is presented in Figure 4-1.

Are fewer reinforcers available to depressives than normals? According to Lewinsohn depressives do engage in fewer pleasurable activities than nondepressives. He has not established, however, whether the low rate of reinforcing activities precedes the depression or whether the depression precedes the low rate of activities. The depressive is also viewed as lacking the social and economic skills necessary to elicit positive reinforcement. For example, a population survey of the incidence of depression revealed that people who are most likely to become pathologically depressed come from the lower social classes and also have an inferior educational background (Levitt & Lubin, 1975).

Coyne (1976) found some further support for Lewinsohn's model. Coyne had normal subjects converse on a telephone with either a depressed patient, a nondepressed patient, or a normal control. The subjects were told that they were free to discuss any topic of mutual interest, that they were simply to become acquainted with the person on the other end of the line. It was found that, following the conversation, subjects who had spoken to depressed patients were themselves significantly more depressed, anxious, hostile, and rejecting. If depressives lack the social skills required to elicit positive feelings from others it becomes more likely that they will be increasingly ignored by others and thereby become less exposed to situations associated with positive reinforcement.

The treatment of depression, according to Lewinsohn, requires forcing the depressed individual to engage in behaviors that will be followed by positive reinforcement. This is accomplished by having the depressed individual increase activities that are associated with positive reinforcement and by acquiring social skills that will facilitate this process. The patient might be required to force himself to engage in a selected number of activities as well as practice communication and self-assertion skills. The available evidence does not strongly support Lewinsohn's position that an increase in antidepressive behaviors will be followed by a decrease in depression. Some studies have reported little improvement following this procedure, whereas other studies have shown depression to increase rather than decrease following the procedure (Blaney, 1977).

It is not always possible to reverse the debilitating effects of a history of low rate of positive reinforcement. Many marital relationships result in depression in one of the members because the couple failed to use positive reinforcement during the "good years." Instead they relied heavily on aversive control to manipulate each other ("What do you do around here all day—sit on your rear end?" "Why can't you be a good husband?" "Get your act together." "Can't you get that kid of yours to shut up?"). The couple may not realize that the prolonged use of this form of communication may precipitate, usually in the member with fewer social skills, an intense depression (McLean, 1976). The pattern may lead to irreversible negative feelings. At the same time, an awareness by the couple of the debilitating effects of aversive control might have prevented the depression in the first place.

Mystery behind the Feelings of Depression

Having examined a number of variables that have been implicated in the etiology of depression, one can say that taken together, these variables point to the importance of understanding the patient's social, interpersonal, and psychological status when attempting to alleviate depression. A more specific understanding of depression is still hampered by a lack of information about the psychobiological processes that maintain the intense and debilitating feelings of the patient.

What processes, for example, make a patient feel as if he or she is "dead inside?" Why do these feelings seem to dissipate with time?

The identification of psychobiological processes that control depression will improve our ability to assist patients in dealing with their affliction. Recent studies have demonstrated that the manner in which a patient holds his facial musculature may even contribute to these processes (Schwartz, Fair, Salt, Mandel, & Klerman, 1976). Distinct patterns of facial-muscle activity are generated when a person simply thinks about depressing experiences. In one experiment 12 normal subjects and 12 depressed subjects were required to generate happy, sad, or angry imagery while EMGs were recorded from different facial muscles (Figure 4-2). Each image produced its own pattern of electromyographic activity, even though this activity was not noticeable to the subject. For the normals, "happy" imagery resulted in decreases in muscle activity about the eye and forehead and increases in activity from muscles about the mouth and jaw. The EMG patterns obtained from the depressed patients were similar in form to the patterns obtained from the normals but were smaller in amplitude. An interesting difference occurred when both groups were asked to think about a "typical day." Under this instruction, the EMG pattern for the normals resembled the pattern obtained under the "think happy" instruction, whereas the pattern for the depressed subjects resembled that obtained under the "think sad" instruction. The differences between normals and depressives could be reduced if both groups were encouraged, not just to "think happy" or "sad," but also to "feel" the image.

From these data Schwartz hypothesized that self-induced cognitive states do elicit discrete bodily patterns of response and that these patterns may act as a major physiological mechanism that allows the image to elicit the subjective feelings associated with different emotions. In terms very similar to the James-Lange theory of emotion, he states:

> A self-regulated internal feedback loop·may be created, when the particular "thought" triggers a specific *pattern* of peripheral physiological activity which is then itself reproduced by the brain, contributing to the unique "feeling" state associated with the image. (1975, p. 320)

Another possibility is that the peripheral physiological activity mediating the feelings of depression comes to operate, for some depressives, independently of any specific negative cognitions or images. More re-

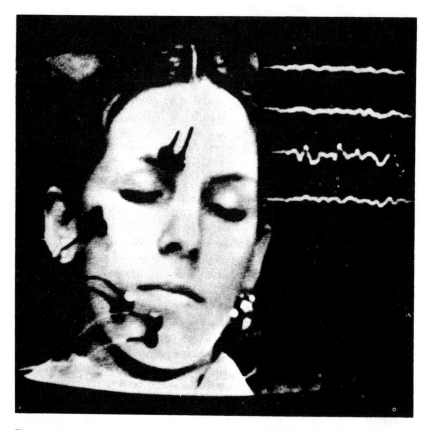

Figure 4-2 Placement of the four pairs of EMG electrodes; superimposed (top right) the oscilliscope tracings of the electromyographic activity from the four facial regions (Schwartz, Fair, Salt, Mandel, & Klerman, 1976). Copyright © 1976 by the American Psychosomatic Society, Inc. Reproduced by permission of the publisher.

search of this nature is required to refine our understanding of the processes mediating the actual feelings of depression.

Suicide

The World Health Organization lists suicide as one of the 10 leading causes of death. It has been ranked even higher as a cause of death among college students. Why so many people choose death as a solution to their problems remains a mystery. According to Lester and Lester (1971), many of the commonsense ideas about suicide are wrong and may be useless or even destructive in dealing with suicidal people. To illustrate, they presented a table of facts and fables about suicide (Table 4-2).

It is likely that no single explanation will ever be found for the many forms that suicide can take. A number of motivations for suicide are mentioned in the literature: aggression turned inward; retaliation by inducing guilt in others; efforts to force love from others; efforts to make amends for perceived past wrongs; efforts to rid oneself of unacceptable feelings; the desire to rejoin a dead loved one; and the desire or need to escape from stress, deformity, pain, or emotional vacuum (Mintz, R. S., 1971).

Broader sociological variables may also influence suicide rates. That is, the larger society may inadvertently legitimize suicide as a means of coping with life's problems. A person who cannot accept being alone, or the guilt associated with some action, or the loss of a loved one may see suicide as a meaningful alternative because in some subtle fashion the larger society has conveyed this very alternative. Even suicide prevention centers, although intended to help individuals through acute emotional times, may contribute to the incidence of suicide in this fashion. In Los Angeles, the incidence of suicide actually increased rather than decreased following the establishment of a suicide prevention center (Weiner, I. W., 1969).

Even newspaper stories may trigger suicidal actions in the already suicide-prone individual. Phillips (1977) examined whether motor-vehicle fatalities increase immediately after publicized suicide stories. He searched two large newspapers in California for front-page suicide stories and then tabulated the incidence of motor-vehicle fatalities for the period immediately following the story. Control periods were selected that contained no publicized suicides, and these were matched to the experimental periods for month of year, day of week, and presence or absence of holiday weekends.

On the average, the number of motor-vehicle fatalities increased by 9.1% in the week after the published suicide stories. Figure 4-3 indicates that the daily fluctuation of motor-vehicle fatalities for the period starting 2-weeks before the publicized suicide and ending 11 days afterward. Observe the rise in motor-vehicle fatalities that occurred following the publicized suicide. Phillips believes that publicized suicide stories stimulate a wave of imitative suicides and that some of these suicides are disguised as motor-vehicle fatalities.

The high suicide rate in college students may reflect the operation of similar sociological variables. One of the commonest explanations of suicide with this group has been the competitive strain of college existence. Writers have emphasized the overly high expectations

Table 4-2   Facts and Fables about Suicide (Lester and Lester, 1971)

These Statements Are NOT True	*These Statements ARE True*
FABLE: People who talk about suicide don't commit suicide.	FACT: Of any ten people who kill themselves eight have given definite warnings of their suicidal intentions. Suicide threats and attempts *must* be taken seriously.
FABLE: Suicide happens without warning.	FACT: Studies reveal that the suicidal person gives many clues and warnings regarding his suicidal intentions. Alertness to these cries for help may prevent suicidal behavior.
FABLE: Suicidal people are fully intent on dying.	FACT: Most suicidal people are undecided about living or dying, and they "gamble" with death," leaving it to others to save them. Almost no one commits suicide without letting others know how he is feeling. Often this "cry for help" is given in "code." These distress signals can be used to save lives.
FABLE: Once a person is suicidal, he is suicidal forever.	FACT: Fortunately, individuals who wish to kill themselves are "suicidal" only for a limited period of time. If they are saved from self-destruction, they can go on to lead useful lives.

FABLE:
Improvement following a
  suicidal crisis means that the
  suicidal risk is over.

FACT:
Most suicides occur within
  three months after the beginning of "improvement,"
  when the individual has the
  energy to put his morbid
  thoughts and feelings into
  effect. Relatives and physicians
  should be especially vigilant
  during this period.

FABLE:
Suicide strikes more often
  among the rich—or, con-
  versely, it occurs more
  frequently among the poor.

FACT:
Suicide is neither the rich
  man's disease nor the poor
  man's curse. Suicide is very
  "democratic" and is represented proportionately among
  all levels of society.

FABLE:
Suicide is inherited or "runs in
  a family" (i.e., is genetically
  determined).

FACT:
Suicide does *not* run in
  families. It is an individual
  matter, and can be prevented.

FABLE:
All suicidal individuals are
  mentally ill, and suicide is
  always the act of a
  psychotic person.

FACT:
Studies of hundreds of
  genuine suicide notes indicate
  that although the suicidal
  person is extremely unhappy,
  he is not necessarily mentally
  ill. His overpowering un-
  happiness may result from a
  temporary emotional upset, a
  long and painful illness, or
  a complete loss of hope.
  It is circular reasoning to say
  that "suicide is an insane act,"
  and therefore all suicidal
  people are psychotic.

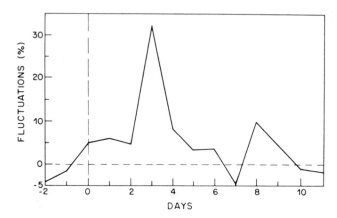

Figure 4-3   Daily fluctuation in motor-vehicle fatalities for a 2-week period
before, during (day 0), and after publicized suicides (Phillips,
1977). Copyright © 1977 by the American Association for the
Advancement of Science. Reprinted by permission of the publisher and D. Phillips.

college students have of themselves and that their parents also had
high expectations of achievement for these students. According to
Hendin (1975) this explanation is simply not supported by the evidence. From his own observations of some 50 suicidal students, he has
concluded that these individuals have adopted a suicidal lifestyle that
represents a kind of suicidal cult. Rather than being intimidated by
the pressures of schoolwork, his students viewed studying as a defense
against suicidal feelings. Death, then, had become a way of life and
their major concern was their own extinction. Their relationship with
their parents is described as a form of death knot in that the only relationship they had was a form of emotional deadness. Following is one
of his student cases:

Case Report: Leon

Leon had lost neither of his parents, although he could be said never to
have had them either. He had gotten along with them by being a drone,
burying himself alone in his room studying, listening to music, and having suicidal thoughts. At 18 he had already been thinking of suicide for
years and in high school had compiled a list of reasons why he should
not kill himself. He enumerated them to me in the mechanical manner
he usually adopted. First, things were so bad that they could only get
better. Second, you had no right to take your life. Third, his parents
had made a great investment in his education and it would cost a lot to
bury him. Fourth, his parents would blame themselves. Fifth, they
would be devastated and would miss him. Since he had been at college
he had added a sixth reason—his friends would feel very bad if he did

it. Leon had been able to resist his suicidal preoccupations during his lonely high school years, but after a few months at college in which he had grown close to his roommates, his need to kill himself became overwhelming. The challenge to his past isolation and deadness from his new friendship was finally pushing Leon toward suicide.

Leon wanted to hold onto his depression far more than he realized. He saw himself as always having been on "the losing side of the law of averages." He gave his dissatisfaction with his own average at college after studying hard all term as cause for his depression and sign of his bad luck. After a college mixer at which he met no one, he rode the subways and stood for a long time at one station in Harlem in a challenge to fate to see if he would be mugged. He considered it a bad omen that two of his favorite professional football teams lost on the day after he was admitted to the hospital. During the time I saw him, after his favorite team won its crucial game, he dreamt that in the last minute they lost.

Leon saw defeat as preferable to victory, but for the most part he sought an impregnability that prevented both. He had a recurring fantasy in which he was a medieval citadel under attack. He drew a map to illustrate the deployment of his protective armies. Areas were indicated in different colors to mark his social, academic, spiritual, and emotional defenses. Most of his forces were concentrated in the academic realm. Leon's map of barricades was a powerful symbol of his emotional state. He felt that he would survive only as long as his defenses held.

Leon saw life as war and himself as the ultimate weapon. It was easier for him to see danger as an outside attack than to see his own destructiveness. After an incident in which his roommates had disappointed him, he dreamt that he was an executioner who had to decide whether people should live or die. He condemned them to death and "some kind of angel came and killed them all." Leon clearly saw himself as the Angel of Death. His suicidal preoccupations and his depression masked an image he had of himself as sitting on a time bomb that was "getting ready to explode." When I questioned him about the anger and destructiveness suggested in the image, he was quick to tell me that the most that would happen was that he would "quietly and nonviolently" kill himself.

Leon's need to hide his anger was bound up with his need not to blame his parents for his problems. He insisted that he had little relationship to them, liked them from afar but was always irritated with them when at home. All of the incidents that he related of his childhood cast his mother in the role of dampener of his or his father's pleasure or excitement. His father handled the situation by being away much of the time, leaving his mother to rule the house. Leon felt that he and his parents had never been able to talk about anything, but expressed no anger or bitterness over this. His suicide note conveyed the quality of his family life.

In a note addressed to both of his parents, Leon wrote that by the time they read it he would be dead and that they were not responsible for his act. (In suicide notes, such statements specifically freeing particular people of any blame or responsibility are usually to be read psychologically as meaning the opposite.) He added that he was depressed and could see nothing coming out of his life. He went on to dispose of his possessions, leaving his tapes and tape recording equipment to his mother and requesting that his favorite tape be buried with him. From beginning to end, Leon's note was about communication from beyond life. He told his parents that it was too late to reach him but went on to leave them equipment which permitted him to speak to them, like the Angel of Death he dreamt he was, as a voice from beyond the grave. In asking to be buried with the tape of melancholy songs he played again and again as accompaniment to his suicidal thoughts, Leon was almost literally asking to be cemented for all eternity in his unhappy, isolated relation to his mother. It was not surprising that his (projective test) stories had the repetitive theme of a parent's affection for a dead son. (p. 205)

Source: Hendin, H. Student suicide: Death as a lifestyle. *The Journal of Nervous and Mental Disease*, 1975, *160*, 204-219, Copyright © 1975 by The Williams and Wilkins Co. Reproduced by permission of the publisher and H. Hendin.

This case illustrates Hendin's thesis that many suicidal students have chosen their course of action as a lifestyle. Their cognitions and behavior are designed to control any enthusiasm over life and to guarantee a form of lifelessness. For these students depression is a form of protective deadness that may even make suicide unnecessary.

Although suicidal individuals need not be suffering from a psychiatric disorder, there is considerable evidence that the incidence of suicide is very high with some forms of psychiatric disorders. Miles (1977) established the percentage of suicide deaths in several psychiatric disorders to be: endogenous depression, 15%; reactive depression, 15%; alcoholism, 15%; schizophrenia, 10%; psychopathic personality, 5%; opiate addiction, 10% or more. These data suggest that suicide is most often a "sequella or complication of various other conditions, and that the majority of suicides are secondary to such conditions." Treatment efforts, then, should be directed at the underlying condition rather than at the suicidal inclination. In broader terms, individuals need to be taught other means for coping with life's problems.

5

Pain and Pain Patients

Although pain is an extremely common patient complaint, it is also one of the least understood symptoms in medicine. It has been said that there are literally hundreds of thousands of individuals who spend their existence seeking relief from unbearable pain. Many of these individuals develop additional physical and psychological problems as a result of the persisting pain. Many of the chronic-pain patients attending pain clinics represent failures of conventional surgical treatment, some of these individuals having had 10-to-15 operations for their pain. Part of this problem originated from the way medicine historically dichotomized pain complaints as being either "organic" or "psychogenic" in nature. Such terms hampered the physician's ability to understand the patient fully. Conversely the same dichotomy created feelings of distrust and hopelessness in many patients. A theoretical objective of this chapter is to present a model that integrates completely both psychological and physiological variables with respect to pain. Practical applications of this model for treating pain patients are also presented.

Complexity of Pain

The notion that psychological variables contribute extensively to the experience of pain is not new. Beecher (1959) describes the physiological component of pain as the sensory component and the psychological component as the reaction component. In many situations he believes that the reaction component is often more important than the sensory component. This belief originated with his observations of wounded soldiers returning from battle during World War II. He was surprised to find that when the wounded men were taken to combat hospitals, only one out of three complained of enough pain to require morphine. Most of the soldiers either denied having pain from their extensive wounds or had so little that they did not want any medication to relieve it. These men were clear mentally, not in a state of shock, and they had not had narcotics recently. According to Beecher, the total situation and its meaning had a great positive influence on the reactive component of their experiences. Tissue damage was simply not interpreted as pain. Civilians with similar wounds obtained during surgery were observed by Beecher to experience much more pain.

Cultural and racial differences in the perception of pain have also been widely demonstrated (Weisenberg, 1977a, 1977b). Cultural variables seem to influence the tolerance of pain rather than the perception of the pain sensation per se. Different cultures have different attitudes toward what pain reactions are appropriate for their group members (under what circumstances it is permissible to cry or to ask for help). Attitudes toward pain have their origin in the family. Studies of dental fears in children have shown that the experiences and attitudes of one's family toward dental care are instrumental in determining the person's anxiety to dental treatment. For example, children with anxious mothers demonstrated more negative behavior during an extraction than children of mothers with low anxiety (Weisenberg, 1977b).

Melzack (1973) is the leading proponent of the view that pain is much more than a simple sensory experience. He has proposed that there are two additional dimensions to the pain experience: the *motivational affective* and the *cognitive evaluative*. The motivational-affective dimension refers to the unpleasant affective or emotional quality that differentiates pain from other sensations. Pain can become overwhelming and disruptive of ongoing behaviors. The cognitive-evaluative dimension refers to higher intellectual processes that influence the perception of pain. Included here would be cultural, social, personality, and situational variables.

Melzack cites considerable clinical evidence to support the notion of a three-dimensional model of pain. One example to which he refers is the rare clinical disorder called *congenital insensitivity to pain*, a syndrome descriptive of individuals that are apparently normal in every respect except they have never experienced pain. The following criteria have been proposed for diagnosing congenital insensitivity to pain: (a) the defect must be present from birth, rather than acquired as a secondary manifestation of a disease process or traumatic injury; (b) the insensitivity to pain must be generalized to all pain stimuli and the entire body; (c) the remaining sensory modalities (touch, warmth, cold, pressure) must be intact.

These individuals are not simply indifferent to pain as are some psychotics; rather, they are insensitive to pain. Potentially painful stimuli are reported as eliciting sensations of "itching," "tingling," or "tickling," rather than as pain.

> The best documented of all cases of congenital insensitivity to pain is Miss C., a young Canadian girl who was a student at McGill University in Montreal. Her father, a physician in Western Canada, was fully aware of her problem and alerted his colleagues in Montreal to examine her. The young lady was highly intelligent and seemed normal in every way, except that she had never felt pain. As a child she had bitten off the tip of her tongue while chewing food, and had suffered third-degree burns after kneeling on a hot radiator to look out of the window. When examined by a psychologist . . . in the laboratory, she reported that she did not feel pain when noxious stimuli were presented. She felt no pain when parts of her body were subjected to strong electric shock, to hot water at temperatures that usually produce reports of burning pain, or to a prolonged ice-bath. Equally astonishing was the fact that she showed no changes in blood pressure, heart rate, or respiration when these stimuli were presented. Furthermore, she could not remember ever sneezing or coughing, the gag reflex could be elicited only with great difficulty, and cornea reflexes (to protect the eyes) were absent. A variety of other stimuli, such as inserting a stick up through the nostrils, pinching tension, or injections of histamine under the skin—which are normally considered as a form of torture—also failed to produce pain. (Melzack, 1973, p. 15)

The seriousness of this disorder contributed directly to the patient's death at the age of 29.

Sternbach (1968) described a similar individual who only experienced pain three times in his life: At the age of 7 he had a headache for a few days after an axe was buried in his skull; at age 14 he experienced brief pain when a surgeon probed for a bullet; and at age 16 there was a report of pain when he received treatment for a broken fibula which "hurt a little." Sternbach suggested that this individual probably experienced no pain during these accidents, but in response to the social demands of the situation, the patient thought it best to indicate some feeling of pain so as not to appear "crazy" or "weird" to the attending physician.

Because the sensory systems of these individuals seem to be intact, Melzack believes their problem must lie with the physiological mechanisms that mediate the motivational-affective and cognitive-evaluation dimensions of pain. He also discusses individuals who, after physically recovering from a pain trauma, suffer extreme pain in the absence of any apparent damage:

> Damage of peripheral nerves in the arms or legs, by gunshot wounds or other injuries, is sometimes accompanied by excruciating pain that persists long after the tissues have healed and the nerve fibres have regenerated. These pains may occur spontaneously for no apparent reason. They have many qualities, and may be described as burning, cramping or shooting. Sometimes they are triggered by innocuous stimuli such as gentle touches or even a puff of air. Spontaneous attacks of pain may take minutes or hours to subside, but may occur repeatedly each day for years after the injury. The frequency and intensity of the spontaneous pain-attacks may increase over the years, and the pain may even spread to distant areas of the body. (Melzack, 1973, p. 16)

Both with respect to congenital insensitivity to pain and chronic pain without tissue damage, the logical expectation of a necessary correlation between subjective experiences and physiology is absent.

Early Experience and Pain

An interesting example of how environmental contingencies may modify pain perception comes from the early work of Pavlov (1927). It is well established that if an aversive stimulus such as electric shock follows the presentation of food, an animal will quickly cease eating in that particular situation. In fact, when placed in the situation, the animal will manifest a variety of emotional responses and frequently will choose to starve. However, what happens if the aversive stimulus precedes the presentation of food? In such cases, Pavlov found that dogs failed to exhibit any emotional responses to electric shock, or skin pricks and burns. Instead, the animals perceived such stimuli as signals meaning that food was on the way. Under these specific conditions, electric shock now evoked salivation and approach behaviors.

In a classic experiment, Melzack and Scott (1957) raised Scottish terriers in isolation cages from puppyhood to maturity. At maturity, these dogs failed to respond normally to a variety of noxious stimuli such as electric shock and a burning match.

> One of the most remarkable features of the restricted dogs was their behavior during and following presentation of the flame. To the astonishment of the observers, seven of the ten restricted dogs made no attempt to get away from E during stimulation, and it was not even

necessary to hold them. The sequence of behavior observed was almost identical for all seven dogs: they moved their noses into the flame as soon as it was presented, after which the head or whole body jerked away, as though reflexively; but then they came right back to their original position and hovered excitedly near the flame. Three of them repeatedly poked their noses into the flame and sniffed at it as long as it was present. (p. 158)

According to Melzack (1973), the abnormal response of these animals was due, not to failure of the sensory conducting system, but to their perception of the tissue damage. That is, the "meaning" of physical damage was absent for these animals.

Do not assume from these examples that all pain is learned. The critical point is simply that most complaints of pain have a large psychological component that contributes directly to the experience of pain. Even newborn infants with limited experience will cry intensely in response to some painful stimuli and yet show minimal reaction to others. Circumcision, for example, elicits a minimal pain response to the cutting action of the scalpel. Melzack (1973) has defined pain as:

a perceptual experience whose quality and intensity are influenced by the unique past history of the individual, by the meaning he gives to the pain-producing situation and by his "state of mind" at the moment. We believe that all these factors play a role in determining the actual patterns of nerve impulses that ascend from the body to the brain and travel within the brain itself. In this way, pain becomes a function of the whole individual, including his present thoughts and fears, as well as his hopes for the future. (p. 48)

From this definition it is apparent that psychological variables play a direct role in the pain expereince.

Physiological Mechanisms

Historically, psychological variables have been viewed as secondary to the sensory aspects of pain. Pain was described as resulting from the stimulation of specific peripheral and central nervous system pathways. The specificity theory of pain had its origin in ancient times.

The best classical description of the theory was provided by Descartes in 1644, who conceived of the pain system as a straight-through channel from the skin to the brain. He suggested that the system is like the bell-ringing mechanism in a church: a man pulls the rope at the bottom of the tower, and the bell rings in the belfry. So too, he proposed, a flame sets particles in the foot into activity and the motion is transmitted up the leg and back into the head, where presumably, something like an alarm system is set off. The person then feels pain and responds to it. (Melzack, 1973, p. 126)

In 1895 von Frey presented a specificity model to explain all sensations. He proposed that the quality of a skin sensation (touch, cold, warm, pain) depends, initially, on the type of *sensory receptor* that is stimulated. Sensory receptors are a class of specialized nerve endings at which physical, chemical, or electromagnetic incoming signals are changed into nerve-action potentials. The difference in structure of these receptors renders them highly sensitive to a specific kind of stimulus and much less responsive to other kinds of stimuli. Von Frey assigned pain to the free nerve endings.

The relationship between the sensation of pain and the activation of free nerve endings was not to prove so simple. First it was found that stimulation of free nerve endings is also capable of eliciting other sensations. The pinna, or outer part of the ear, contains basically only free nerve endings, and yet when this area is appropriately stimulated, the individual experiences warmth, cold, touch, itch, or pain. The cornea, which is the transparent outer covering of the eye, also has only free nerve endings as receptors; yet it, too, is sensitive to warmth, cold, touch, and pain (Lele & Weddell, 1956).

An alternative approach to that of viewing specific receptors and fibers as mediating pain was that of viewing the overall pattern (rather than the kind) of fiber being stimulated. Within this model, pain may occur with any kind of stimulation as long as the stimulation is excessive. Thus, anything very hot, very cold, or pressing very hard on the skin, or a very bright light to the eyes, causes pain. If pain is due to excessive stimulation of other kinds of sensation, then there is no stimulus-specific modality of pain. According to this theory, the many differences in the discharge characteristics of nerve fibers are the source of the various kinds of sensation we experience. For example, the discharge patterns of a rapidly adapting receptor and of a slowly adapting one are different. The spatial and temporal discharge patterns of the peripheral nerve fibers and the fibers connecting to them within the central nervous system may represent a code that, being finally decoded, produces different kinds of sensation. A certain group of fibers contributes to more than one kind of sensation. From this perspective (called the *pattern theory* of pain), the differences in quantity (rather than quality) of peripheral nerve-fiber discharge produce the differences in quality of sensation. The pattern theory is able to account for the fact that a minimal tactile stimulus of the cornea causes a feeling of touch, whereas a stronger tactile stimulus causes a pain, by assuming that the same kind of nerve fibers are discharging and that the difference in sensation is due to an increased discharge and spatial summation. The pattern theory ruled out any naming of peripheral nerve fibers according to the sensation experienced (Nathan, 1976).

The most recent physiological research points to a number of structures within the nervous system that contribute to pain. It is the interplay between these structures, however, that is critical in determining if and to what extent a specific stimulus leads to pain. Pain is no longer viewed as resulting from the straight-through transmission of impulses from the skin to the brain. This view has major implications for our understanding of the pain patient.

Specialized peripheral fibers that are maximally responsive to pain stimuli are known to exist. Two groups of nerve fibers have been implicated: the A-delta fibers, which are the slowest of the myelinated fibers; and the unmyelinated C fibers. Some investigators believe that the A-delta fibers mediate immediate or sharp pain, whereas C fibers mediate slow, diffuse, dull or aching pain. One class of A-delta and C fibers respond maximally to mechanical stimulation and are labeled *mechanical nociceptors*. A second class of A-delta and C fibers respond maximally to intense mechanical and temperature stimulation and are called polymodal nociceptors. The term *nociceptor* has replaced the older term *pain receptor* in order to emphasize that these sensory units contribute to, rather than create, the pain experience.

Sensory fibers enter the spinal cord through the dorsal horns. Sensory neurons within the dorsal horn are packed into several layers or laminae (Figure 5-1). These layers contain cells that are especially responsive to pain stimuli (that is, activation of A-delta and C fibers). Two basic types of nociceptive cells are believed to exist within the different laminae. The first type are referred to as *Class 1* nociceptive cells and they receive input only from A-delta and C fibers. The second type are referred to as *Class 2* nociceptive cells, and their activity is not specific to A-delta and C fiber input, but they respond maximally in the presence of such input. Their activity is greatest when the peripheral stimulus is sufficient to cause pain (Liebeskind & Paul, 1977). Laminae II through III contain the cells that comprise the substantia gelatinosa. These cells are of central importance to Melzack's gate-control theory of pain, which is examined in the following section. Descending impulses from higher brain centers are also known to be capable of inhibiting activity in the dorsal horn neurons. Sensory input therefore can be modulated at the spinal level.

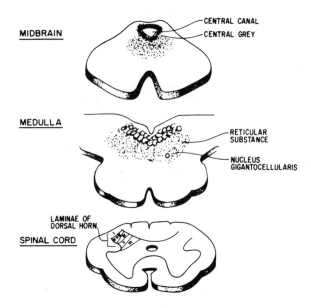

Figure 5-1   Cross sections of spinal cord and brainstem depicting structures
involved in the mediation and inhibition of pain.

Currently, brainstem structures are receiving attention from pain
researchers, and some of the recent findings are quite exciting. For
example, clusters of cells or nuclei have been identified within the
brainstem that when stimulated lead to the experience of pain. Other
clusters of cells have been identified that when stimulated block the
experience of pain. In addition, naturally produced substances with
morphinelike qualities have also recently been identified within
brainstem structures.

A cross-sectional view of two levels of the brainstem is presented
in Figure 5-1. At the lowest level is the medulla, which is actually an
extension of the spinal cord. The medulla is comprised of white-
matter fiber tracts that carry motor and sensory impulses between the
brain and the spinal cord, and intermingled white and gray matter
called *reticular substance*. Various cells of different types and sizes
lie among the meshwork of interconnecting reticular fibers. One clus-
ter of cells that is known to be involved in pain is called the *nucleus
gigantocellularis (NGC)*. Stimulation of these cells is known to lead to
aversive behaviors that are similar to those elicited by pain stimuli.
Both rats and cats will attempt to avoid such stimulation (Casey,
Keene, & Morrow, 1974). Many NGC cells are also maximally responsive to activation of A-delta and C fibers.

The midbrain, or as it is often called, the *mesencephalon*, lies between the pons and the hypothalamus. The midbrain central gray matter and, at a more cranial level, the periaqueductal gray matter are known to possess cellular mechanisms that influence the perception of pain. The term *periaqueductal* is derived from *peri*, meaning "around," and *aqueduct*, meaning "pipe" or "duct." It describes the portion of brain tissue surrounding the ventricles containing the cerebrospinal fluid. This duct is continuous with the spinal cord and at the spinal level is called the *spinal canal*.

Electrical stimulation of cells within the midbrain central gray matter not only blocks pain behaviors but also inhibits the activity of NGC cells that were previously responsive to pain stimuli (Morrow & Casey, 1976). Stimulation of brainstem structures that leads to the inhibition of pain responses is called *stimulation-produced analgesia (SPA)*. It has been produced from regions in the medulla, through regions in the midbrain, to the lower limbic structures (Liebeskind & Paul, 1977). Its analgesic effects are often equal to the analgesic effects of morphine because it is capable of blocking all manifestations of pain, from spinal reflexes to learned avoidance reactions. A few seconds of stimulation may produce an analgesic effect that lasts a few hours. The analgesic effect is often isolated in that the stimulated animal ignores a pinch to one limb and responds maximally with pain to a pinch on the other limb. Other normal behaviors, such as eating, are not necessarily interfered with.

Liebeskind and Paul observed a number of other parallels between SPA and morphine. An important site of morphine's analgesic effect, like SPA, appears to be the central and periaqueductal gray matter. Morphine when applied directly to the central and periaqueductal gray matter exerts more powerful analgesia than when applied elsewhere. Both morphine and SPA suppress nociceptive responding in dorsal horn cells. Organisms develop tolerance to SPA and morphine and also show cross-tolerance between morphine and SPA. Tolerance to a drug is said to result when a given dose produces a smaller effect than it did initially. A final similarity between morphine and SPA is their reduced effectiveness in the presence of the drug naloxone, which blocks the actions of morphine and has also been found to block the effects of SPA.

Further support for the existence of specific nociceptive mechanisms within the brainstem comes from the recent discoveries that the brain produces morphinelike substances. Hughes and his colleagues (Hughes, Smith, Kosterlitz, Fothergill, Morgan, & Morris, 1975) have discovered an endogenous morphinelike substance within the brain that they have called *enkephalin*. This substance is produced within the central gray matter and if injected into animals produces analgesia. Similarly, Li, Chung, and Doneen (1976) have isolated a substance within the human pituitary gland, which they have named *B-endorphin*, that also has morphinelike properties.

In summary, in examining the mechanisms of pain from the periphery to the brainstem, a degree of physiological specificity can be observed at all levels. Specificity at higher cortical levels is poorly understood, although efforts are being made to isolate nuclei within the thalamus that are specific to pain. In fact, the surgical destruction of such nuclei (called a *thalamotomy*) is being used to treat some forms of chronic pain. Although no structures—receptors, fiber tracts, spinal cells, or brainstem mechanisms—respond only to pain stimuli, structures exist at each level that respond maximally in the presence of pain stimuli. What does all this mean? According to Liebeskind and Paul (1977), it means that although all these mechanisms contribute to the experience of pain, none in isolation is sufficient to account for the experience of pain. Peripheral receptors, sensory fibers, and spinal nociceptive cells probably contribute to the sensory aspects of pain, whereas brainstem mechanisms contribute to the motivational-affective component. Cerebral mechanisms controlling the cognitive-evaluative component remain to be identified.

Where then does pain originate? From the above perspective, pain reflects the outcome of many peripheral and central nervous system structures and therefore cannot be isolated to one specific set of structures. Melzack (1973) has supported this position with his statement that the idea of a pain center in the brain is utter nonsense, "unless virtually the whole brain is considered to be the pain center, because the thalamus, hypothalamus, brainstem reticular formation, limbic system, parietal cortex, and frontal cortex are all implicated in pain perception."

This holistic model of pain, combined with the recent discoveries of morphinelike substances within the brain, may prove to be extremely important for developing behavioral programs to treat pain.

> We think it likely that all mammals possess a set of powerful and endogenous centrifugal mechanisms of pain control within the brainstem. Lower animals may have little access to these systems except under the most dire circumstances, such as during strong appetitive, aggressive, or self-protective drive states, and especially during the goal-directed behaviors associated with these states. In man, however, it may be that there are better developed pathways of access . . . to these brainstem systems. Thus, our cognitive capacities to think, to believe, and to hope enable us, probably all of us under the appropriate conditions, to find

and employ our pain inhibitory resources. The important challenge in the years to come for behavioral scientists involved in pain research will be to explore and ultimately bring under control those precise circumstances and techniques that will reliably enable people to make use of these resources when needed. (Liebeskind & Paul, 1977, p. 54)

Gate-control Theory of Pain

The *gate-control theory* of pain was introduced by Melzack and Wall (1965) to account for: (a) the high degree of physiological specialization of receptors, nerves, and spinal tracts in the central nervous system; (b) the direct influence of psychological processes on pain perception and response; and (c) the persistence of clinical pain after healing.

Basically, the gate-control theory proposes that a neurophysiological mechanism in the dorsal horns of the spinal cord acts like a gate that can increase or decrease the flow of nerve impulses from peripheral fibers to the central nervous system. Somatic input is therefore subjected to the modulating influence of the gate before it evokes pain perception and response. The degree to which the gate increases or decreases sensory transmission is determined by the relative activity in large-diameter (A-beta) and small-diameter (A-delta and C) fibers and by descending influences from the brain. When the amount of information that passes through the gate exceeds a critical level, it activates the neural areas responsible for pain experience and response.

A schematic of the gate-control theory of pain is shown in Figure 5-2. The model is based on the following propositions:

1. The transmission of nerve impulses from the periphery to spinal cord transmission cells is modulated by a spinal-gating mechanism in the dorsal horns. The spinal-gating mechanism is contained within the cells of the substantia gelatinosa. When stimulated, these cells produce an inhibitory effect on the transmission cells.

2. The spinal-gating mechanism is influenced by the relative amount of activity in large-diameter and small-diameter fibers: Activity in large fibers tends to inhibit transmission (close the gate), whereas small-fiber activity tends to facilitate transmission (open the gate). From Figure 5-2, it can be seen that large-diameter fibers increase the inhibitory effect of the spinal-gating mechanism, whereas small-diameter fibers decrease its inhibitory effect.

3. The spinal-gating mechanism is influenced by nerve impulses that descend from the brain. Thus, cognitive processes such as atten-

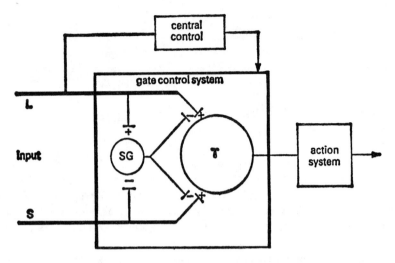

Figure 5-2   The gate-control theory of pain; (L) large-diameter fibers; (S) small-diameter fibers; (SG) spinal-gating mechanism; (T) spinal cord transmission cells (Melzack & Wall, 1965). Copyright © 1965 by the American Association for the Advancement of Science. Reprinted by permission of the publisher and R. Melzack.

tion, anxiety, anticipation, and past experience are able to exert their effects directly on pain processes. Their overall effect is conceptualized as a central control trigger. The central control mechanism is not relegated to the secondary role of simply modifying the sensation of pain. Instead, this mechanism is involved in identifying signals from the body, evaluating these signals in terms of prior experience, and determining whether the action system responsible for pain perception and response is activated.

4. When the output of the spinal cord transmission cells exceeds a critical level, it activates the action system. The action system consists of those neural areas that underlie the complex patterns of behavior and experience characteristic of pain.

The small (A-delta and C) fibers play a highly specialized and important role in this theory. Rather than acting as "pain fibers," they activate the transmission cells directly and contribute to their output. The activity of high-threshold small fibers, during intense stimulation, may be especially important in raising the transmission-cell output above the critical level necessary for pain. They are also believed to facilitate transmission (open the gate) and thereby provide the basis for summation, prolonged activity, and spread of pain to other body areas. According to Melzack, the cells of the substantia gelatinosa

(Laminae II and III of the dorsal horn) appear to be the most likely site of the spinal-gating mechanism. These cells receive axon terminals from many of the large- and small-diameter fibers. The substantia gelatinosa runs the full length of the spinal cord on each side. Activity in the large fibers is assumed to activate the cells of the substantia gelatinosa and thereby indirectly inhibit the activity of the central transmission cells. In contrast, activity in small fibers inhibits the activity of the substantia gelatinosa and thereby further facilitates their effects on the cells of the dorsal horn.

The gate-control theory led to the development of a technique for artificially stimulating the nervous system for the relief of pain. Electrical stimulators have been devised that can be used on or beneath the skin surface, or that can also be implanted near the spinal cord. The electricity is applied in the vicinity of areas where pain is perceived or in the region of major nerves serving these areas. The brief stimulation of these nerves often produces relief from severe pathological pain for durations that outlast the period of stimulation, often by hours, and less often by days or weeks. Melzack (1975) observed a patient in whom a pain of several years' duration suddenly vanished for the first time a few days after a single treatment. The pain then returned in a sporadic fashion but could be quickly abolished with the peripheral-nerve stimulator. Not all patients benefit from this form of treatment, and when effective, the relief is usually temporary (Long, 1976; Melzack, 1975). Electrical stimulation is believed to activate large-diameter fibers and thereby "close the gate" at spinal or higher levels.

Phantom Limb Pain

Most amputees report feeling a *phantom limb* almost immediately after amputation of an arm or leg. The phantom limb is usually described as having definite shape that resembles the real limb before amputation. It is reported to move through space in much the same way as the normal limb would move when the person walks, sits down, or stretches out on a bed. At first, the phantom limb feels perfectly normal in size and shape, but as time passes, the phantom limb begins to change shape. The arm or leg becomes less distinct and may fade away altogether. Sometimes, the limb is slowly "telescoped" into the stump until only the "hand" or "foot" remain at the stump tip.

Only a small percentage of amputees report pain in the phantom limb. The pain tends to subside and eventually disappear in most of them. In 5% to 10%, however, the pain is severe and may become worse over the years. It may be occasional or continuous and is described as cramping, shooting, burning, or crushing. The pain is felt in definite parts of the phantom limb. A common complaint, for example, is that the phantom hand is clenched, fingers bent over the thumb and digging into the palm, so that the whole hand is tired and painful (Melzack, 1973). Position your hand in this manner for a few seconds to experience how intense the pain must be for these unfortunate individuals.

If the pain persists for long periods of time, other regions of the body may become sensitized so that merely touching these new "trigger zones" will evoke spasms of severe pain in the phantom limb. Almost anything from urination to emotional upset may set off the pain reaction. Moreover, some patients experience relief for days, weeks, and sometimes permanently after a *sympathomimetic block* (injecting an analgesic into the sympathetic ganglion). This is the case even though the pharmacological effects are lost after only a few hours.

Melzack (1974) proposed an explanation of phantom limb pain in the context of the gate-control theory. He postulated the existence of a *central biasing mechanism* within the brainstem reticular formation that exerts an inhibitory influence at all levels within the sensory system. If through the loss of a limb a large number of sensory fibers are destroyed, the inhibitory influence of this mechanism will decrease, making it more likely that a pain response will occur to almost any stimulus. Melzack believes there are several lines of evidence in support of this hypothesis. First there is fiber loss when the end of a nerve is disconnected from the receptor—as is the case with amputation. Second, the fibers that eventually regenerate into the stump tend to have small diameters. Third, there are, as we have seen, powerful inhibitory mechanisms within the central gray structures of the reticular formation.

One criticism of this model is that increased sensitivity to pain is not always the result of an increased ratio of small- to large-diameter fibers. Although some patients suffering from hypersensitivity to innocuous stimuli do show a selective loss of large-diameter fibers, other patients who are equally pain sensitive to innocuous stimuli show a selective loss of small-diameter fibers (Nathan, 1976).

Melzack believes that the resultant decreasing influence of the central biasing mechanism could also facilitate the development of self-sustaining activity in neurons at spinal, thalamic, and cortical levels. This activity would account for the persistence of pain in the absence of an external stimulus. Moreover, adjacent neuron pools normally activated by other body areas might also begin to acquire self-reverberatory characteristics. This would account for the spread of pain to adjacent or distant areas. Also the anesthetic block of sensory input might shut down the activity in the self-sustaining neuron loops, thereby providing relief beyond the time taken for the analgesic to wear off. Another possibility is that the attachment of a prosthetic limb would, by increasing the use of the stump, produce a pattern of input from the muscles that also shuts down the firing of these self-sustaining neuron pools. Even the psychological relief of pain might be achieved through cortical effects on the central biasing mechanism.

Acupuncture

Acupuncture therapy originated in ancient China some 2,000 years ago. Originally, acupuncture was based on the theory that all vital organs of the body are connected through tubular systems or meridians that radiate underneath the skin. Life energy, or "ch'i," was believed to flow through the meridians, and its excess or deficit produced pain and disease. The insertion of needles into points along the meridians served to correct imbalances in the life energy. There is absolutely no evidence to support the meridian theory, and even the Chinese do not consider the meridian theory as a reasonable explanation for the effectiveness of acupuncture.

Acupuncture sites located in the ear and face are shown in Figures 5-3 and 5-4. Do the sites make a difference or would the same effect occur regardless of where the needles are placed? According to Wall (1972), some Chinese physicians believe strongly in the importance of placing the needles in the correct sites. He visited an acupuncture school in Bangkok and discovered that the final examination required the student to identify the correct sites on a bronze statue with holes. The whole statue was covered with plaster prior to the exam and the student had to insert a needle into the hole without bending it on the bronze. At the same time, not all Chinese surgeons are concerned about the precise needle sites. Taub (1976) provided an example of one surgeon who allowed his patients to choose the site of needle placement.

Experimental support for the importance of classical acupuncture sites is mixed. Katz, Kao, Spiegel, and Katz (1974) found that the use of the correct acupuncture points relieved pain in 10 of 13 patients; the use of random sites relieved pain in only 3 patients. Kepes, Chen, and Schapira (1976) found no difference in the pain relief produced by acupuncture administered at the classical sites versus

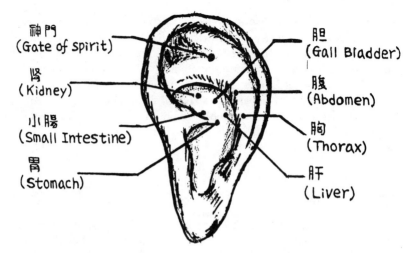

神門
(Gate of spirit)

胆
(Gall Bladder)

肾
(Kidney)

腹
(Abdomen)

小腸
(Small Intestine)

胸
(Thorax)

胃
(Stomach)

肝
(Liver)

Figure 5-3   Acupuncture sites located in the ear (Frost, Kim, Hsu, & Orkin, 1976). In Bonica, J. J. & Albe-Fessard (Eds.), *Advances in Pain Research and Therapy* (Vol. 1) New York: Raven Press, 1976. Copyright © 1976 by Raven Press, Publishers/New York.

acupuncture administered at random sites. The investigators also examined the effects of manual stimulation versus electrical stimulation of the needles. The data analysis showed that across all subjects excellent-to-good results were obtained in 19.2% to 26.9% of patients,

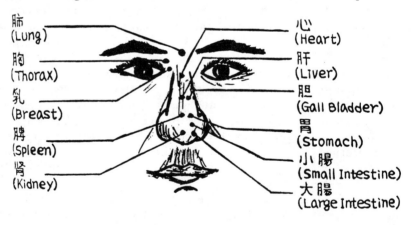

肺
(Lung)

心
(Heart)

胸
(Thorax)

肝
(Liver)

乳
(Breast)

胆
(Gall Bladder)

脾
(Spleen)

胃
(Stomach)

肾
(Kidney)

小腸
(Small Intestine)

大腸
(Large Intestine)

Figure 5-4   Acupuncture sites located in the face (Frost, Kim, Hsu, & Orkin, 1976.) In Bonica, J. J. & Albe-Fessard (Eds.), *Advances in Pain Research and Therapy* (Vol. 1) New York: Raven Press, 1976. Copyright © 1976 by Raven Press, Publishers/New York.

fair in 29.1% to 39% of patients, and none in 34% to 51.6%. No group differences between the sites (classical versus placebo) or between the methods of stimulation (manual versus electrical) were observed.

Some investigators believe that acupuncture achieves its effects primarily through psychological mechanisms. In China, the psychological state of the patient is a major determinant in making the decision to use acupuncture as a surgical anesthetic.

> Acupuncture anesthesia as practiced in China today is predicated on careful physical and psychological selection of patients. They must be in generally good health. They must be emotionally stable; that is, capable of lying motionless, awake, on an operating table for several hours. They essentially volunteer for the procedure, and compulsion, in the sense of physical or pharmacological coercion, is not used. Patients have heard of acupuncture anesthesia through Communist Party organs, from their friends, or from other patients in the hospital, and, of course, are familiar with acupuncture in medicine. School children are taught to accept needling as harmless, beneficial, and politically correct. In general, those patients selected have also been found to tolerate preliminary acupuncture testing, painful to Western observers. (Taub, 1976, p. 743)

Katz et al. observed that pain patients who benefit most from acupuncture are also highly hypnotizable. Patients who are not easily hypnotizable do not benefit from acupuncture treatment. In spite of this correlation, the authors do not believe that acupuncture and hypnosis operate through identical mechanisms. They observed that the overt behaviors of patients undergoing acupuncture and hypnosis treatments are distinct. The hypnotized patient is concentrating fully on ignoring the pain and is therefore unresponsive to everything in the immediate environment. The patient undergoing acupuncture treatment, on the other hand, is in complete contact with the external environment, as is evidenced by his ability to carry on normal conversations while the treatment is being administered. Also patients that have received both hypnosis and acupuncture feel that they are entirely different techniques. In summary, it is not known why this interesting relationship between hypnotizability and the effectiveness of acupuncture exists. Possibly, in susceptible patients, both acupuncture and hypnosis succeed in closing the gating mechanism, with acupuncture exerting its effect primarily through one mechanism and hypnosis exerting its effect primarily through another mechanism.

Mayer, Price, Barber, and Rafii (1976) found support for the hypothesis that acupuncture and hypnosis operate through different mechanisms. They compared the degree to which injections of the narcotic-antagonist naloxone reduced analgesia produced through acupuncture and hypnosis. Initially, experimental pain was induced in subjects by electrical stimulation of a tooth. A pain threshold was established for each subject by increasing the voltage until the subject reported the electrical stimulus as painful. One group of subjects was then given acupuncture and another group of subjects was hypnotized. Pain estimates were obtained, followed by the administration of naloxone to both groups. Acupuncture increased the pain thresholds (level of electrical stimulation perceived as painful) by 27%, whereas hypnosis increased pain thresholds by 85%. Clearly, hypnosis proved to be a more effective technique than acupuncture for inducing analgesia to the electrical stimulus.

Following the naloxone injections, the acupuncture group's pain threshold fell dramatically. Naloxone had no effect on the pain thresholds of the hypnosis group. The authors concluded that acupuncture, unlike hypnosis, probably achieves its effect by causing the release of endogenous morphinelike substances from the central and periaqueductal gray matter. Hypnosis probably achieves its analgesic effects through higher cortical mechanisms.

Although acupuncture may be capable of producing short-term analgesia and anesthesia, it is not a proven technique for treating persistent complaints of pain. Levine, Gormely, and Fields (1976) examined the analgesic effects of acupuncture in patients with chronic pain without nerve damage and with chronic pain associated with objective evidence of nerve damage. *Chronic pain* was defined as having persisted for more than 6 months. The majority of patients, although showing some initial relief from pain, eventually reported that the pain returned to pretreatment levels. In some patients the treatment itself produced more severe pains. All patients eventually requested the termination of needle-puncture treatment. Other researchers (Murphy, 1976) have also found the pain relief following acupuncture treatment to be short-lived.

Hypnosis

Hypnosis is currently experiencing a revival in clinical medicine. The technique is being used to assist in the control of pain associated with cancer, childbirth, and surgery. Numerous illustrations are available that attest to the power of hypnosis to assist patients during these crises. Following is an example illustrating the subjective experiences of a hypnotized patient during childbirth:

A 32-year-old physician who had had two previous pregnancies asked if we would use hypnosis during her third pregnancy. Her obstetrician was in agreement, as her first two pregnancies were marked by prolonged labor of about eighteen hours accompanied by much distress and pain. She responded well to hypnosis and was seen once a week during her pregnancy. Her labor started at 9:00 A.M. and hypnosis was induced immediately. Three hours later she delivered a normal 7½-pound male child. Some of her recorded comments were "I feel relaxed—no tensions, no fears, no anxieties . . . I know the pain perception should be pretty rough at this point . . . but I am comfortable . . . very comfortable . . . just a dull pain . . . like having a period and yet I normally have a low pain tolerance . . . I should be perceiving pain but I'm not . . . I almost feel like a drunk, relaxed, lethargic, but my brain is functioning so clearly, only a tight band about my abdomen occasionally . . . I just don't give a damn!"

She did not require nor was she given any anesthetic other than hypnosis during labor and the repair of the episiotomy. Her final comment was "No one could ask for an experience in which the pain was so intense during my first two deliveries and yet completely blocked this time." (Hilgard & Hilgard, 1975, p. 113)

The most publicized application of hypnosis has been in the context of alleviating surgical pain. Some of the most dramatic examples of hypnosis come from this application:

In 1829, prior to the discovery of anesthetic drugs, a French surgeon, Dr. Cloquet, performed a remarkable operation on a 64-year-old woman who suffered from cancer of the right breast. After making an incision from the armpit to the inner side of the breast, he removed both the malignant tumor and also several enlarged glands in the armpit. What makes this operation remarkable is that, during the surgical procedure, the patient, who had not received any drugs, conversed quietly with the physician and showed no signs of experiencing pain. During the surgery, her respiration and pulse rate appeared stable and there were no noticeable changes in her facial expression. The ability of this patient to tolerate the painful procedures was attributed to the fact that she had been mesmerized immediately prior to the operation. (Barber, Spanos, & Chaves, 1974, p. 79)

This case is one of the earliest reports of painless surgery with mesmerism, or as it is now called, hypnotism.

The general view today is that cases such as the above represent rare, rather than typical, outcomes of what can be expected from hypnosis. In fact, Barber et al. believe that the majority of these dramatic reports represent exaggerations of what actually happened.

For example, the proponents of hypnosis often cite the work of Esdaile as clear proof of the power of hypnosis. In the mid-nineteenth century Esdaile claimed to have performed major surgery on over 300 patients using only hypnosis as the analgesic. He also maintained that the surgery was painless. But was this the case? Barber et al. reexamined Esdaile's report and found that although many of the patients verbalized no pain during surgery, several of them showed "convulsive movements of the upper limbs, writhing of the body, distortion of the features giving the face a hideous expression of suppressed agony."

Hilgard (1975) believes that the scientific literature has simply moved beyond the stage of needing to refer to dramatic illustrations, either in support of or against hypnosis. He maintains that there are sufficient data showing the usefulness of hypnosis in treating pain conditions associated with burns, cancer, migraine, obstetrics, dental extractions, and surgery. He does not propose that hypnotic techniques be viewed as an alternative to chemical analgesics and anesthetics. The techniques are, however, a useful supplement in some cases in which the anesthetics may be dangerous or in which the patient is excessively anxious. Success with hypnosis as the sole anesthetic depends on how highly hypnotizable the patient is, and highly hypnotizable patients are in the minority. The majority of patients are, however, sufficiently hynotizable to warrant the use of the technique as an adjunct to chemical treatment. At the preoperative stage, hypnosis can help reduce the anxiety, tension, and worry associated with the impending operation. During the operation, hypnosis can be used to produce analgesia and anesthesia—especially in cases in which heavy doses of chemicals might be dangerous. Postoperatively, hypnosis may facilitate the convalescence period by reducing the need for narcotics and by raising the morale of the patient.

State-Nonstate Issue

Until very recently, the major theoretical issue in the hypnosis literature was whether or not hypnosis led to a unique or altered state of consciousness. Barber has been one of the major antagonists of those who take the position that hypnosis produces a unique state of mind or consciousness. Interest in the issue has declined, but the issue is far from being settled.

According to Barber, proponents of the unique-state position view the hypnotic state as being similar to the psychological state of the sleepwalker. The argument goes that both states create a person who has little contact with his surroundings, a low level of awareness, and amnesia upon awakening. The sleepwalker is also totally unresponsive to his environment. If told to awaken, the sleepwalker will not respond. In order to bring him out of this state, he must be shouted at or physically throttled. The sleepwalker has no recall for events that took place during a sleepwalking episode.

Barber believes that similarities between the hypnotized person and the sleepwalker are only superficial and that they are in fact two different states. Unlike sleepwalkers, hypnotized subjects are responsive to environmental stimuli, as evidenced by their ability to respond to the hypnotist's suggestions. Also, hypnotic subjects do not forget the events occurring during a hypnotic session if they are, in fact, told to remember what happened. Finally, hypnosis is not associated with any known unique brain-wave pattern.

Barber and his colleagues have devoted years of research to support their position. Age regression, for example, has always been considered to be uniquely associated with hypnosis. Thus hypnotized subjects are capable of behaving just as if they were 4-month-old infants. Barber believes that a control subject who is asked to simulate the role of a child can do so to the same extent as the person that has been hypnotized. Also the behaviors of hypnotized subjects tend to be somewhat superior to the actual behavior of infants or children at the specified age or to the subject's original performance at the earlier age. Examples of subjects that become deaf with the suggestion of deafness are subject to similar criticisms. Barber has shown that the hypnotized person, although not behaviorally responding to noise stimuli, does in fact hear these stimuli. To demonstrate this, he used a method called *delayed auditory feedback*.

Auditory feedback is a procedure whereby a person wearing earphones speaks and hears his own voice simultaneously. In delayed auditory feedback, the voice feedback is delayed a fraction of a second so that the person hears what he has just said rather than what he is saying. An individual with normal hearing will quickly become confused and begin to mispronounce words under this condition. A deaf individual is not affected. Barber has shown that hypnotized individuals behave more like normals than like deaf people under delayed auditory feedback. That is, they begin to stammer and slow down their speech, which indicates they are, in fact, hearing the stimulus. Sometimes, when deafness has been induced and the experimenter asks, "Can you hear me?" some subjects will respond, "No, I can't hear you." These observations certainly suggest that hypnosis consists of nothing more than a form of role playing.

If hypnosis does not resemble a trancelike state, then what kind of state does it resemble? Barber believes that a better analogy for hypnosis is that of becoming engrossed in an interesting novel, play, or movie. When reading a good novel, for example, the person becomes totally involved. He does not have contradictory thoughts such as "This is only a novel" or "This is only make-believe." Instead, he experiences the drama and the emotion that is contained in the book. From Barber's position, it is just as misleading to explain the experiences of the hypnotized subject by saying that he is in a hypnotic trance as it is to explain the experiences of the book reader by saying that he is in a hypnotic trance.

This view of hypnosis is consistent with the description of the good hypnotic subject. People vary tremendously in their responsiveness to hypnotic instructions. According to Hilgard and Hilgard (1975), the good subject is one who is able to engage freely in *imaginative involvement*. Such a person is able temporarily to set aside ordinary reality and become completely absorbed in an imaginative experience, whether it be reading, acting, or listening to music. Those individuals who can relate to such experiences are the most hypnotizable, whereas those who seldom have such experiences are the least hypnotizable.

Hilgard and Hilgard (1975) have devised a test, the Stanford Hypnotic Clinical Scale (SHCS), designed to determine a subject's susceptibility to hypnotic instructions. Thus, once the subject has been hypnotized, he is asked to imagine various happenings, such as the following:

> All right, then . . . please hold both hands straight out in front of you, palms facing inwards, hands about a foot apart. Here I'll help you. (Take hold of hands and position them about a foot apart.) Now I want you to imagine a force attracting your hands toward each other, pulling them together. Do it any way that seems best to you—think of rubber bands stretched from wrist to wrist, pulling your hands together, or imagine magnets held in each hand pulling them together—the closer they get the stronger the pull. . . . As you think of this force pulling your hands together, they will move together, slowly at first, but they will move closer together, closer and closer together as though a force is acting on them . . . moving . . . moving . . . closer, closer. (p. 214)

Hypnotizable subjects are easily able to perform such tasks, whereas nonhypnotizable subjects are not. Only a few subjects are highly hypnotizable or not hypnotizable at all; the majority of individuals lie between these extremes.

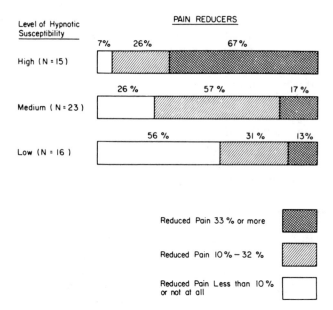

Figure 5-5   Relation of reduction of pain achieved by hypnotically suggested
analgesia to susceptibility to hypnosis (Hilgard, 1975). Copyright
© 1975 by Elsevier/North-Holland Biomedical Press, Amsterdam. Reprinted by permission of the publisher and the author.

Responsiveness to hypnosis is closely related to how effective the
technique is in reducing pain. The relationship between hypnotizability and pain reduction is shown in Figure 5-5. This illustration shows
how much reduction of pain can be expected given the level of hypnotizability of the individual. The hypnotizability of the patient is a
variable that should be assessed before hypnosis is used in clinical applications.

Hidden Observer

Hilgard and Hilgard (1975) have observed a somewhat paradoxical
situation with hypnotized subjects that have been exposed to painful
stimuli under analgesic instructions. Although the subjects verbally
report little or no pain to the stimulus, concomitant physiological indexes (heart rate, blood pressure) tend to be elevated beyond normal
levels. They began to wonder whether their hypnotized subjects were
really hurting less or whether they were simply denying or ignoring

the pain. A partial answer to the question came during a classroom demonstration of hypnosis. A student had been hypnotized to experience total deafness. Loud sounds made close to his head and direct questions made to him failed to elicit any response. Apparently he was "deaf." At this point in the demonstration, a student in the class asked if it could be possible that "some part" of the subject might be aware of what was happening. Recognizing that this was a good question, the experimenter then asked the hypnotized subject to signify with his index finger if there was some part of him that was aware of what was taking place. To his surprise, the subject immediately raised his index finger. Apparently the hypnotized person does remain in contact with the environment at some level of consciousness. This concealed awareness has been labeled by Hilgard and Hilgard as the *hidden observer* phenomenon.

The Hilgards have studied the hidden observer effect in several experiments. One of the studies required a hypnotized subject to place one arm in a bucket of ice water while under the suggestion of analgesia in that arm. The activity of the other arm was to be kept from awareness. The subject was instructed to report her pain sensations on a scale ranging from 0, for no pain, up to 10, for a very severe pain. The subject was instructed to feel no pain, and the technique was successful inasmuch as she verbally reported a pain rating of 0 throughout the experiment. She had also been instructed under hypnosis to use the same numerical rating scale for the hand that was out of awareness, but she would not be aware of what the hand was writing. While she was overtly reporting 0 pain, the hand that was out of awareness was writing scale values for increasing covert pain as follows: 2, 5, 7, and 9. The hidden observer was reporting essentially normal pain while the hypnotized part of the subject was experiencing no pain at all. Not all subjects who are able to achieve hypnotic reduction of pain have access to covert pain. For those who do, Hilgard believes that this aspect of the pain experience has been hidden by a kind of amnesic process. The subject, upon removal of the hypnosis, will not recall reporting the covert pain, unless instructed to do so.

The Hilgards believe that in some way the human mind is capable of operating from several independent communication channels, in this case from an overt and a covert channel. In some unknown way, one channel is able to operate outside awareness of the other channel. They give an example of a hypnotized patient who had been given suggestions that his left arm was analgesic and insensitive and that his right arm would write automatically and the subject would not be aware of what he was writing. When the experimenter pricked the left (anesthetic) arm several times with a hypodermic needle, the other hand wrote, "Ouch, damn it, you're hurting me." After a few minutes, the subject, oblivious to what had happened, asked when the experiment was going to begin.

A similar phenomenon has been observed with patients who have had surgery performed under hypnotic analgesia. Chertok, Michaux, and Droin (1977) found that patients were able to recall, at a later date, the events that took place in the operating theater. Following the surgery, at a later date, two patients were rehypnotized and ask to describe the bodily sensations associated with their previous surgery. Both patients were capable of recalling the sensations but did not feel that these sensations were terribly painful. One of the patients described the sensations associated with tooth extraction as follows:

> I don't know, I don't know any more. There were little . . . I felt sort of little twinges . . . I'm not sure . . . Yes, maybe three or four times—I'm not sure. Something like little twinges in the jaw—and then I think I woke up after that, and then you were telling me that it was over. . . .
>
> Oh, no—I felt something, I felt that something was being placed in my mouth. It reminded me of the time when my dentist took impressions for my dentures, but it wasn't so unpleasant anyway, it wasn't painful. And after that I think I woke up; but I only had one thought on awakening: "When are you going to start, and get it over?" And you told me: "It's all over". (p. 92)

Following the model of the hidden observer, the authors concluded that hypnotic analgesia modified both sensory pain and associated suffering while at the hidden level the sensory pain was still experienced. They also cited an experiment by Cheek (1964) who found that patients undergoing surgery under general anesthesia were able to recall the conversations between members of the operating team. One obvious lesson from these illustrations is to be careful about what is said in the presence of an anesthetized patient.

Hilgard (1975) also reported an experiment that is relevant to the state-nonstate issue. Proponents of the nonstate position have argued that pain reduction from direct suggestion is similar to the reduction observed following hypnotic induction. The experiments supporting this argument have not controlled for the hypnotizability of the subjects involved, however. Thus the comparisons probably included some subjects that were not hypnotized and, as well, some highly hypnotizable subjects who drifted into hypnosis under the suggestion instructions. The suggestion condition used in these experiments demands considerable subjective involvement and differs from hypnosis only in that formal induction procedures are not used. The subject is not told that he will become relaxed, fall asleep, and then enter a unique hypnotic state. It might be instructive to examine what he is told under "suggestion instructions." The following instructions were taken from an experiment reported by Spanos, Barber, and Lang (1974):

> I want you to succeed in not being disturbed by the weight by doing the following. Try to the best of your ability to imagine and think of your right hand as numb and insensitive. Think of your right hand as unable to sense any pain or discomfort. Please try to think of your hand as numb and insensitive as if it were a piece of rubber, until I take the weight off your finger. Other students were able to think of their hand in this way and it isn't as hard as it seems. What I want you to do is to control your thoughts and think continuously that your right hand has no feeling. Keep thinking that it is unable to feel any pain or discomfort. Continue to think of your hand as without pain, discomfort, or feeling of any kind. Please try to the very best of your ability to think continuously and to imagine vividly that your hand is numb, insensitive, and like a piece of rubber until the weight is off. Now keep thinking and vividly imagining that your right hand is becoming more and more numb and insensitive. (p. 148)

After reading this passage, it is easier to appreciate Hilgard's point that under such instructions, highly hypnotizable subjects might drift into hypnosis.

Hilgard used a variant of the hidden observer technique to compare the effectiveness of direct-suggestion and hypnotic-induction procedures in controlling pain responses to the cold pressor test. Only highly hypnotizable subjects were used, and they were instructed not to enter hypnosis under the suggestion instructions. Under the suggestion condition, the subjects first reported their overt response to the cold stimulus. Next they were hypnotized and asked to give a restrospective report of the pain experience under automatic talking (rather than automatic writing) instructions. In the hypnotic-analgesia condition, the subjects gave verbal reports of the overt pain experienced and tapped out covert pain ratings on a computer key.

The reduction in overt pain was far greater under the hypnotic-induction condition than under the suggestion condition. Covert pain, although reduced in intensity from the normal waking condition, was experienced equally under the hypnosis and suggestion conditions. Apparently, if subjects are carefully selected, hypnosis is capable of reducing pain to a greater extent than suggestion—at least at the overt level. Hilgard believes that suggestions may reduce pain by modifying the emotional response to the pain (that is, by teaching the individual to relax in the presence of pain), whereas hypnosis actually blocks a major portion of the pain response from awareness.

Chronic-pain Patients

Fortunately, most of us have not experienced intense and chronic pain. In fact, the experience of pain is usually short-lived and reversible. Also, commonly occurring pains that result from a toothache, cuts, or bruises are easily traceable to some specific cause such as failure to seek professional assistance or to care sufficiently for oneself during some activity. Chronic pain, however, quite often has no identifiable cause for the individuals afflicted:

> We ask what we have done to deserve such pain, and think back to make a connection between some action of ours and the onset of the pain. We implore others to help us, to take away the hurt. We promise that once the pain is removed we will be different—we will be kinder to others, do good works. We beg for forgiveness, we say we are sorry. We ask God for help, we ask Him to save us, and swear we will be faithful in going to church. As the intensity of the pain increases, as we experience greater agony, our thoughts are less specific and our pleas more disorganized. We are ready to promise anything, if only someone will help. Finally we feel only the pain, we have no thoughts, and our cries become wordless moans. (Sternbach, 1968, p. 83)

The situation for chronic-pain sufferers has been depicted as one in which hopelessness and despair over their endless suffering predominates in their lives, with only death providing relief:

> Pain patients frequently say that they could stand their pain much better if they could only get a good night's sleep. They feel as though their resistance is weakened by their lack of sleep. They never feel rested. They feel worn down, worn out, exhausted. They find themselves getting more and more irritable with their families, they have fewer and fewer friends, and fewer and fewer interests. Gradually, as time goes on, the boundaries of their world seem to shrink. They become more and more preoccupied with their pain, less and less interested in the world around them. Their world begins to center around home, doctor's office, and pharmacy. (Sternbach, 1974, p. 7)

This passage suggests that pain, if prolonged, changes the afflicted individual's perceptions, preoccupations, and activities. Once such changes occur, the new behavioral patterns may be more instrumental in eliciting the sensation of pain than was the original physical trauma.

There is some evidence to support the notion that chronic-pain patients manifest distinctive psychological characteristics and that these characteristics influence their response to treatment. Sternbach, Wolf, Murphy, and Akeson (1973b) compared the *Minnesota Multiphasic Personality Inventory* (MMPI) responses of a group of acute-pain patients (less than 6 months) with the similar responses of a group of chronic-pain patients (more than 6 months). The MMPI is a clinical test that is used for classifying patients into diagnostic categories. The MMPI profiles for the acute and chronic patients are presented in Figure 5-6. The average score for the normal population is defined as 50, and scores 2 or more standard deviations above the

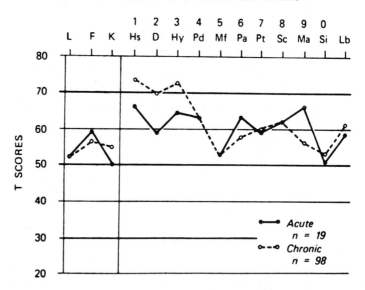

MMPIs -- ACUTE vs. CHRONIC LOW BACKS

Figure 5-6 Comparisons of MMPI profiles of acute and chronic low back-pain patients; major differences occurred on the first three clinical subscales: (Hs) Hysteria, (D) Depression, and (Hy) Hypochondriasis (Sternbach, Wolf, Murphy, & Akeson, 1973b). Copyright © 1973, Academy of Psychosomatic Medicine. Reprinted by permission of the publisher.

mean (70 and higher) are considered to be clinically significant. The two groups differed significantly on the first three scales, which are *Hypochondriasis* (undue concern over health and bodily symptoms), *Depression* (feelings of hopelessness), and *Hysteria* (multiple physical symptoms for which there is no known physical basis). The three scales in combination comprise the *neurotic triad*, and those with chronic pain obtained clinically significant scores, whereas the acute-pain patients were within normal limits. This finding suggests that, during the initial stages of their illness, the chronic patients would have had a more normal-looking profile and that their present neurotic disturbances reflect a preoccupation and extension of the pain symptoms.

Organic versus Psychogenic Pain

It is important to understand that a diagnosis of organically caused pain does not rule out the relevance of psychological variables for any particular patient. That is to say, a positive neurological examination may yield only a small part of the answer in terms of understanding the patient's pain complaints. Until recently, there was a tendency to view organic pain as one kind of pain and psychogenic pain as another kind of pain. The term *psychogenic* was taken to mean "due to psychological causes," which implied that the patient was "imagining" his pain or that it was not really pain simply because an organic basis could not be found. Psychogenic pain is not experienced differently, however, from that arising from physical disease or injury. Psychogenic and organic pain both hurt the same. Moreover, as seen in the context of the gate-control theory, the experience of pain may be elicited by psychological events through the postulated central control trigger. Thus, even when some physical damage has previously occurred, the combination of past experience and present emotional experience can induce the original pain experience. An example of this point is a patient who, although he had recovered from a physically produced pain, continued to experience a burning pain whenever he became depressed. When he was cheerful, the pain abated, and when he was depressed, the pain returned.

In short, the lifestyles of both organic and nonorganic pain patients may become similar across time as these individuals attempt to cope with their affliction. Sternbach, Wolf, Murphy, and Akeson (1973a) compared the MMPI profiles of low back-pain patients who showed positive neurological signs (muscle atrophy, decreased sensation, diminished tendon reflexes) with the MMPI profiles of a group of similar patients that did not manifest neurological damage. The profiles for the groups were similar, with both scoring high on *Hysteria*, *Hypochondriasis*, and *Depression*.

These data suggest that surgical treatment alone might not prove effective in alleviating pain if in fact the pain has become a central focus for the patient. Support for this notion has been provided by Blumetti and Modesti (1976), who found that patients suffering from intractable back pain benefited far less from surgical intervention if they scored high on the *Hysteria* and *Hypochondriasis* subscales of the MMPI. Patients that were within normal limits on these two scales showed greater benefits from surgery.

It is apparent, then, that excessive bodily concerns may become a central attitude of *both* organic and psychogenic pain patients. Sternbach (1974) has observed that the mean age of the patient in almost all of the pain studies is about 42 years.

> In our Western culture this is the time when one is well into middle age, when childen are maturing and husband and wife are again the centre of each other's attention, and when one has usually reached the limits of occupational success. In all of these areas there are bases for disappointment and discouragement. Middle age is also the time when anxiety-provoking stresses occur. Friends die of heart attacks. One reads of famous persons, younger than oneself, being treated for cancer. Parents die, and one wonders whether (and when) one will die of the same disease. With the advancing years there is a clearly noticeable increase in uncomfortable physical sensations; joints ache, muscles stiffen, more foods are harder to digest, and sleep comes less easily and is less restful. (p. 35)

As a result of difficulties at work or at home, the individual may begin to experience feelings of resentment and self-pity. He will also be more likely to focus on physical sensations and interpret these as a sign of illness.

According to Engel (1959) individuals that are likely to develop this hypochondriacal response pattern are characterized by the following features: (a) prominent guilt feelings that tend to be relieved by the experience of pain; (b) a family history of violence and punishment that predisposes the patient to use pain to expiate guilt feelings; (c) a personal history of suffering, defeat, inability to tolerate success, and a tendency to solicit pain with a large number of injuries, operations, and painful examination; (d) great anger and hostility toward others, which is rarely expressed directly, but instead is turned in on the self and is experienced as pain; (e) strong conflict over sexual impulses that are usually unconscious and expressed only indirectly and that, with aggressive and guilty feelings, are symbolized by the appearance of pain; and (f) the development of pain to reflect the loss of another person. Although these predisposing characteristics may or may not have an empirical basis, there is no question that chronic-pain complaints can become the focus of lifestyle for some individuals.

Sternbach (1974) proposed that a distinction be made between the sensation of pain and the behavioral characteristics of pain patients. Pain patients, he believes, should be viewed as a class of individuals possessing common characteristics much as anxious or depressed individuals are assumed to possess identifying characteristics. The distinction has theoretical and practical value for increasing our understanding of the dynamics of these patients. An immediate theoretical gain of the distinction is that it becomes possible to view psychogenic and organically based chronic-pain patients as possessing similar characteristics.

All kinds of problems arise when the complaints of chronic-pain patients are not viewed in a holistic fashion. Initially, the chronic-pain patient will probably have consulted a family physician or a general practitioner, who after a period of time will have referred the patient to a specialist. After having been hospitalized and told that the disease is not treatable, the patient may seek out different specialists. Or the patient may have surgery that produces relief, but in the long run, the pain might return to its former intensity. Consequently, the patient will be placed on dosages of a combination of medication and instructed to return for follow-up visits at frequent and regular intervals. As time passes, the required dosages increase and further problems develop. At this time, a psychologist or psychiatrist might enter the scene. Quite often the patient will react with hostility because he knows that he is not crazy or imagining his pain. A typical patient's response is to say, "How can it all be in my head when I hurt here?" The psychiatrist might say that the pain is "psychosomatic" or that it is not, but in either case, nothing of value to the patient will come out of this interchange. Unfortunately, the patient must continue this cycle because, "Who knows?—maybe something will be found." At this point, too, he might read in a popular magazine of the successful treatment of cases similar to his through hypnotism or acupuncture. Although such treatments may help for a while, the pain eventually returns. According to Sternbach, this cycle goes on every day in thousands of pain clinics and doctors' offices across the country. He feels that this happens, primarily, because we do not recognize the self-identity of the pain patient.

Pain Games

Thomas Szasz (1968) first used the term *painmanship* to characterize the interaction that occurs between pain patients and physicians. In the game of painmanship, the physician's aim is to confirm
his or her professional identity by being able to identify the cause of
the pain and to relieve the patient's suffering. The patient's aim, on
the other hand, is to confirm his identity as a painful, suffering person
by presenting the physician with undiagnosable pain and unrelievable
suffering. Szasz contends that it is as unreasonable to expect the
patient to give up his identity and career as it is to ask the physician
to do so.

Although Szasz was describing psychogenic pain patients,
Sternbach (1974) believes that such a pattern characterizes large
numbers of organically based pain patients as well. He feels that this is
a most dangerous situation because the patient will not let doctors be
and will insist on medical and surgical intervention in order to
legitimize his role as a professional invalid. Moreover the game is
not engaged in for entertainment. There is no assumption that the
patient (or doctor) is aware of what he is doing. The game is actually a
lifestyle developed over a period of time designed to confirm a particular self-concept. Thus, it is similar to the games played by others to
confirm their roles as psychologist, alcoholic, physician, nurse, drug
addict, or schizophrenic.

The pain game begins when the following transaction occurs between the patient and the physician:

> *Pain Patient*:   I hurt, please fix me. (But you can't.)
> *Doctor*:   I'll fix you.
>   Procedures are performed; these fail, and relief is again de-
> manded; the doctor admits failure, a referral is made and/or more pro-
> cedures are performed, which fail, etc. The transaction is completed
> when the following exchange occurs:
> *Pain Patient* (in righteous indignation):   Another incompetent quack.
> *Doctor* (defensively):   Another crock. (Sternbach, 1974, p. 55)

Examples of specific pain game players are the *addict* who consumes
multiple drugs and constantly complains of a distaste for drugs or the
home tyrant who would be much more responsible at home—if only
the pain were not so intense.

The concept of behavioral games has been accused of being cyni-
cal because it implies that the pain experience is a form of a put-on.
For example, Szasz (1968) has depicted the hypochondriacal person
as having a bachelor's degree in pain; the more seriously disabled in-

dividual who has had multiple encounters with surgical operations as having a doctor's degree in pain; and the patient usually described as suffering from "intractable" and "unbearable" pain (but no bodily illness) as having a Nobel Prize in pain. Each kind of individual is likely to have as his medical partner a correspondingly qualified expert in pain: the beginner in pain, the general practitioner; the advanced student, the general surgeon; and the champion, a neurosurgeon. However, Szasz is using humor to emphasize the seriousness of the matter. The roles associated with these "careers" are as real as any behavior can be. Moreover, the analysis of a patient in terms of role behavior increases our understanding of their pain complaints. Chapter 7 contains an examination of behavioral treatment techniques that are currently being used to modify such behaviors and an assessment of the extent to which these techniques lead to a reduction in the actual suffering of chronic-pain patients.

Psychopharmacology

Beginning in the 1950s the use of drugs to control mood and behavior disorders increased at a fantastic rate. In fact, many individuals believe that our society has become largely drug dependent. In this chapter, the concern is not with drug abuse per se but with the theoretical rationale implicit in the use of medication to alter behavioral disorders. Psychoactive or mood-modifying compounds are often advertised as "adjuncts" to therapy only, but the same advertisement will imply that the drug is capable of treating or "curing" the patient within the medical sense of the term. For example, diazepam, or Valium, is advertised as providing "prompt relief of psychic tension, anxiety, apprehension and agitation" and also as capable of reducing "somatic symptoms and depressive symptomatology secondary to psychic tension."

Although physicians are skeptical of such advertisements, many patients are convinced of the drug's powers. In fact, patient demands for prompt relief of psychological difficulties for themselves and their children constitute the major reason for the heavy prescription of psychopharmacological compounds. At the same time there is a poor understanding of what can be expected from psychoactive drugs. Because behavioral disorders are under the control of a multitude of variables, it is unreasonable to expect a total cure from the drug alone. Moreover, the theory and the application of drugs that affect behavior require a model different from that underlying the use of drugs associated with the organic disorders.

Principles of Drug Action

Basic principles of drug action have been established for the peripheral nervous system, and similar principles of drug action are assumed to hold for the central nervous system as well. In Chapter 2 the peripheral nervous system was described as consisting of the somatic motor system and the autonomic nervous system. The somatic system consists of nerves that regulate the skeletal muscles in the body, whereas the autonomic nervous system is a system whose nerves control intestinal muscle, cardiac muscle, and glands. Drugs exert their effects primarily at synaptic sites throughout the nervous system. The synapse is the gap that separates the axonal membrane of one neuron from the dendritic membrane of an adjacent neuron. Synaptic junctions also occur between neuronal endings and the muscles being innervated.

Transmission of a Nerve Impulse

When a nerve-action potential (NAP) reaches the end of an axon, a chemical compound or transmitter is released from the axon into the synaptic space (Figure 6-1). The process by which an impulse is transmitted across a synapse may be analyzed in a series of steps. First, there is the arrival of the nerve action potential at the axonal ending. Within the axonal ending, there are a number of small sacs called *synaptic vesicles*. The chemical compound, or transmitter, is stored within these small vesicles. With the arrival of a nerve impulse, the second step takes place, which is the release of the transmitter into the synaptic space. The transmitter substance diffuses across the synaptic space and combines with specialized receptor substances on the adjacent dendrite (called the *postjunctional membrane*).

The concept of receptive substance or drug receptor is used by pharmacologists to explain how transmitter molecules, once diffusing across the synaptic cleft, combine with the postjunctional membranes. A receptor is considered to be a specialized material or chemical complex located within the postjunctional membrane. Drug receptors have a high degree of specificity for certain drug molecules. This drug-receptor specificity is used to account for the observation that slight variations in the chemical structure of a drug may have a profound effect on the cell's response to the drug. For example, amphetamine and methamphetamine are both powerful stimulants of

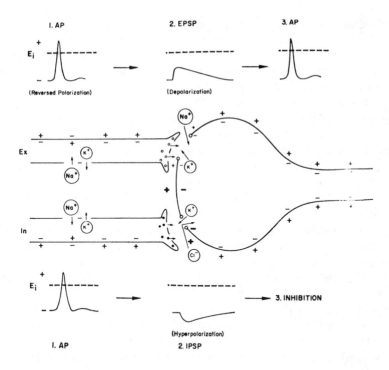

the central nervous system, but methamphetamine is slightly different in chemical structure from amphetamine, a difference that causes it to be a more potent stimulant (Julien, 1975). It is assumed that methamphetamine "fits" the receptor better than amphetamine and produces a greater change in the postjunctional cellular membrane.

Following the interaction of the transmitter molecule with the receptor, one of two kinds of changes take place. Some transmitters decrease the postjunctional membrane potential producing what is called an *excitatory postsynaptic potential (EPSP)*. Assume that during the resting state the interior of the postjunctional membrane is -70 millivolts (one thousandth of a volt) to the exterior. Also assume that once this voltage difference reaches -40 millivolts, the postjunctional neuron fires. An excitatory postsynaptic potential means that the postjunctional membrane is somewhere between -70 and -40 millivolts. It is called "excitatory" because it will now take less of a stimulus to initiate a nerve-action potential down the postjunctional neuron. The other change that can take place is called an *inhibitory postsynaptic potential (IPSP)*. The postjunctional membrane becomes selectively permeable to smaller positive ions and negative ions, and as a result the interior becomes more negative (further away from the threshold value) than it was during the resting state. It will now take a stronger stimulus to initiate a nerve-action potential. Whether the neuron fires is determined by a continual interplay between these excitatory and inhibitory influences.

The final step in the transmission of an impulse across a synapse involves the destruction of the transmitter itself. After the transmitter has performed its job, it must be immediately removed in order to allow the neuron to repolarize. The removal is accomplished by the release of an enzyme that destroys the transmitter substance by breaking it down into its constituent parts. An example of a transmitter is acetylcholine; acetylcholinesterase is the enzyme that breaks acetylcholine down. Norepinephrine, serotonin, and dopamine are other transmitters.

Sites of Drug Action

Within the peripheral nervous system there are four major synaptic sites of drug action: (a) skeletal muscles; (b) smooth muscles, cardiac muscle, and glands innervated by the parasympathetic division of the autonomic nervous system; (c) autonomic ganglia; and (d) smooth muscles, cardiac muscle, and glands innervated by the sympathetic division of the autonomic nervous system. *Acetylcholine* is the transmitter found at autonomic ganglia, parasympathetic post-ganglionic nerve endings, some sympathetic postganglionic nerve endings, and somatic postganglionic nerve endings. *Norepinephrine* is the transmitter found at most sympathetic postganglionic nerve endings. Acetylcholine and norepinephrine are also found within the central nervous system. Drugs that mimic the actions of acetylcholine are called *cholinergic drugs* or *cholinomimetics*. Drugs that mimic the actions of norepinephrine are called *adrenergic drugs* or *sympathomimetics*.

There are several ways in which a drug might operate within the nervous system: (a) the direct action of a drug resulting from its ability to combine with a cholinergic or adrenergic receptor on a neuron and thus either initiates excitation or inhibition, (b) a direct action of a drug to block a receptor and thus prevent the synaptic transmitter from having any action, (c) an indirect action whereby a drug would release the synaptic transmitter from an axon terminal of one neuron and thus initiate excitation or inhibition in the next neuron, (d) an indirect action by which the drug inhibits the synthesis of a synaptic transmitter within a neuron and thereby blocks synaptic transmission, and (e) an indirect action by which the drug prevents the storage of the synaptic transmitter in the neuron and thus makes it unavailable for release.

Classification of Psychopharmacological Drugs

Prior to the 1950s, drugs with specific psychological therapeutic effects were not in use. That is, centrally acting drugs were classified as nonspecific depressants or nonspecific stimulants. Barbiturates were widely used as depressants, and amphetamines were widely used as stimulants. Their effects were nonspecific in the sense that all behaviors were either decreased or increased. The barbiturates, for example, did not specifically suppress symptoms of anxiety; rather, they induced a general anestheticlike effect. Then, in the 1950s, several drugs were discovered that seemed to have specific psychotherapeutic effects. The drug reserpine, an extract of the plant *Rauwolfia serpentina*, generated the initial interest in specific drug effects (Harvey, 1971). Reserpine and (soon after) chlorpromazine were discovered to decrease the excessive agitated behavior of psychotics at dosages that did not decrease normal consciousness or impair intellectual functioning. These major tranquilizers, as they were called, were found to be highly effective in altering behaviors associated with schizophrenia. In addition, minor tranquilizers such as chlordiazepoxide (Librium) and meprobamate were found to be of value in the treatment of neurotic disorders. Also, specific drugs were identified for the treatment of depression.

Following these demonstrations of relative drug specificity, a number of behaviorally based classification systems of centrally acting drugs emerged. Representative of these systems is the following (Jarvik, 1967):

I. *Psychotherapeutic drugs*

　A. *Antipsychotics.* These drugs are used primarily to treat major psychoses, such as schizophrenia, manic depressive psychoses, and senile psychoses. The phenothiazines (Thorazine) are the best known family of antipsychotic drugs.

　B. *Antianxiety drugs.* These are used to combat insomnia, induce muscle relaxation, treat neurotic conditions, and reduce psychological stress. The barbiturates and the benzodiazepines are two classes of antianxiety drugs.

　C. *Antidepressant drugs.* These are used in the treatment of psychiatric depression. The monoamine oxidase inhibitors (such as Parnate) fall in this category.

II. *Psychotogenics.* These drugs produce changes in mood, thinking, and behavior. The resultant drug state may resemble a psychotic state, with delusions, hallucinations, and distorted perceptions. These drugs have little therapeutic value.

III. *Stimulants.* These drugs elevate mood, increase confidence and alertness, and prevent fatigue. Many diverse drugs may serve as stimulants including amphetamine, caffeine, and nicotine.

IV. *Sedatives and hypnotics.* Most of these drugs produce general depression (sedation) in low doses, and sleep (hypnosis) in larger doses. They are used clinically to treat stress, anxiety, and insomnia. The barbiturates are the best known representatives of this class.

V. *Anesthetics, analgesics, and paralytics.* General anesthetics act centrally to cause a loss of consciousness. Analgesic drugs, many of them addicting, typically produce euphoria and stupor and are effective pain relievers. Well-known analgesics are aspirin and morphine. Paralytic drugs (such as curare, succinylcholine) act primarily at the neuromuscular junction to produce muscular paralysis.

Drug–Behavior Interactions

The excitement surrounding the advent of the tranquilizers, antidepressants, and antipsychotics was generated by their apparently greater selective effects as compared with the effects of previously employed drugs. These demonstrations of specificity gave new impetus for the belief that behavioral disorders did in fact have a strictly biological basis. Biochemical researchers reasoned that if the behavioral and physiochemical effects of a drug were identifiable, then it should be possible to identify the physical systems mediating the observed behavioral changes.

The hoped-for one-to-one relationship between chemistry and behavior was to prove to be naïve, for it quickly became evident that the behavioral effects of psychopharmacological compounds were often variable and unpredictable. In some cases small dosages of a drug could not be distinguished from the effects of administering an inactive compound such as sugar. In other instances, the same drug might produce stimulation in one case and depression in another. Moreover, researchers discovered that the drug effect, at the physiological level, is also influenced by the ongoing activity of the involved organ. For example, the effect of amphetamine on the small intestine is dependent on the predrug activity of the intestinal muscle. During digestive activity, amphetamine may cause relaxation of the intestine, but if the intestine is already relaxed, amphetamine may produce contraction. Greater difficulties were encountered at the behavioral level. Researchers found that the behavioral effect of a drug is also influenced to a great extent by the ongoing behavior of the recipient.

In studying drug–behavior interactions with animals, researchers have relied heavily on the learning concept of schedules of reinforcement. In formal terms the concept of *schedule of reinforcement* is defined as a statement of the contingencies upon which reinforcement depends. There are four basic schedules of reinforcement used in animal research, two of which are based on the number of responses and the other two on the passage of time. The two based on number of responses are *fixed-ratio* (FR) and *variable-ratio* (VR) schedules of reinforcement. The two based on time are called *fixed-interval* (FI) and *variable-interval* (VI) schedules. On a fixed-ratio schedule, a specific number of responses are required before reinforcement is administered. An FR-10, for example, would require that 10 responses be made, whereas an FR-25 would require 25 responses be made before reinforcement is administered. A variable-ratio schedule requires an average number of responses be made with the number changing from trial to trial. Thus an animal on a VR-10 would be rewarded on the average after the 10th response; sometimes it would be after the 5th; other times after the 12th response; and so on. Interval schedules require that a period of time elapse before a response is reinforced. With fixed-interval schedules, the time period is constant; with variable interval schedules, the length of time between reinforcement varies from one reinforcement to the next, but around some average duration. To illustrate, a rat on an FI-10 is reinforced for the first bar press that occurs 10 seconds after the last reinforced bar press. A rat on a VI-10 is reinforced for the first bar press that occurs on an average of 10 seconds or more but the interval is sometimes 5 seconds, sometimes 20 seconds, and so on.

Dews (1955) demonstrated that the effect of a drug is partially determined by the type of schedule on which the organism is trained. He used the drug pentobarbital, which is generally classified as a central nervous system depressant. Pigeons were tested under two different schedules of reinforcement. Under one, the bird was required to peck at a stimulus key 50 times for reinforcement (FR-50). The second schedule required the bird to wait 15 minutes before pecking (FI-15). After receiving low doses of pentobarbital, pigeons made fewer responses on the FI-15 schedule than they did after being injected with saline; but the same dosage of pentobarbital actually produced an increase in response rate under the FR-50 schedule. This experiment demonstrated clearly that the behavior of the organism modified the action of the drug, and this interaction must be taken into account in attempting to predict drug-administration outcomes.

Although the research of Dews (pecking rates of pigeons) is hardly characteristic of the clinical setting, certain variables influencing drug response at the human level have been studied. The stimuli influencing human behavior are often those produced by other individuals, and such social influences have proved to markedly affect drug response. For example, in one experiment four persons in the same room were told they would each receive a sleeping pill (barbiturate). In fact, three did receive the barbiturate, but one received amphetamine. The three subjects receiving the barbiturate became drowsy and sat about quietly, but so did the subject that had received amphetamine (Harvey, 1971). This study indicated that the effect of amphetamine was more powerfully determined by the social influence of the experimenter and by the behavior of the other three subjects than by the drug itself.

This research calls to mind the cognitive-label theory of Schachter (Schachter & Singer, 1962). In fact, Schachter has explained the positive benefits reported from smoking marihuana within his cognitive-label theory. At the physiological level, marihuana produces physiological arousal, associated with an increase in heart rate, a slight rise in blood pressure, minimal changes in blood sugar and metabolic rate, dryness of the mouth, tremor, and increased sensory sensitivity. In and of themselves, according to Schachter, such bodily changes could just as equally be labeled "sick" as "high." He believes that the individual must learn to label these changes as pleasant and this process takes time. Many novice smokers, after receiving detailed instructions, wait for the euphoria to set in and to their dismay nothing happens. At first the novice will experience new sensations ("My legs feel rubbery"). With the assistance of the continued laughter and giggling from the experienced users, the novice will eventually transform these sensations into euphoric cognitions. The drug-produced "high," within this framework, is truly a psychobiological experience.

These examples illustrate the tremendous complexities associated with predicting the behavioral effects of psychoactive drugs. It is necessary to understand not only the drug-produced changes in physiochemistry but also how these changes *interact* with the individual's current situation and learning history. Thus drugs do not create new behavior but only influence existing behavior.

Placebo Effects

Our current understanding of subject and environmental variables that are interactive with drug-produced effects comes largely from studies dealing with the placebo effect. *Placebo* is Latin for "I shall please" and is defined as "any component of therapy that is deliberately or knowingly used for its nonspecific, psychologic, or psychophysiologic effect, or that is used unknowingly for its presumed or believed specific effect on a patient, symptom, or illness, but which, unknown to patient and therapist, is without specific activity for the condition being treated" (Shapiro, 1976, p. 796). An important aspect of this definition is that a therapeutic procedure may be used with or without knowledge that it is a placebo, including treatments given in the belief that they are not placebos.

According to Shapiro (1976) the placebo effect is the main reason that many forms of primitive treatment techniques used throughout the history of medicine were effective.

> Psychologic factors in illness and treatment have always been important in medicine and were recognized by Hippocrates and also by Galen who insightfully observed, "He cures most successfully in whom people have the greatest confidence." He then estimated that 60% of patients had emotional rather than physical symptoms, a figure that is close to the contemporary estimate of 50 to 80%. Despite the psychologic sensitivity of Galen and Hippocrates, all of the drugs used in their treatment were placebos.
>
> Treatment was primitive, unscientific, for the most part ineffective, and often shocking and dangerous. Patients were given every known organic and inorganic substance including blood from almost every animal and nearly all excretions from humans and animals.
>
> Some famous treatments used for centuries bore unique names such as the royal touch, Egyptian mummy, bezoar stone, mandrake, Theriac (with 37 to 63 ingredients) and mattioli (with 230 ingredients), the last two requiring several months to concoct, and a unicorn's horn which sold for as much as the equivalent of $250,000. Galen's elaborate pharmacopoeia contained 820 animal, vegetable, and mineral substances all of which were worthless. Medical reasoning was primitive: lung of the long-winded fox was given to consumptives; fat of a hirsute bear was prescribed for baldness; mistletoe, a plant that grows on the oak which cannot fall, was specified for the falling sickness. . . . Throughout medical history patients were purged, puked, poisoned, punctured, cut, cupped, blistered, bled, leeched, heated, dehydrated, frozen, sweated, and shocked.
>
> Useful drugs or procedures appeared infrequently in medical history and even then were usually forgotten by succeeding generations. For thousands of years physicians prescribed what we know were useless and often dangerous medications. This would not have been possible were it not for the fact that physicians did in some way help their patients. Today we know that the effectiveness of these procedures was due to psychologic factors that are often referred to as the placebo effect. (p. 794)

Even in modern times, the placebo effect remains an important component of treatment. After reviewing 15 studies, Beecher (1959) concluded that placebo medication successfully reduced pain in approximately 35% of the patients studied. Evans (1974) reviewed 13 more recent studies and concluded that an average of 36% of patients achieve relief from pain after ingesting a placebo. It has also been stated that 35% to 45% of all current prescriptions are for substances that are incapable of having an effect on the condition for which they are prescribed (Bok, 1974). Many mood-modifying drugs seem to appear and then quickly disappear, almost like fashions. All forms of treatment rely on the placebo effect to some extent. X rays, vitamins, antibiotics, and even surgery all have a placebo component, which in some cases may account totally for the improvement.

Controlling for the Placebo Effect

Drug researchers have generally preferred to ignore the effects of drug–behavior interactions and operate as if the drug-produced effects are independent from subject variables. For example, the standard procedure for testing a drug's effectiveness is to perform an experiment using a *double-blind crossover design.* In this design one group receives the placebo substance during the first experimental period and during the second period is switched to the active substance. A second group begins the experiment with the active substance and is switched to the placebo during the second period of the experiment. Neither the experimenter nor the subject knows the nature of the compound being administered at any particular session. Thus expectancies on the part of the experimenter and the subject are controlled. At the end of the experiment the drug code is broken. The placebo effect is then subtracted from the drug effect, and the observed differences are attributed to the medication. For example, if 60% of the subjects are observed to improve under the drug condition and 40% are observed to improve under the placebo condition, the drug effect is assumed to be 20%.

There are two arguments against assuming that it is possible to view drug-produced changes and subject-produced changes as being independent in operation. Not informing a subject as to what he has ingested does not rule out subject variables but rather creates a kind of guessing game in which the subject is not certain whether he should or should not feel better. This relates to the second argument, which is the observation that clinical studies that have failed to use double-blind procedures usually report success rates four-to-five times in excess of studies that have used double-blind procedures. In short it is the interaction between drug effects and placebo effects that is critical and not the drug effect or the placebo effect in isolation.

Why have researchers ignored the interactive effects between placebo variables and drug-produced changes? The placebo effect has always had negative connotations in psychology and medicine. Discussions of the placebo effect in psychology and medical texts are usually in terms of control groups for psychotherapy and chemotherapy. Shapiro (1971) found that physicians and therapists are far more likely to find placebo effects in the work of others than in their own work. In a definition of the placebo, surgeons excluded surgery, in-

ternists excluded active medicine, and psychotherapists and psychoanalysts excluded psychotherapy and psychoanalysis.

The negative view of placebo phenomena has at its basis the mis-
taken belief that placebo effects are "unreal." The assumption is that if
a patient improves simply by "wanting to" or by following a psychological suggestion, this is evidence that he wasn't really ill in the first place
(Ullmann & Krasner, 1969). It is important to realize that the definition of the placebo effect includes actual physiological changes and is
not restricted to psychological changes. Sternbach (1964) demonstrated experimentally that physiological changes do occur under
placebo conditions. He had six students take part in a "drug" experiment consisting of three experimental sessions. The subjects were told
that they would have to ingest three different pills that had different
effects on the activity of the stomach. The following instructions were
associated with each pill:

> *Stimulant (+).* This pill is a stimulant to the stomach. You'll feel
> your stomach churning pretty strongly in a few minutes, and it'll reach a
> peak in about 15 minutes, at which time you'll feel some cramps. Then
> it'll wear off gradually, and be gone in another 15 minutes.

> *Relaxant (−).* This pill relaxes the stomach. You'll feel your
> stomach full and heavy in a few minutes and it'll reach a peak in about
> 15 minutes, at which time you'll feel bloated. Then it'll wear off gradu-
> ally, and be gone in another 15 minutes.

> *Placebo (0).* This pill has no effect. We use it for a control, a
> placebo essentially, to see the effects of just taking a pill on stomach ac-
> tivity. You won't feel anything. (p. 70)

In actual fact, the "pill" swallowed in all cases was a small magnet
used to measure the rate of gastric peristalsis. Four of the six subjects
showed gastric changes that were in the instructed directions. That is,
their intestinal activity decreased under the *relaxant* condition and
increased under the *stimulant* condition. This study demonstrated
that external placebo manipulations do produce changes that are
manifest at the physiological level.

Variables Influencing the Placebo Effect

Shapiro (1971) has identified some of the psychosocial variables
that enhance a placebo's effectiveness. Some of these variables are
subject or patient variables, whereas others are situational or staff variables.

Patient variables. Are some patients particularly susceptible to the placebo effect? The answer to this question has usually been sought within the framework of suggestibility, the idea being that some individuals are more suggestible than others. It has not been an easy matter to measure suggestibility because different measures of suggestibility do not correlate (Shapiro, 1971). Moreover, it is not likely that there is a pervasive trait of suggestibility inasmuch as patients who fail to respond to a placebo in one study may respond positively in another. Other personality traits have been used to describe placebo reactors. Some of the trait adjectives that have been used in the past include compliant, neurotic, religious, dependent, and emotionally labile. However, the recognition that the placebo response is highly situation-specific has led to the general conclusion that there is no such person as a *universal placebo reactor*.

The best situation predictor of a positive placebo response is the degree of anxiety manifested by the subject at the time of the investigation. Subjects manifesting a high degree of anxiety prior to placebo administration exhibit a greater placebo reaction than less anxious subjects. Relevant here are Beecher's (1959) observations concerning the differential effectiveness of placebos in controlling experimental and clinical pain. Experimental pain is usually inflicted on university students as part of a research study and is induced by electric shock, heat, thumbscrews, or some other such apparatus. He found the placebo to be 10 times more effective in relieving pain of clinical origin than pain of experimental origin. Interestingly, he also found morphine to be more effective in alleviating clinical pain than experimental pain. Beecher believes that the greater response occurred in the clinical situation because this situation is associated with a high level of anxiety and personal involvement.

> Great wounds with great significance and presumably great reaction are made painless by small doses of morphine, whereas fleeting experimental pains with no serious significance are not blocked by morphine. The difference here in the two situations would seem to be in difference of significance of the two wounds. Morphine acts on significant pain, not on the other. (p. 164)

In a later article, Beecher (1975) proposed a "new principle of drug action," which is that some drugs are only effective in the presence of an appropriate mental state.

Another patient variable is the degree of confidence that the patient has in the physician and the procedure. Park and Covi (1965) found that patients will improve even if they know they have been given a placebo—the critical variable being the patient's faith in the attending physician. They selected 15 patients suffering from chronic anxiety and a host of somatic symptoms and provided each with the following instructions:

> Many different kinds of tranquilizers and similar pills have been used for conditions such as yours, and many of them have helped. Many people with your kind of condition have also been helped by what are sometimes called "sugar pills," and we feel that a so-called sugar pill may help you, too. Do you know what a sugar pill is? A sugar pill is a pill with no medicine in it at all. I think this pill will help you as it has helped so many others. Are you willing to try this pill?

All but one of the 15 patients agreed to try this new "treatment" for a period of 1 week. The patients' symptomatology was assessed prior to and following the placebo period. The major assessment device was a 65-item symptom checklist that was completed by the patient and the treating psychiatrist. The patients themselves reported an overall decrease of 41% in their symptoms, which, according to the authors, was a greater improvement rate than they had previously observed with patients on active drugs. A postexperimental interview revealed that 8 of the patients simply ignored the paradoxical instructions and assumed that the pill actually contained a drug. Some of these patients even manifested side effects. Of the 6 patients that were convinced the pill was a placebo, some attributed their improvement to the physician and others to an awareness that they could help themselves. At the end of the study, 5 patients wished to continue the placebo treatment and 2 others felt no need for additional treatment.

I. Mintz (1977) described a female schizophrenic patient who became dependent on a placebo. Initially, the patient was dependent on antidepressant medication. She was consuming between 25 and 35 10-milligram antidepressant tablets per day. It was arranged to have the patient's husband gradually substitute placebo tablets for the active tablets until the patient was consuming 2 active tablets along with 25-to-30 placebo tablets. The patient reported no awareness of the deception.

Staff-situational variables.   Interest in and optimism for the patient on the part of the medical staff are known to enhance the placebo effect. It has been found that the physician's personal interest and not his or her competence was the major variable determining whether a patient liked his doctor (Shapiro, 1971). Enthusiastic physicians are also known to obtain more improvement in patients suffering from psychological disorders than less enthusiastic physicians. Interest in the treatment procedure is also an important variable. It is this interest that accounts for the universal effectiveness of any new therapeutic procedure. The treatment of chronic patients with a new drug, for example, is likely to create renewed hope for and interest in the patients. The staff might now show optimism toward the patients and begin treating them as humans once again. This change in attitude probably contributes in a major way to the drug's effectiveness. With new treatment regimens, there is usually a very high degree of emotional and intellectual involvement, and as a result the involved patients undoubtedly receive far more attention than is usually provided. Interest in drug treatment has been associated with successful treatment of depressed patients, bleeding ulcers, and hypertension. Other situational variables include the prestige of the physician and the setting and even the color, size, and shape of the drug capsules.

State-dependent Learning

It would be a mistake to conclude, from the preceding discussion, that placebo variables are the primary determinant of a drug's effectiveness. Although placebo variables, or to use a better term, *cognitive variables*, are important in determining the reaction to a drug, the drug-produced physiological changes are equally important to the overall reaction. A concept from psychopharmacology that is useful for understanding how drug variables interact with psychological variables in determining the final response outcome is called *state-dependent learning*. State-dependent learning is a psychopharmacological concept that views the properties of psychoactive drugs within a stimulus-response framework (Heistad, 1957). The drug-produced state is an integral part of the total stimulus-response complex controlling human behavior.

A widely quoted study illustrating state-dependent learning in rats was conducted by Overton (1964). Rats were trained under a drug or nondrug condition to escape from unavoidable shock in a T-maze. Each animal was dropped into the electrified center arm of the maze, and the shock remained on until the animal reached the correct arm of the maze. Following the training trials, the rat was given a daily test trial during which both arms of the maze were accessible. During the test trials the rat could escape the shock by choosing either arm.

One group of rats was trained to run to the right goal box after receiving a saline injection (nondrugged state). Then there followed 28 test trials (1 per day) that alternated between nondrug and drug states. For the drug trials each animal received a heavy dose of pentobarbital (central nervous system depressant). As presented in Figure 6-2, the subjects in this group (labeled Group 1) regularly turned right when tested while nondrugged but responded randomly when tested during the drugged trials. Group 2 was trained to turn left while drugged. Once again, the subjects performed well during the test trials only when the state was similar to that used during training. The rats in Groups 3 and 4 were first trained to turn toward one goal box in one state, then trained to turn toward the other goal box while in the other drug state, and finally tested as before. Group 3 received 6 training trials to the right goal box while nondrugged, then 15 training trials to the left goal box while drugged. Group 4 received 15 training trials to the left goal box while drugged, followed by 6 training trials to the right goal box while nondrugged. Figure 6-2 reveals the high degree of dissociation that occurred during the test trials.

Overton (1964) found that clear-cut dissociation between drug and nondrug states only occurred when the animals were heavily drugged. The drug dosage used in his study was sufficient to initially produce anesthesia in the animals, and training was delayed until each animal had recovered sufficiently to regain mobility. If the drug dose was too low, Overton found that learning transferred to the nondrug state. In fact, Overton performed additional experiments that demonstrated the amount of transfer of training between the nondrug state and the drug state increased regularly as the dose used to establish the drug state was decreased. In most animal experiments the state-dependent learning effect has only been partial, with the effect being determined by dosage, type of drug employed, and kind of task.

Connelly, Connelly, and Phifer (1975) demonstrated that the state-dependent learning effect could be overridden by pairing a tone with foot shock in training and then sounding the tone during the test trials. That is, with the tone on during test trials, the animals chose the arm reinforced during training (and hence paired with the tone), regardless of their drug state during the test trials. The authors hypothesized that the tone was a strong emotional stimulus that initiated some brain process that mediated transfer between the drug states. That is, the tone served as an emotional memory prompter that facilitated the retrieval of learned information as the drug states varied.

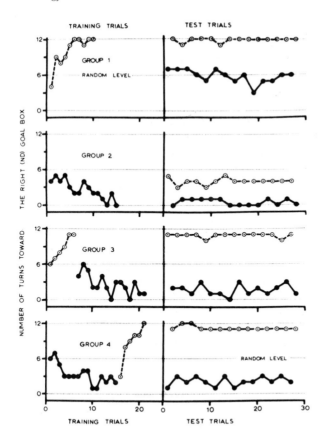

TRAINING TRIALS   TEST TRIALS

Figure 6-2   Performance in the T-maze during training trials and subsequent
test trials; rats alternately drugged (D) and nondrugged (ND)
during daily test trials; sodium pentobarbital administered before drug trials (solid circles) and saline administered before
nondrug trials (dotted circles) (Overton, 1964). Copyright 1964
by the American Psychological Association. Reprinted by permission.

There are very few studies dealing with state-dependent learning
in humans, and it is not clear to what extent the phenomenon occurs.
Leavitt (1974) provided an anecdote in which one of his friends stayed
awake all night to prepare for a morning examination. He ingested
amphetamines to help him keep awake. By morning he felt that he
was ready, but when it came time to take the exam, he was a complete
blank. Fischer (1975) provided a similar anecdote of a man who when

intoxicated could easily find the home of a certain woman but when
sober had no idea of where she lived.

Bustamante, Rossello, Jordan, Pradera, and Insua (1968) demonstrated, experimentally, that state-dependent learning does occur
in humans. Students were required to learn and retain nonsense syllables across a 3-day experimental period. A nonsense syllable is a
meaningless three-letter unit consisting of a vowel between two con-
sonants, such as "wev" and "cas." It is used in memory research to
control for the possible confounding effects of familiarity, difficulty,
and previous experience. They divided their subjects into five experimental groups: (a) a control group that received a placebo on
three alternate days; (b) a group that received alternatively across the
3 days amphetamine, placebo, and amphetamine; (c) a group that received placebo, amphetamine, and placebo; (d) a group that received
amobarbital, placebo, and amobarbital; and (e) a group that received
placebo, amobarbital, and placebo. On the first day of the experiment,
the subjects were required to ingest their respective pills and learn a
list of nonsense syllables, followed by a recall test. On the second day,
they again consumed their pill and were required to write down the
syllables remembered from the previous day. The same experimental
procedure was followed on day 3. The results of the experiment are
presented in Table 6-1. The placebo group showed a progressive decrease in recall over the three sessions. The drug-placebo groups
all showed a drop in recall on the second test day and a strong recovery in recall on the third and final test day. Bustamante, Jordan, Vola,
Gonzalez, and Insua (1970) were able to replicate these findings in a
second study. This time they added two additional control groups that
received the same drug across all 3 days. These two groups exhibited
forgetting curves similar to the curve observed for the all-placebo

Table 6-1   Number of Syllables Recalled by Subjects across Different Drug
Conditions (Bustamante, Rossello, Jordan, Pradera, & Insua,
1968)

	Means of Test A	*Means*		
		Day 1	*Day 2*	*Day 3*
PLA-PLA-PLA (control)	6.2	6.8	3.2	2.4
AMPH-PLA-AMPH	5.8	5.3	3.2	5.0
PLA-AMPH-PLA	6.2	6.7	2.8	5.2
AMO-PLA-AMO	5.5	4.8	2.8	5.2
PLA-AMO-PLA	5.8	7.0	3.0	5.6

group of the first study. Possibly alternating between drug and non-drug test conditions in some way protects the acquired information and facilitates its later retrieval under the drug condition that prevailed during learning.

Other investigators have not been so successful in demonstrating state-dependent learning in humans. Aman and Sprague (1974), for example, were unable to demonstrate state-dependent learning in hyperactive children. To account for the discrepancy between their negative findings and the positive results of Bustamante et al., they proposed that the drug dosage used by the latter investigators might have been the critical variable. They suggested that the dosage used by Bustamante et al. was higher than clinically recommended dosages and that stimulants administered within clinically recommended ranges are not likely to produce state-dependent learning. Overton (cited in Harvey, 1971) has also suggested that state-dependent learning is unlikely to be convincingly demonstrated in man because of the high dosages required to produce the effect.

> The likelihood of finding totally dissociated learning in man is somewhat reduced by the delirium produced by high doses of anesthetic and anticholinergic drugs. Whereas rats continue to learn many tasks easily right up to a lethal or anesthetic dose of these drugs, high doses produce in man a defect in memory consolidation such that learning apparently ceases. Under these circumstances a human subject has a sort of ongoing amnesia and becomes unable to remember most events within a few seconds or minutes after they occur. Apparently, to obtain dissociated learning, one must select a level low enough so that such a delirium is not produced, and this dose level may be too low to produce total dissociation. (p. 81)

Although state-dependent learning is not easily demonstrable with humans, the concept has value in explaining what can be expected of psychoactive drugs in the clinical situation. Any treatment procedure that changes the internal stimulus conditions so that they are different from the stimuli that were associated with a pathological response during the learning process will reduce the strength of that pathological response. For example, an external fear-eliciting stimulus will elicit a weaker fear response under the drug state because of drug-produced changes in physiological stimuli. Conversely, however, a learned pathological response that has been reduced by drug-associated stimuli may reappear at full strength if the internal stimulus conditions that prevailed during the learning of the response are reinstated following the discontinuation of the drug. This model may explain why many patients can function with the aid of drugs but cannot function in their absence. For these individuals, there is simply no transfer from the drug-produced state to the nondrug state.

Focus of Symptoms

Within the framework of state-dependent learning, drug-produced physiological changes represent only one of several complex events controlling behavior. If psychological difficulties are present to a great degree, one might expect the change produced through the drug to have minimal therapeutic impact. Some recent research suggests that a key determinant of a psychoactive drug's ability to control anxiety is the patient's focus of concern with respect to his symptoms.

Tyrer (1976) found antianxiety medication to be more effective in calming patients with *somatic* anxiety than patients with *psychic* anxiety. His distinction between somatic and psychic anxiety was based on the perception of symptoms by patients rather than on actual presence or absence of symptoms. That is, both groups manifested similar cognitive and physiological symptoms but the perceived importance of the symptoms was different across the two groups. One group focused on their bodily symptoms, whereas the other group focused on their psychological problems. Illustrative examples of both classes of patients follow.

Somatic Anxiety Patients

Mr. P. L. (aged 32)—A patient with severe anxiety and hypochondriasis ever since adolescence. Had nocturnal enuresis in childhood, persisting until the age of 21. Admitted to hospital aged 23 for treatment of persistent anxiety and preoccupation about his physical health. He was convinced that he had cardiac disease and this was investigated on several occasions in hospital with negative results. His symptoms persisted after discharge and he continued to be concerned about his cardiac function. During attacks of palpitations, he feared he would die, and this was his chief complaint on entry to the study. His inability to maintain social relationships and a steady occupation added to his symptoms. . . .

Mrs. A. B. (aged 21)—A young woman who first developed acute attacks of panic four months before assessment. . . . Onset of attacks followed physical assault on the patient during which she received a head injury. Attacks of panic many times a day, preceded by flushing, dizziness, and palpitations. Although she related the onset of symptoms to her assault in temporal terms she maintained that they occurred as a consequence of her bodily symptoms. (p. 100)

Observe that, although psychological variables are mentioned by both patients, their primary concern is with bodily symptoms. Both patients responded well to antianxiety medication.

Psychic Anxiety Patients

Mr. C. H. (aged 52)—A postman who had long suffered from low self-esteem, anxiety, and phobic symptoms. First developed these when aged 27 and attended a psychiatrist at this time. Social fears became more intense in the year before assessment and he also developed a fear of heights. . . .

Miss C. M. (aged 39)—A secretary who had experienced social anxiety and attacks of trembling for two years. These attacks occurred in company, particularly in the presence of eligible unmarried men. She blamed these attacks on her failure to find a suitable marriage partner. Had been generally anxious and irritable for many years. (p. 101)

The focus of concern for these two patients is on psychological difficulties. Antianxiety medication was not effective in alleviating their symptoms.

A similar differential outcome might be expected to occur with patients receiving antidepressant medication. As seen in Chapter 4, the focus of concern for reactive depressives is primarily on negative interpersonal events, whereas the focus of concern for endogenous depressives is primarily on negative subjective and bodily feelings. Endogenous depressives might benefit more, at least in the short run, from antidepressant medication.

Phenothiazines and Schizophrenia

The hallucinations, agitations, and delusions characteristic of schizophrenic patients have been brought under considerable control with psychoactive drugs. The phenothiazine derivatives such as chlorpromazine are the most popular drugs for the control of psychotic behavior. Chlorpromazine was first used to reduce autonomic changes associated with surgical stress. In 1952 it was tested on schizophrenic patients and produced dramatic effects. Currently, nearly all schizophrenic patients are receiving phenothiazines or some other antipsychotic compound for their disorder. Phenothiazine treatment does reduce or remove disordered associations in thinking. Other symptoms such as hallucinations and delusions also diminish with treatment. Over 100 double-blind studies have tested the efficacy of chlorpromazine and other antipsychotic drugs. In nearly all of these studies the antipsychotic drugs proved superior to placebo in the treatment of schizophrenic patients (Davis & Casper, 1977).

Phenothiazines are not simply supersedatives, inasmuch as they are not efficacious in alleviating anxiety. They seem to have some degree of specificity for schizophrenia, although the precise mode of action is unknown. Phenothiazines may work by blocking receptor sites for the neurotransmitter actions of dopamine, which is a catecholamine found in the brain (Snyder, 1974). Research is currently focused on the neuronal tracts that use dopamine as a transmitter in the brain. In spite of the short-term effectiveness of the phenothiazines in controlling the symptoms of schizophrenia, there is increasing evidence that their long-term usage may lead to serious physical complications. Prien, Caffey, and Klett (1973) have documented the following symptoms as being strongly suspected side effects of prolonged antipsychotic drug administration: (a) tardive dyskinesia (defect in voluntary movement such as speech distortion, facial distortions, inability to maintain normal posture); (b) opaque deposits in the cornea, lens, and retina; (c) electrocardiogram abnormalities; and even the possibility of (d) sudden death. There is also a growing concern that long-term medication may contribute to institutionalism by reducing drive, initiative, and planning ability in the chronic patient.

What happens to the patient when the antipsychotic drugs are discontinued? There are numerous studies (reviewed by Prien & Klett, 1972) that indicate that drug discontinuation leads to the reappearance of the psychotic symptoms. Although a few studies have found relatively low relapse rates (5% to 25%), most studies have found regression in at least 40% of the patients taken off medication. Several studies reported relapse rates exceeding 70%. Patient variables such as diagnosis, duration and severity of illness, age at onset, and level of social adjustment have all been examined as possible predictors of regression following drug discontinuation, but without success.

Given that schizophrenia is not purely an organic disorder, then state-dependent learning theory would predict such an outcome inasmuch as the behaviors occurring under drug stimuli cannot be expected to transfer automatically to the nondrug state for the majority of patients. There is some evidence that patients who have received relatively low dosages of medication during hospitalization show less incidence of relapse after drug discontinuation than do patients receiving high doses of medication. This observation too is supportive of the state-dependent learning theory because the total stimulus change occurring between the drug and nondrug conditions would have been less dramatic for the patients receiving low doses of phenothiazines.

Stroebel (1972) suggested that the transfer from the nondrug to the drug state might be facilitated by the gradual withdrawal of the medication. Greenberg and Roth (1966) tested this hypothesis with schizophrenics by gradually substituting placebo for active medication over a 48-week period. During the first 8 weeks, placebo was substituted for medication 1 day a week. Every 8 weeks thereafter 1 placebo day was added to the weekly regimen. At the end of 48 weeks, when patients were receiving one-seventh of their original medication, only 1 of 21 patients had relapsed. However, when all active medication was withdrawn, clinical deterioration was rapid; 57% of the patients had to be returned to active medication within a 20-week period. Greenberg and Roth concluded that most patients apparently need medication but that the majority are currently receiving much higher quantities than is necessary. Prien, Caffey, and Klett (1973) have reached a similar conclusion. Based on the results of two studies involving the intermittent drug treatment of schizophrenics, they proposed that it is possible to substitute a placebo for active medication 2-to-3 days a week without producing a serious deterioration in the patient's behavior. In fact, even a 4-day abstinent period did not lead to a dramatic reoccurrence of psychotic symptoms.

It is apparent that simply withdrawing medication (even gradually) does not lead to long-term recovery. To obtain long-term effects, one would suspect that the drug control of normal behavior would have to be *actively* programmed into environmental and patient controls of the same behavior. In the above studies, the patients were uninvolved because the drugs were discontinued without their awareness under double-blind conditions. There is also some evidence that psychotic patients under phenothiazine medication in the community are still suffering from their symptoms and also are able to make only a marginal adjustment to the community setting. In a 10-year follow-up study by Gurel (1970) of over 1,000 discharged schizophrenic patients, it was found that these patients showed little change in postdischarge symptomatology and few were able to maintain employment. Four out of five patients were eventually readmitted. Outpatient treatment consisted solely of medication.

Without programming the transfer of control, state-dependent learning theory would predict the possibility that psychotic behavior might even transfer to the drug state. Stroebel believes that this is exactly what is currently happening. In the past decade there has been a decreased use of facilities for long-term patient treatment and an increased reliance on short-term outpatient treatment. Stroebel claims that there is a new group of chronic psychotic patients that are continually being readmitted to hospitals after stopping medication. Many of these patients also no longer respond to the standard antipsychotic drugs. It is possible that as a result of repeated drug–nondrug transitions and poorly administered drug regimens, the psychotic behaviors have transferred to both the drug and nondrug conditions, thereby making the patient drug-insensitive. There is a therapeutic movement under way *actively* to combine psychosocial intervention with chemotherapy, and the results of the early efforts appear much more promising than the dismal therapeutic benefits obtained through medication alone. At the same time there is evidence that social therapy and psychotherapy in the absence of chemotherapy are not effective in treating schizophrenia, a finding that emphasizes the necessity of combining behavioral and chemical treatment techniques.

Drug Dependence

The term *drug dependence* refers to a condition in which the user has a compelling desire to continue taking the drug either to experience its effects or to avoid the discomfort of its absence (Levine, 1973). The term *drug dependence* has recently been substituted for the term *drug addiction*. Pharmacologists typically view drug dependence as having two distinct and independent components: psychological dependence and physical dependence. Psychological dependence refers to the mental symptoms (craving, anxiety, restlessness, irritability) associated with the drug withdrawal, whereas physical dependence refers bodily symptoms (ache, cramps, vomiting, sweating) associated with the withdrawal of the drug.

Physiological dependency is assumed to occur from drug-produced changes at the physiochemical level. One hypothesis is based on the concept of *disuse supersensitivity* (Jaffe, 1975). It is proposed that if a drug operates by reducing physiochemical activity within specific nervous system structures, these same structures, with continued disuse, become hypersensitive to all neurotransmitters to which they previously responded. Upon withdrawal of the drug, there is an immediate hyperactivity from these structures. A similar hypothesis is based on the notion that drugs selectively block certain pathways within the nervous system, which results in the appearance of a number of redundant pathways. With drug withdrawal, activity in the primary pathway summates with activity in the redundant pathways, which again results in hyperexcitability of the structures involved. In time, the redundant pathways disappear, leading to the concomitant disappearance of the withdrawal symptoms.

Both personality and learning variables have been used to explain psychological dependence. Efforts to isolate the "addictive personality" have met with no more success than efforts to isolate the "placebo personality." Concepts from learning theory, however, have provided much more promise. For example, it has been known for over 70 years that the effects of morphine can be conditioned. Pavlov described the occurrence of this phenomenon as follows:

> It is well known that the first effect of a hypodermic injection of morphine is to produce nausea with profuse secretion of saliva, followed by vomiting, and then profound sleep. Dr. Krylov, however, observed when the injections were repeated regularly that after 5 or 6 days the preliminaries of injection were in themselves sufficient to produce all the symptoms—nausea, secretion of saliva, vomiting and sleep. Under these circumstances the symptoms are now the effect, not of the morphine acting through the blood stream directly on the vomiting centre, but of all the external stimuli which previously had preceded the injection of morphine. The connection between the morphine itself and the various signals may in this instance be very remote, and in the most striking cases all the symptoms could be produced by the dogs simply seeing the experimenter. Where such a stimulus was insufficient it was necessary to open the box containing the syringe, to crop the fur over a small area of skin and wipe with alcohol, and perhaps even to inject some harmless fluid before the symptoms could be obtained. The greater the number of previous injections of morphine the less preparation had to be performed in order to evoke a reaction simulating that produced by the drug. Dr. Krylov was able to demonstrate these facts quite easily in my laboratory. In a series of experiments specially adapted to the purpose he showed that the phenomena described are absolutely identical with conditioned reflexes. The experiments readily lend themselves for lecture demonstration. . . . The dog has repeatedly been injected with morphine on previous occasions, and is now held quietly on the table by an attendant who has never had anything to do with injecting the morphine. When the experimenter approaches, the dog gets restless and moistens its lips, and as soon as the experimenter touches the animal, severe nausea and profuse secretion of saliva begin. (cited in Lynch, Stein, & Fertziger, 1976, p. 47)

Lynch and Fertziger (1977) proposed a model of drug dependence that incorporates both physiochemical and learning variables. In a previous report (Lynch, Stein, & Fertziger, 1976) they observed that dogs conditioned to morphine are highly resistant to extinction. For example, dogs quickly developed a tachycardia (increase in heart rate) to a tone paired with morphine injections. The heart-rate response to the tone persisted even after 3 months of discontinuation of the morphine. After the 3-month period, they were surprised to dis-

cover that a single injection of the narcotic antagonist naloxone after
the tone elicited a full-blown withdrawal response. The dogs suddenly
began to retch and show behavioral signs of restlessness and hyperactivity.

Why did this happen? According to Lynch and Fertziger, the
original conditioning of the tone with morphine led to a form of
nervous system modification such that the tone acquired the power to
release endogenous analgesic substances such as enkephalin and
B-endomorphin. The conditioned stimulus then may have been eliciting the release of endogenous substances all throughout the extinction period. The administration of naloxone blocked this physiochemical reaction to the tone. This explanation, if correct, illustrates the
powerful relationships that may be formed between environmental
and physiochemical variables. It also has obvious implications for the
treatment of drug addiction in humans, as the possibility exists that
psychosocial stimuli in the addict's environment are also capable of
triggering the release of these substances.

Whitehead (1974) believes that conditioning may be the basis of
withdrawal symptoms in heroin addicts. He observed that a high percentage of addicts suffering an attack of withdrawal symptoms experience a stressful life event prior to their onset. Heroin usage, he
argues, begins for social reasons involving pleasure-seeking motives
and the need for peer acceptance. Eventually, its use becomes an effective means for the addict for reducing unpleasurable stimulation
(post-Christmas fix, postargument fix), and finally, its use is also motivated by an intense fear of experiencing the abstinence or withdrawal
syndrome. Through conditioning, the withdrawal symptoms may become associated with the stress-induced emotional reactions. Thus the
reappearance of a stressful event may elicit an unextinguished
learned stress response, part of which is the withdrawal symptom.
This theory is consistent with his observations that the withdrawal
syndrome occurs primarily in the early months of rehabilitation and
also that its onset and offset coincide with the onset and remission of
stress.

Adjuncts to Self-control

The preceding discussions have emphasized the role of integrating
environmental and cognitive variables into formulations concerning
drug effectiveness. It follows that the complete treatment of a behavioral disorder requires more than the administration of a drug. In

one sense the treatment requires transferring the control of the disorder from the drug to the patient.

Many patients seeking help do so because they feel they have lost control over their difficulties and also because they believe that it is the responsibility of the professional to alleviate the problem, as clearly demonstrated with chronic-pain patients. Patients clearly have an expectation that something external (psychotherapy or medication) is required to bring about symptomatic relief. J. E. Singer (1974) provided a humorous analogy with the following description of Walt Disney's classic film *Dumbo*.

> Dumbo is the titular hero of an animated cartoon motion picture. He is a small, young elephant with very large ears. Eliding those aspects of the plot not of relevance to the point at issue, it develops that Dumbo, while asleep, can fly, by flapping his ears like a bird's wings. When awake, he is land bound, just like any other elephant; his friends, the birds, are unable to persuade the nonsomnolent Dumbo that he is that unlikely creature, a flying elephant. One of the birds eventually plucks a routine feather from among those covering his own rump. He presents it to Dumbo together with an elaborate story which describes the feather as a magical one. The feather purportedly has the power of enabling its bearer to fly; to lend plausibility Dumbo is told that the magic feather is the means by which birds teach their young to aviate. Dumbo accepts the gift and attributes flying-inducing power to the feather. Holding it in his trunk, he is able to fly. Eventually, Dumbo loses the feather and once again, is unable to voluntarily fly. When his friends are, at last, able to convince him that the feather was not really magical, Dumbo is finally able to fly by himself. (p. 5)

The analogy between Dumbo's belief in the magic feather and a patient's belief in the magic of medication is possibly unfair, but maybe it is not.

In the section on the placebo effect, the Park and Covi (1965) study showed that patients who knew that they had received a placebo, but still improved nonetheless, attributed their success to the realization that they could change themselves. Most patients, under treatment, however, are unwilling even to entertain such a possibility because such an admission would mean that they are not really in need of help.

Davison and Valins (1969) hypothesized that subjects who are led to believe that changes in their own behavior result not from a drug but from some internal change would be more likely to maintain the changes upon withdrawal of the drug. To test the hypothesis, they had volunteers believe that they would be given a drug that affected skin sensitivity, as measured by the threshold of tolerance to electric shock. Skin sensitivity or shock threshold was first determined, followed by the administration of the drug "parataxin," which in fact was a placebo. The threshold determinations were then repeated, but the shock intensities were secretly halved by the experimenter. Thus a shock rated as a 5 on the second determination was only half the intensity of the shock with the same rating obtained during the first determination. The subjects, therefore, were deceived into thinking that the drug had increased their ability to tolerate electric shock. Next, half of the subjects were told that they had in fact received a placebo and the remainder were assured that the drug effects would wear off in a minute or so.

A second experimenter then entered and explained that his experiment also involved determinations to electric shock. The subjects were then asked to rate a third series of shocks. Subjects who attributed their changes during the second series of shocks to the effects of the drug tolerated less shock than they did during the initial series. Subjects who were led to believe that their improvement must have been due to some internal variable tolerated more shock before reporting pain during the third administration than they did during the first administration. If an individual believes that he, rather than an external force, is responsible for engaging in a behavior that is inconsistent with his own belief, his belief is more likely to change and become consistent with the behavior.

Patients' dependency on medication often prevents them from even considering the possibility that they might in fact be able to gain control over their symptoms. The following case study, provided by Levendusky and Pankratz (1975) illustrates this phenomenon.

> Mr. X. was a 65-year-old retired army officer with a history that included significant military achievement, a productive teaching and research career, and numerous social accomplishments. Medically, the patient had had frequent abdominal operations for gallstones, postoperative adhesions, and bowel obstructions. At the time of his voluntary hospitalization, he was complaining of continued abdominal pain, loss of weight, and social withdrawal.
>
> A mental status exam revealed an oriented, intact man with excellent higher mental functions. His mood was somewhat depressed, and he was unkempt and had poor personal hygiene. He explained because of the difficulty of controlling his abdominal pain over the past 2½ years, it had become impossible for him and his wife to remain socially active. For example, to control his pain while in social situations with friends, he would often assume awkward or embarrassing postures.

The patient's reliance on Talwin (Pentazocine, a weak narcotic antagonist with some narcotic-like properties) had begun more than 2 years prior to the current treatment. It had been initially prescribed to control pain following abdominal surgery. Mr. X was convinced that this medication was essential for the control of pain and he had spent considerable effort adjusting dosage to his optimal level of 1.25 cc, self-administered intramuscularly, six times daily. Because of the resultant excessive tissue and muscle damage, it had become difficult to find injection sites. The patient insisted that any less than 1.25 cc was almost useless and that more was of no additional value. He had read the early drug literature and was quick to cite evidence that Talwin was not addictive. In addition, Mr. X had no difficulty obtaining his medication by prescription.

Mr. X's primary goal for therapy was to "get more out of life in spite of my pain." He also verbalized the need to control Talwin, but had become highly resistant to any change in his medication regime. (p. 165)

Initially, the treatment program for Mr. X consisted of self-controlled muscle relaxation. Also, he learned to visualize his pain sensations as "tightening steel bands," which he could "loosen" through relaxation. Although he agreed to a time-contingent rather than a pain-contingent medication schedule, he was unwilling to have the Talwin dosage of 1.25 ml altered in any manner. Levendusky and Pankrantz decided to reduce the dosage of Talwin secretly by gradually subisituting a placebo. Within 5 days, Mr. X was, unknowingly, receiving pure placebo four times daily. Eventually, the patient was told of the switch, and although angry, he attributed his improvement to the imagery training and relaxation. At the time of discharge, Mr. X still experienced abdominal pain, but he now had more control over its intensity.

It is not good practice to use deception to accomplish a therapeutic objective. Deceiving patients is not to be recommended under any circumstances (Bok, 1974). The Levendusky and Pankratz case study prompted several comments on the use of deception in a treatment setting (Kelman, 1975). Although the comments were not totally negative toward the experimenters' procedure, the critics all agreed that there were inherent dangers in the use of deception. For example, if the self-control training had not worked, the patient might have lost faith in the Talwin. Also, the use of deception can undermine the therapist-patient relationship. That is, even though the deception was for the patient's "own good," he will no longer be able to fully trust the therapist and thereby harm future efforts at therapeutic intervention.

Once patients learn to recognize the necessity of taking a more active role in their recovery, such forms of deception will become unnecessary. Behavioral interventions (discussed in the next chapter) can be used to teach patients the skills necessary for self-control.

7

Behavioral Techniques
in Medical Practice

The nature of medical practice demands that any treatment procedure, physical or psychological, be effective in assisting patients to recover from their afflictions. In recent years psychologists have developed a number of specific treatment techniques that show promise of meeting this demand. Historically, the main form of psychological treatment in medicine was psychoanalysis. Psychoanalysis, with its orientation toward total restructuring of the personality, was not geared toward assisting patients with specific medical complaints. The majority of current techniques are subsumed under the broad label of behavior therapy. This chapter outlines the basic principles of behavior therapy and illustrates as well the application of these principles to medical disorders.

What is behavior therapy? The diversity of techniques associated with behavior therapy makes this a difficult question to answer, for these techniques now range from biofeedback to group therapy. Any therapeutic technique, regardless of its theoretical orientation, can be considered part of behavior modification, just as long as the technique adheres to certain criteria. The following two criteria are commonly used to define behavior therapy. First, behavior therapy represents a broad spectrum of clinical procedures that are based on the experimental findings of psychological research. Second, behavior modification relies extensively on an objective and measurable outcome (Mahoney, Kazdin, & Lesswing, 1974).

During the 1950s and early 1960s, a number of behavior therapists did attempt to adhere to a rigid theoretical doctrine known as *behaviorism. Behaviorism* has been defined as "the doctrine that the behavior of man and animal can be fully understood without the use of explanatory concepts referring to states of actions of consciousness, namely by studying only observable behavior" (Locke, 1969, p. 1,000). The doctrine was first proposed in 1913 by an American psychologist named John Watson. Behavior therapists now recognize that such a model is not workable in that any meaningful explanation of human actions requires reference to conscious phenomena. They continue, however, to direct their efforts toward environmental variables and specific behaviors. The emphasis on the environment reflects their belief that many behaviors are largely under environmental control. This emphasis is especially important for the health professional because in many instances health professionals constitute a large part of the environment of patients. Consequently their actions and reactions toward patients have a powerful influence on patient behaviors. Learning to use this control properly enhances the health professional's ability to deal with patients and their concerns in an effective manner.

Environmental variables have always been considered important determinants of behavior by animal psychologists but only with the recent advances of behavior therapy has the importance of these variables to the human condition been recognized. Initially there was a tremendous opposition to this approach mainly because all behavioral and psychosomatic disorders were viewed in psychoanalytic terms. Disorders were seen as "symptomatic" of some underlying psychic conflict. Behavior therapists began, however, to demonstrate, with hospitalized psychiatric patients in particular, that profound changes in behavior could often be achieved through simple manipulations of the patient's existing environment.

The following case study by Haughton and Ayllon (1965) represents one of the first demonstrations that environmental manipulations can influence behavior. The patient, a female schizophrenic, had been hospitalized for a period of 23 years. She was considered to be so cognitively impaired as to be totally unaware of her surroundings. Her behavioral repertoire consisted of lying in bed, walking about the ward, eating, and going to the bathroom. The one activity that she seemed to enjoy was cigarette smoking. The therapists wished to assess whether this patient was indeed as unresponsive to the environment as her lack of behaviors indicated. They decided to try to teach her a simple response, which in this case was holding a broom. The ward personnel were instructed to withhold cigarettes from the patient until she held the broom. One staff member handed her the broom, and while she held it another staff member rushed forward with a cigarette. Next, she was given, for holding the broom, a poker chip that could be exchanged later for a cigarette. The patient quickly learned the response and held the broom throughout the day. In fact, she became quite aggressive if another patient attempted to handle the prized broom. Why did the therapists make the patient learn such a response? Certainly the demonstration had no therapeutic value but it did serve to show that even severely disturbed patients are responsive to their environment.

Following this and other demonstrations, clinical psychologists looked to learning theories for principles that might be used to enhance their understanding of the environmental influences on behavior. Learning theorists had known for years that there are two different ways in which behaviors are related to environmental or stimulus events. First there is *respondent behavior*, which is behavior that is controlled by preceding stimulus events. *Respondent conditioning* is another term for *classical conditioning*, a model developed by I. Pavlov. Second, there are behaviors called *operants,* which are influenced by what happens following the behavior. *Operant behaviors* change or "operate upon" the environment. *Operant conditioning* was developed by B. F. Skinner. The difference between the two models of learning is illustrated in Figure 7-1.

In the course of his research on digestive processes (for which he received the Nobel Prize in 1904), Pavolov was bothered by the observation that his experimental dogs not only salivated with the place-

RESPONDENT OR CLASSICAL CONDITIONING

AFTER SEVERAL PAIRINGS THE INITIALLY NEUTRAL CS PRODUCES THE UCR

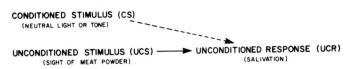

CONDITIONED STIMULUS (CS)
(NEUTRAL LIGHT OR TONE)

UNCONDITIONED STIMULUS (UCS) ⟶ UNCONDITIONED RESPONSE (UCR)
(SIGHT OF MEAT POWDER)   (SALIVATION)

OPERANT CONDITIONING

AFTER SEVERAL REINFORCEMENTS OF THE CR, THE CS SERVES AS A SIGNAL TO PERFORM THE
LEARNED RESPONSE (CR) IN ORDER TO OBTAIN REINFORCEMENT

CONDITIONED STIMULUS (CS) ⟶ CONDITIONED RESPONSE (CR) ⟶ REINFORCEMENT
ANY SIGNAL   ANY RESPONSE   (FOOD, WATER, PRAISE, ETC)
WHICH THE ORGANISM CAN DISCRIMINATE   WHICH THE ORGANISM
                                  CAN PHYSICALLY EXECUTE

Figure 7-1 Models of learning: classical conditioning and operant conditioning.

ment of meat powder in the mouth but quickly learned to salivate as soon as they heard Pavlov approaching the lab. Being a good physical scientist, he recognized that he was losing control over the experimental stimulus. At first he and his colleagues tried to solve the problem by imagining what the dog was "experiencing." He was cautioned, however, against trying to study this phenomenon from a mentalistic framework, and instead he chose to identify the external events (conditioned stimuli) that were responsible for these "psychic" secretions.

Phobias and Classical Conditioning

Few human behaviors are acquired in accordance with the principles of classical conditioning, and for this reason behavior modifiers have directed most of their attention to operant conditioning. Excessive fears or phobias represent behavior disorders that have been analyzed within the framework of classical conditioning. Watson and Rayner's (1920) famous experiment with an 11-month-old boy is frequently cited as a model for the conditioned acquisition of a phobia. First, the child was shown a white rat toward which he displayed no fear. Whenever he reached for the rat to play with it, however, the experimenter made a loud noise (the unconditioned stimulus) by striking a steel bar behind the child's head, which caused the child to become afraid (the unconditioned response). After several such associations between the steel bar and the white rat, the child became afraid at the sight of the white rat alone (the conditioned stimulus). Other attempts to demonstrate the acquisition of fear via classical conditioning have not been successful. For example, English (1929) attempted to condition fear in a 14-month-old girl by pairing the presentation of a duck with a loud noise. After 50 trials, no conditioned response to the duck was established.

Some clinically reported phobias do fit the model of classical conditioning. Individuals have been known to become phobic over driving after being involved in a serious accident. Other clinical phobias, however, are definitely not acquired in such a painful fashion. Many individuals with severe fears of snakes, germs, airplanes, and heights report to clinicians that they have no particularly unpleasant experiences with any of these objects or situations (Meyer & Crisp, 1970).

Another difficulty with the classical conditioning model of phobias concerns the nonarbitrary nature of objects that children and adults are afraid of. Classical conditioning does not deal with the content of fears; the model merely suggests that any neutral stimulus, when paired with a painful unconditioned stimulus, can acquire fear-eliciting properties. People with fear of being alone at home at night do not, however, generally develop fears toward stimuli in physical proximity such as their toothbrush and their pajamas. In addition human phobias tend to follow recurrent themes that in many cases originate in childhood. Common fears include themes of darkness, being left alone, snakes, insects, storms, heights, and enclosures (Agras, Sylvester, & Oliveau, 1969).

In spite of the confusion associated with the precise origin of phobias, it has become possible to treat these disorders with a technique that is based on the principle of counterconditioning. Success in this area has demonstrated that it is not always necessary to understand the cause of a disorder in order to treat the disorder. In counterconditioning, a response (R_1) to a given stimulus (S) is eliminated by eliciting a different behavior (R_2) in the presence of that stimulus. An early clinical demonstration of counterconditioning was reported by Mary Cover Jones (1924). She successfully eliminated a little boy's fear of rabbits by feeding him in the presence of a rabbit, beginning with the animal several feet away and gradually moving it closer on successive occasions. In this fashion the fear (R_1) produced by the rabbit (S) was "crowded out" by the stronger positive feelings associated with eating (R_2).

Some 30 years later, Joseph Wolpe (1958) developed a similar technique called *systematic desensitization*, which is based on the learning principle of reciprocal inhibition. The term *reciprocal inhibition* simply means that the occurrence of a response antagonistic to anxiety in the presence of anxiety-eliciting stimuli will weaken the bond between the anxiety response and those stimuli. The clinical procedure then consists of three distinct stages: (a) training in muscle relaxation, (b) construction of the fear hierarchy, and (c) counterconditioning.

Muscle relaxation is the "response" that is usually taught to oppose the anxiety response. The idea of muscle relaxation is communicated in the following manner:

> Even the ordinary relaxing that occurs when one lies down often produces quite a noticeable effect. It has been found that there is a definite relationship between the extent of muscle relaxation and the production of emotional changes opposed to those of anxiety. I am going to teach you how to relax far beyond the usual point, and this will enable you to "switch on" at will the greatest possible emotional effects of an "anti-anxiety" kind. . . .
> I am now going to show you the essential activity that is involved in

obtaining deep relaxation. I shall again ask you to resist my pull at your
wrist so as to tighten your biceps. I want you to notice very carefully the
sensations in that muscle. Then I shall ask you to let go gradually as I
diminish the amount of force I exert against you. Notice as your
forearm descends that there is decreasing sensation in the biceps muscle. Notice also that the letting go is an activity, but of a negative kind—
it is an "uncontracting" of the muscle. In due course, your forearm will
come to rest on the arm of the chair, and it may seem to you as though
relaxation is complete. But although the biceps will indeed be partly
and perhaps largely relaxed, a certain number of fibers will still be con-
tracted. I shall therefore say to you, "Go on letting go." Try to continue
the activity that went on in the biceps while your forearm was coming
down. It is the act of relaxing these additional fibers that will bring
about the emotional effects we want. Let's try it out and see what happens. (Wolpe & Lazarus, 1966, p. 61)

The second step consists of identifying the fear-eliciting stimuli
and, once identified, arranging the stimuli in a hierarchy from least
threatening to most threatening. If the patient has multiple fears with
different themes, a separate hierarchy is constructed for each theme.
The third step of counterconditioning involves having the patient initially imagine the least threatening stimulus in a specific hierarchy
while deeply relaxed.

The following case study (Rardin, 1969) represents a successful
application of the technique:

The client was an 18-year-old single female in the first year of a nursing
program. . . . The client indicated that she had been fearful of blood
and generally squeamish for several years but her fears had not been a
serious concern until she entered nursing—a career goal for her since
childhood.

Her reaction to blood and possible physical injury varied from
moderate discomfort to dizziness and nausea depending on the topic
and circumstances. The immediate concern was her reaction to the
films shown in nursing classes which vividly depicted various medical
conditions. On a number of occasions, she had to put her head down or
leave the room. She felt that she would faint or vomit if she continued to
observe the film. This reaction was interfering with her performance
in the classes in which the films were shown, and the nursing faculty was
beginning to question her suitability for the profession. (p. 125)

A fear hierarchy was constructed that included items involving blood
that resulted from surgery, injury, and childbirth. After training in
muscle relaxation and a few sessions of counterconditioning in the
clinic, the patient was encouraged to practice imagining the scenes

while relaxing at home. After 6 weeks of training, the patient reported being able to tolerate increasing exposure to blood in hospital situations. At the end of one year, she found herself being able to cope with the most threatening event on the hierarchy.

Systematic desensitization has proved to be a useful technique for assisting patients with phobias and other anxieties. There is some question, however, as to whether it works for the reasons stated by Wolpe (that is, counterconditioning through reciprocal inhibition). Ryan and Gizynski (1971) asked their patients why they thought systematic desensitization was effective and received replies such as "I felt she [therapist] was involved with me and that I would hurt her if I quit. . . ." and "[I] felt like he [therapist] needed to feel it was a success." Several studies have shown that neither training in muscle relaxation nor the construction of a graded hierarchy are necessary conditions for treatment success. The cognitive element of imagining the feared events and the rehearsing of antifear responses provides the patient with feedback that enables him to cope with the fears. Unlike counseling, in which the patient is simply told that he "should not" be so afraid or is given reasons for his fears, systematic desensitization provides the patient with specific skills for reevaluating his position.

Concepts of Operant Conditioning

Operant behavior refers to a class of behavior that is controlled by stimulus consequences. This fundamental relationship that exists between behavior and the events following the behavior represents the essence of operant psychology. Knowing how to use this relationship in a therapeutic manner represents the essence of behavior modification. That is, if the occurrence of a particular behavior (or "symptom") is controlled by consequences with which it has been associated, it becomes possible to change the consequences that follow or fail to follow a particular behavior.

Positive Reinforcement

In operant psychology a *reinforcer* is only defined in terms of its effects on behavior. A *positive reinforcer* is any event that increases the frequency of a behavior that it follows. From the example of the broom-holding schizophrenic, a cigarette may be defined as a positive reinforcer only because the frequency and strength of a behavior (broom holding) increased following the administration of a cigarette.

If the behavior had not occurred, the cigarette could not have been considered as a reinforcer. Again, a reinforcer cannot be defined independently of its effect on behavior. The definition of reinforcement is circular, but at the same time this definition provides the practitioner with tremendous flexibility in identifying reinforcers for any particular patient.

Operant psychologists speak of two categories of positive reinforcers: primary reinforcers and secondary reinforcers. *Primary reinforcers* are unconditioned in the sense that the individual does not have to learn their reinforcing value. Food and water are examples of potential primary reinforcers (potential because their presentation is less likely to produce behavior in an individual that is not hungry or thirsty). *Secondary reinforcers* refer to a class of stimuli that are assumed to have acquired their reinforcing value through repeated pairings with primary reinforcers. Praise, recognition, attention, and approval are examples of social stimuli that are classed as secondary reinforcers. Secondary reinforcers are used extensively in behavior modification treatment programs.

Some people object to the suggestion that interpersonal behaviors can be used to change or "control" a patient's behavior. In fact, this objection is at the core of accusations that behavior therapy is unethical and strips the patient of self-determination. The problem with such criticism is that it fails to recognize that all of our actions have an influence on the individuals in our immediate environment. Quite often, this influence goes unnoticed. Mikulic (1971) found, for example, that nurses in an extended-care setting were inadvertently reinforcing dependent behaviors (patients asking others to do everything) as opposed to independent behaviors (patients doing things for themselves). During my clinical training, I experienced a similar situation while on tour of a physical rehabilitation unit. The staff brought forth a male stroke patient and placed him on an exercise bicycle. He was instructed to exercise while the staff and I moved to an adjacent area for coffee. As we chatted about the weather and other trivia, the patient peddled a few revolutions, stopped, looked over, peddled a few more revolutions, looked over, and collapsed. No one from the staff observed this little drama. After coffee, the patient was hoisted to his chair and returned to the ward. A smile or some other secondary reinforcer delivered while he was exercising might have had a marked effect on his morale and rehabilitation.

Behavior therapists have demonstrated that many medical symptoms are often unintentionally reinforced by people in the afflicted individual's immediate environment. Consciously or unconsciously, the individual may learn that attacks are followed by predictable consequences: alarmed reactions on the part of family members, sympathy, medication, or the avoidance of routine responsibilities. These consequences, despite their intended helpful effect, are reinforcing to the individual and so increase the frequency, severity, or duration with which the symptoms occur. Neisworth and Moore (1972) described a case involving a 7-year-old asthmatic boy who was especially susceptible to attacks that occurred at bedtime. The hypothesis was that parental attention to the problem was positively reinforcing the behavior. The parents were advised to discontinue all attention and administrations of medicines during bedtime asthmatic attacks. The child was put to bed with the usual affectionate interactions between parents and child. Once the bedroom door was closed, however, no further interaction occurred until morning. The child was also given monetary reinforcement for coughing less frequently. The results of the intervention procedure are presented in Figure 7-2. The initial effect of the intervention program was to increase the

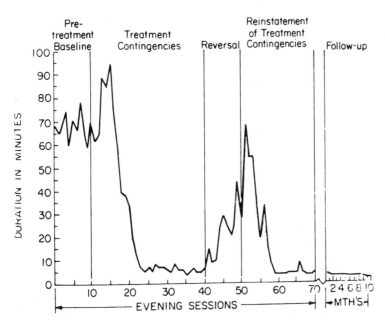

Figure 7-2 Duration of bedtime asthmatic responding as a function of contingency changes (Neisworth & Moore, 1972). Copyright © 1972 by Academic Press, Inc. Reproduced by permission of the publisher and J. T. Neisworth.

duration of coughing and wheezing. By day 23 the behavior reached a low that remained somewhat stable. To demonstrate that positive reinforcement was actually influencing the frequency of asthmatic attacks, the experimenters then reversed the contingency to that which existed prior to their intervention. The parents were instructed to resume their pretreatment behavior by providing attention and medication during asthmatic episodes. Lunch money was not withdrawn but simply provided on a noncontingent basis. As Figure 7-2 shows, the asthmatic attacks increased quickly and then reversed again with the reinstatement of the treatment contingencies.

The authors point out that this study does not purport to obviate organic factors in the etiology or maintenance of asthmatic responses. Rather, it pinpoints the dramatic role that environmental contingencies may have in the amplification and attenuation of the problem.

Negative Reinforcement

Negative reinforcement refers to an increase in the frequency or strength of a response following the removal of a negative event or stimulus. Negative reinforcement, like positive reinforcement, leads to an increase in behavior. The cessation of a patient's continual complaining, moaning, and demands for medication is an example of negative reinforcement when these behaviors result in a hospital staff providing attention and medication solely in order to terminate the patient's behaviors. The patient is positively reinforced with attention and medication while the staff member is negatively reinforced by the cessation of the complaining.

Kushner (1970) gave an example of how negative reinforcement. was employed to treat a patient suffering from hysterical anesthesia.

> A 39-year-old male patient had been involved in an accident in which an elevator dropped suddenly about 4 feet. Although he walked away from the scene he complained of an ache in his back and within 24 hours was admitted to the hospital complaining that he had no feeling in his lower body from the point of an old incision just below the navel downward. He did not respond to pin pricks or other tactual stimulation in this area. Physical examination revealed no apparent neurological impairment and electromyograms indicated normal muscle potentials. He was confined to a wheel chair since he could not walk without grasping wall, or rails for support. (p. 41)

The patient was connected to two sets of shock electrodes. One set of electrodes was attached to his fingertips, a region of the body from which he reported no loss in sensation. The other set of electrodes was placed on various body sites that were insensitive to stimulation. A push button was placed in his other hand. The treatment procedure involved presenting a mild shock to the various anesthetized sites. If the patient failed to press the button (indicating awareness of the shock) within 3 seconds, a more severe shock was delivered to his fingertips.

During the first session, shock was delivered only to the anesthetized sites and the patient showed very little awareness of the shock. His behavior changed dramatically, however, when the fingertip shock was added to the procedure. Within four sessions the patient was pressing the button on every trial in response to every anesthetized site stimulated. At the end of the fourth session, the patient got out of his wheel chair and walked back to the ward. In this example, the negative reinforcer was the fingertip electric shock and the response reinforced was pressing the button and finally walking away from the situation.

Punishment

Punishment refers to the presentation of an aversive stimulus after a response has occurred. The effect of punishment is to decrease the behavior producing the stimulus. Punishment is more effective when the aversive stimulus immediately follows the response. As punishment is delayed, its effect is greatly reduced. The ineffectiveness of delayed punishment is apparent in the persistence of most behaviors that are injurious to health. Failure to exercise, smoking, excessive drinking, aggressive-competitive lifestyles are all associated with behaviors that produce immediate positive reinforcement, but their punishing consequences do not appear for years after the behaviors have been initiated.

Behavior modifiers do not recommend the use of punishment. Punishment often produces undesirable emotional side effects. An excessively punished child, for example, may learn to avoid the parent that distributes the punishment. Also the person acting as the punishing stimulus serves as a model for aggressive behaviors in the person being punished. If punishment is used, it should only be used in combination with positive reinforcement for an alternative behavior.

An example of the clinical use of punishment comes from a case study by Kushner (1970). A 17-year-old girl was referred to the behavior modification unit with the complaint of uncontrollable sneezing. The girl had previously been examined by a number of medical specialists. The problem was not felt to be a neurological, allergic, or psychiatric basis. The sneezing was quite serious inasmuch as a baseline study of the behavior indicated that she was sneezing at a rate of once every 40 seconds (Figure 7-3). The *baseline period* is a methodological component of the behavioral analysis of any behavioral disorder. It refers to a pretreatment measure of the problem behavior. In addition it often includes an assessment of the environmental events that are maintaining the behavior. The baseline data provides the clinician with a reference for evaluating the effects of environmental change on the problem behavior. To treat the behavior disorder, a punishing stimulus was made contingent upon sneezing. A microphone placed around the patient's neck was connected to shock electrodes attached to her fingers. With each sneeze, the microphone triggered an uncomfortable shock to the fingers. As shown in Figure 7-3, the sneeze-shock contingency resulted in the rapid disappearance of the sneezing behavior. During a posttreatment follow-up, some 13 months later, the problem had not reappeared.

Lang and Melamed (1969) used punishment to reverse persistent vomiting in a 9-month-old infant. The infant consistently vomited 10-to-15 minutes after each feeding. The mother believed that the onset of the vomiting coincided with a period during which there was some family friction concerning the proper care of the child. Exten-

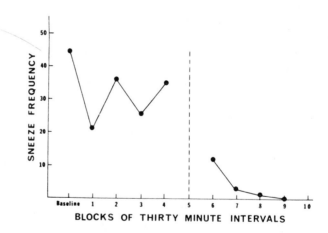

Figure 7-3   Effect of punishment on frequency of sneezing (Kushner, 1970). Malcolm Kushner. Faradic Aversive Controls in Clinical Practice. In Charles Neuringer, Jack L. Michael, *Behavior Modification in Clinical Psychology*, © 1970, p. 40. Reproduced by permission of Prentice-Hall, Inc. Englewood Cliffs, New Jersey.

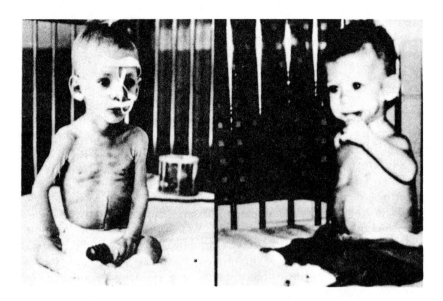

Figure 7-4   (Left) Vomiting infant during the observation period just prior to treatment; (right) on the day of discharge from the hospital, 13 days after the first photo (Lang & Melamed, 1969). Copyright 1969 by the American Psychological Association. Reproduced by permission.

sive neurological examinations revealed no organic basis for the condition. Dietary changes combined with the administration of anti-nauseant medication produced no relief. Intensive nursing care designed "to establish and maintain a one-to-one relationship and to provide the child with warm, friendly, and secure feelings" had to be abandoned because it was increasing the infant's anxiety.

The infant, shown in Figure 7-4, was clearly in a critical condition, and it was decided to use punishment as a last resort to save his life. EMGs recorded from the chin and throat muscles indicated the presence of vigorous throat activity immediately prior to each vomiting sequence. A nurse was instructed to observe the infant for this activity and to signal as soon as it appeared. With the signal, a brief electric shock was delivered to the infant's leg. After two 1-hour sessions of this procedure, the infant rarely vomited. In addition, the nursing staff reported a progressive decrease in his vomiting during the rest of the day and the night. The infant quickly gained weight and was discharged from the hospital within a few days. During a follow-up 1 year later, the parents reported that their child was eating well and the vomiting had not recurred. This study indicates that punishment, when used carefully and under controlled conditions, represents a useful clinical technique for modifying behavior disorders.

Extinction

Operant extinction refers to a reduction in response frequency following the discontinuation of reinforcement. Behavior that is no longer followed by positive or negative reinforcing consequences will cease. The ignoring of whining behaviors in a child or the ignoring of negative self-statements in an adult will eventually lead to a disappearance of these behaviors. During the initial stage of extinction the behavior to be extinguished often increases rather than decreases—a phenomenon called *extinction burst*. A whining child, for example, that is suddenly ignored may not immediately stop whining. Instead the whining may increase in intensity and be accompanied by a temper tantrum. If these behaviors do not produce a response on the part of the adult, such as attention, they will soon disappear. Unfortunately, the whining behaviors often do produce a response after a period of time and are thereby strengthened. When using extinction, the key to success is consistency.

Extinction should not be used in isolation. It can, however, be used effectively with positive reinforcement for alternate acceptable behaviors. Thus if staff attention is withdrawn from a patient whose complaints are groundless, the same attention should be shifted to reinforcing behaviors that will assist the patient in his recovery.

Time out

Time out from positive reinforcement is a technique that is used primarily to alter disruptive behaviors in children. The child is simply removed from the environment that is maintaining his disruptive behavior. In classrooms, for example, disruptive behavior is often maintained by attention from peers, regardless of any actions the teacher might take. Time out involves placing the child in another room for a brief period such as 10 minutes.

Nordquist (1971) described the use of time out to control tantrum behavior in a 5-year-old boy. The boy refused to follow instructions and was especially difficult to handle before bedtime. His tantrum behavior consisted of screaming, kicking, throwing objects, hitting the parents, and occasionally hitting his younger sister. The boy also was a frequent bed wetter. Spanking, reasoning, threats, and isolation were methods the parents had used without success.

Home observation of parent-child behavioral interactions revealed that when the boy was cooperative the parents often retired to a place in the home where they could converse quietly or read the paper, but they quickly responded to disruptive behavior. The parents were instructed to discontinue negotiating with the boy and threatening him on the grounds that such attention probably helped to maintain his disruptive behavior. They were instructed to use the time-out operation by placing the boy in a corner in his bedroom whenever he refused to follow a parental command and cause him to remain in the corner for 10 minutes. All enuretic behaviors were ignored. Not only did the oppositional behavior decrease, but so did the bed-wetting.

With this child, one immediately thinks of the Freudian notion that his bed-wetting represented a form of symbolized aggression—in fact, bed-wetting has been called "revenge enuresis." One other possibility, however, is that prior to the behavioral intervention program, the boy's parents had low reinforcer value. Following the use of time out and the other instructions, their social reinforcement value may have increased dramatically. With this change, the bladder-muscle tension took on new meaning. The boy apparently now learned to associate bladder tension with self-initiated voiding because social reinforcement was made contingent on this behavior.

Shaping

The basic premise of operant psychology is that the required behavior must occur before it can be reinforced. In many instances, the required behavior simply does not occur. Either the behavior has never been acquired, or the behavior, although present in the individual's repertoire, has a baseline frequency of zero. *Shaping* is a procedure that is used in these circumstances. It begins with reinforcing the best approximation available and then gradually altering the reinforcement contingency so that closer and closer approximations of the desired behavior are required.

Shaping is a very useful technique for designing and implementing behavior modification programs in physical rehabilitation. O'Neil (1972) described the use of shaping in combination with other behavioral techniques to treat a 5-year-old girl suffering from right spastic hemiparesis, a spastic muscle weakness on the right side of the body. The disorder was attributed to a brain cyst that had developed prior to birth.

> Nancy displayed several developmental deficits in relation to other 5-year-old children. She had not learned to crawl, creep, or stand independently, and was unable to walk even while holding on to furniture. She had learned to sit without support and she displayed reciprocal leg motion. Her usual method of locomotion was to scoot on the floor in a sitting position, using her left hand and both feet to propel herself. She displayed a limited vocabulary and did not combine words. However, she appeared to be under verbal instructional control and she generally complied with instructions.
>
> Nancy's mother had been told by the child's physician that she would never walk. However, the child was becoming too heavy to be carried and her mother had refused a wheelchair for her, fearing that she would become dependent on it and never learn to walk. Both the mother and the center personnel were very interested in trying some other mode of locomotion which would be more suitable for outdoor activity than scooting. (p. 182)

The treatment procedure had as its objective training the child to walk with only the aid of a crutch. The different behaviors that were to be shaped or built upon the child's customary scooting form of locomotion were:

1. holding on to a cabinet and pulling up to a kneeling position
2. holding on to a cabinet and pulling up to a standing position
3. walking along the cabinet while holding on with a hand
4. walking while using only a forearm crutch for support

Combinations of social reinforcement (praise), material reinforcement (marbles) and edible reinforcement (ice cream) were used to reinforce the required behaviors. The ice cream proved to be the most powerful reinforcer and was used to shape the different behaviors. The other reinforcers were given more freely to maintain the child's interest in the treatment program. The outcome of the procedure is shown in Figure 7-5. During the baseline observation period, scooting was the primary form of locomotion when the child was asked to approach the experimenter. During sessions 43–60, a spoonful of ice cream was given when the child pulled up to her knees. In sessions 61–75, ice cream was made contingent upon her pulling up to feet. During sessions 76–90, ice cream was given only for steps

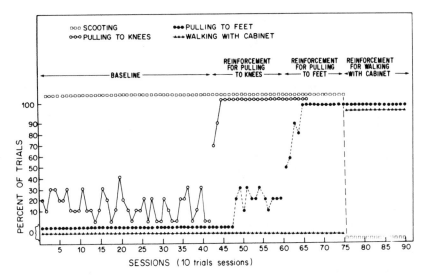

Figure 7-5 Percentage of trials each session that child engaged in scooting, pulling up to knees, pulling up to feet, and walking with cabinet support during baseline period and during reinforcement period (O'Neil, 1972).

taken while holding onto the cabinet. Each of the required behaviors was eventually performed.

The last step of the program involved teaching the child to walk with the aid of a crutch. She could not use her right hand to hold a crutch so she had to be taught to support her body and walk with a single crutch. The experimenter used a combination of prompts and fading to teach the girl this difficult task. In behavior modification, *prompts* refer to events that precede a behavior and help initiate or maintain it. Telling a patient to take his medication is an example of a prompt. *Fading* refers to the gradual withdrawal of prompts, once the behavior is firmly established. In this application, the prompts involved physically guiding the child's walking behavior. Initially she was reinforced for walking while the experimenter supported her with the aid of a harness. The harness support was gradually faded to hand support, fingertip support, stick support, weighted-crutch support (to assist her balance), and finally to crutch support alone.

The procedure was effective in teaching the girl to walk with the aid of a crutch. This study illustrates that motor disturbances associated with organic disorders are under a degree of environmental control. The fact that a child once labeled as a hopeless case could now walk speaks to the significance that behavior modification has for physical rehabilitation.

Stimulus Control

This discussion of operant principles in behavior modification has focused on what happens following the occurrence of a behavior. The concept of *stimulus control* refers to the observation that stimuli present at the time of reinforcement also acquire control over our behaviors. Almost all human behavior is under some form of stimulus control. In more specific terms, a stimulus that signals that the appropriate response will lead to reinforcement is called a *discriminative stimulus*. A response that has been established in the presence of a specific discriminative stimulus is usually much more powerful than a response that is not under specific stimulus control. For example, some students find it extremely difficult to study at home in the quiet atmosphere of their bedrooms. The bedroom is not a strong discriminative stimulus for studying and, in fact, this setting is strongly associated with competing responses such as daydreaming and sleeping. Thus an individual might enter the bedroom with great expectations of reading several chapters, and after a few minutes in the presence of powerful competing discriminative stimuli (magazines, bed) a cognitive haze sets in and the individual is suddenly asleep.

Stimulus control is now recognized as a major variable in understanding patient compliance and noncompliance. When a patient fails to follow a prescribed medical regimen, he is said to be "noncompliant." Estimates of patients that fail to follow their physician's orders range from 30% to 50%. Until recently, the majority of efforts directed toward improving compliance have focused on educating the patients about the nature of their illness and the dangers of failing to follow the outlined treatment procedures. There is little evidence that a patient's knowledge about his illness is related to compliance with associated treatment regimens (Sackett, 1976).

Recently, researchers have shifted their emphasis from studying patient variables involved in compliance to stimulus variables that control or fail to control compliant behaviors (Barofsky, 1976; Zifferblatt, 1975). Within the behavioral framework, compliance is defined in terms of specific target behaviors. This procedure prevents the physician from describing what he wants in vague terms that the client is likely to forget immediately upon leaving the physician's office. Once the target behavior is identified, the next step consists of determining those stimulus or environmental events that lead to the occurrence and nonoccurrence of the behavior. A patient diary or log can be used to identify important cues that either facilitate or hinder the occurrence of the target behavior. By establishing specific cues for performing the required behavior, such as keeping medication in a specific location, the future occurrence of these cues will be more likely to elicit the required behavior.

Observational Learning

Many behaviors are acquired through witnessing the experiences of other people's behavior and its consequences for them. To refer to this class of learning, a variety of terms are used including *imitation, modeling, vicarious learning,* and *observational learning.* Bandura (1969) described the clinical possibilities of observational learning as follows:

> One can acquire intricate response patterns merely by observing the performance of appropriate models; emotional responses can be conditioned observationally by witnessing the affective reactions of others undergoing painful or pleasurable experiences; fearful and avoidant behavior can be extinguished vicariously through observation of modeled approach behavior toward feared objects . . . ; inhibitions can be induced by witnessing the behavior of others punished; and finally, the expression of well-learned responses can be enhanced and socially regulated through the actions of influential models. Modeling procedures are, therefore, ideally suited for effecting diverse outcomes including elimination of behavioral deficits, reduction of excessive fears and inhibitions, transmission of self-regulating systems, and social facilitation of behavioral patterns on a group-wide scale. (p. 118)

Observational learning may partially explain the acquisition of emotional responses in the absence of previous experience with a noxious physical stimulus (as required by the classical conditioning model of fears and phobias). Jones (1924) demonstrated the role of observational learning in the acquisition of a fear response. A child who had no fear of rabbits was placed in a pen with a rabbit along with a second child who was quite fearful of the rabbit. The first child developed toward the rabbit an immediate anxiety reaction that persisted for several days. Jones was also able to treat a fearful reaction by placing one child with a fear of rabbits in the proximity of other children who were playing freely with a rabbit. The child with the initial fear was soon playing with the rabbit along with the other children.

Responses acquired through modeling are not always performed. The difference between acquisition and performance was demonstrated in a study by Bandura (1965). Children observed a filmed model who exhibited aggressive behaviors (hitting and kicking a large doll). For some children witnessing the film, the model's aggressive behavior was punished; for others, the aggression was rewarded; and for a third group, no consequences followed the model's aggressive behavior. The children were then given the opportunity to perform the observed aggressive behavior of the model. The children displaying the least aggression were those who observed the model's behavior being punished. To assess whether all the children had learned the response nonetheless, an attractive incentive was then offered for reproducing the model's responses. Now all the children behaved equally aggressively.

There are several other variables known to influence the extent to which modeled behavior is performed. Observers imitate models who are similar to themselves more than models who are less similar. Prestige and power attributed to the model are additional characteristics that facilitate the modeling effect, mainly because these attributes serve as a cue that positive effects are likely to follow the modeled behavior.

Filmed modeling procedures have been successfully used to reduce hospital and surgery-related anxieties in children. In an elaborate study, Melamed and Siegel (1975) showed one of two films to children (aged 4 to 12) about to undergo elective surgery for tonsillectomies, hernias, or urinary-genital tract difficulties. The experimental group of children witnessed a film entitled *Ethan Has an Operation*. The film depicts a 7-year-old child who has been hospitalized for a hernia operation.

> This film, which is 16 minutes in length, consists of 15 scenes showing various events that most children encounter when hospitalized for elective surgery from the time of admission to time of discharge including the child's orientation to the hospital ward and medical personnel such as the surgeon and anesthesiologist; having a blood test and exposure to standard hospital equipment; separation from the mother; and scenes in the operating and recovery rooms. In addition to explanations of the hospital procedures provided by the medical staff, various scenes are narrated by the child, who describes his feelings and concerns that he had at each stage of the hospital experience. Both the child's behavior and verbal remarks exemplify the behavior of a coping model so that while he exhibits some anxiety and apprehension, he is able to overcome his initial fears and complete each event in a successful and

nonanxious manner. Meichenbaum (1971) has shown that film models who are initially anxious and overcome their anxiety (coping models) result in greater reduction in anxiety than models who exhibit no fear (mastery models). (p. 514)

The control group of children witnessed a film of similar interest value but totally unrelated to the hospital situation.

Physiological, self-report, and observational measures of the children's situational anxiety were obtained prior to the surgery and again 3-to-4 weeks after the surgery. The children who had witnessed the hospital-related film showed less anxiety than the control group of children on all measures taken both preoperatively and postoperatively. Another interesting aspect to this study is that both groups of children had also received the standard hospital preoperative and counseling procedure. A nurse had explained to all the children, with pictures and demonstrations, what would happen on the day of surgery. Each child was also visited by the surgeon and anesthesiologist. This procedure was not as effective as the peer-modeling film.

Peer modeling may be especially important with young children because, under many circumstances, it is easier for a child to understand another child than it is for a child to understand an adult. Until a child reaches the ages of 10 to 13, he cannot perceive issues of health and illness from an adult perspective. How do young children perceive health and illness? Bibace and Walsh (1977) examined this question with three groups of children: 3- to 6-year-olds; 7- to 9-year-olds; and 10- to 13-year olds. Each child was asked to respond to a series of health-related questions: Were you ever sick? How did you get sick? How did you get better? What is a headache? What is a heart attack? What are measles? What is pain? and so forth. The researchers found that each age group gave qualitatively different kinds of answers to these questions.

The 3-year-olds usually did not understand the question and gave no response or some totally unrelated response:

Cancer is like the wizard.

The 4- and 5-year-olds described illness in terms of sensory impressions:

Headache is from the wind.
Heart attack is when some people beep the horn.

The 5- and 6-year-old children were still preoccupied with sensory explanations, but the sensory phenomena were less remote from the child's body. Their responses reflected *contagion explanations*:

A headache is from leaning against something.
A cold is from other people.
A heart attack is when you chew something and the heart gets hard.

The 7- to 9-year-old children began to differentiate between what is internal and external to the self. For younger children in this group, the cause of illness is perceived at the surface of the body. The cause of illness is through physical or moral contamination of the body. The concrete form of thinking is apparent in the way the children link cause and effect, usually through some form of touch:

Germs are kissing someone.
Headache gets better when you rub something on your forehead.
Measles are little bumps on your stomach.
Cancer is smoking without your mother's permission.

The 9- and 10-year-olds within this group begin to internalize causes of illness within the body. These children, however, cannot specify in detail the internal physiological processes and tend to rely on analogies:

A cold is when the cold air gets inside you.
A heart attack is the heart beats too fast.
Cancer is from smoke getting into your lungs.

A truly adult understanding of illness began to appear with the 10- to 12-year-olds. These children see that the source and nature of the illness is due to a specific physiological dysfunction:

A heart attack is when the heart stops pumping blood.
Cancer—you can be born with it.

In these children, the link between illness and causes of illness is seen in physical terms. The older 13-year-olds understand that illness may also have a psychological cause:

A heart attack is when you are all nerve racked.
A headache is when you're all nervous and weary.

This innovative study is significant in several respects. Responses of children observed by health professionals in medical settings should be viewed less as "quaint" or "cute" explanations and more in terms of the cognitive stage that the child is at. By doing so, it becomes possible to provide medical explanations that are in line with the child's thinking processes. Also, the health professional may be better able to communicate to the parent why a child fears a medical procedure that to the parent appears to be harmless.

Stress-inoculation Training

A technique proposed by Meichenbaum (1976) for modifying stress-related reactions is based on the principle that the individual must be taught to modify his "internal dialogue" or cognitions. The technique parallels very closely the underlying philosophy of rational emotive therapy. Ellis (1973) believes that many people have problems because of what they say to themselves. They feel that it is necessary always to be totally competent, that they have no control over their feelings, that they must rely on others who are stronger, or that they cannot overcome the effects of past misfortunes. As a result they harbor irrational beliefs involving self-hatred, hostility, worthlessness, and inadequacy. The goal of rational emotive therapy is to provide patients with methods of self-evaluation that are incompatible with their irrational beliefs.

The patient may not even be aware that irrational beliefs are the basis of his disorder. Many behavioral and physiological disorders become so automatic that they operate totally outside of consciousness. A good example of such automaticity comes from actors who can cry on command. They first learn to accomplish this by vividly recalling the cognitive details of a sad situation and then with practice omitting more of the details, until they are finally able to elicit tears solely by recalling the sensations around the corner of the eyes when they were crying (Miller, 1978). By adopting the reverse procedure, it becomes possible to use cognitions to focus the patient on his maladaptive responses and thereby reverse the automaticity of the sequence.

The stress-inoculation program begins with an educational phase that is designed to provide the patient with a conceptual framework for understanding the nature of his problem. The goal of this phase is to train the patient to talk to himself differently about his problem— to analyze the problem rather than simply to manifest a panic reaction. With phobic patients, for example, Meichenbaum uses Schachter's cognitive-label theory of emotion. The patient is told that his fear reaction seems to involve two major elements: (a) physiological arousal including increased heart rate, sweaty palms, rapid breathing, and bodily tension, and (b) anxiety-engendering thoughts, images, and self-statements such as "I'm really nervous; I'm sweating; others will see it; I can't handle this." The patient is then taught to use the physiological and psychological cues associated with the stress response to trigger a variety of coping responses.

> Sweaty palms, increased heart rate and respiratory rates, and muscular tension now [become] allies, bell ringers, cues to use the coping techniques for which they had been trained. The physiological arousal that the client had previously labeled as totally debilitating anxiety and fear, the harbinger of further behavior deterioration leading to feelings of helplessness, [is] now relabeled as eagerness to demonstrate his competence, as a desire to get on with a task, and as a sign to cope. The result [is] a change to a sense of "learned resourcefulness," replacing a sense of "learned helplessness." In other words, the client learns to respond to the same physiological cues when they do arise with different cognitions. . . . The shift in cognitions in itself may mediate a shift in autonomic functioning. (Meichenbaum, 1976, p. 250)

In some respects this theory sounds like the power of positive thinking advocated in many popular books. The problem with such books is that they seldom explicitly detail precisely how the subject is to change his or her behaviors; consequently, little behavioral change actually occurs. With this technique, the patient is instructed in the use of specific phrases and behavioral skills. The patient is also forced to practice the application of these skills. The importance of practice and rehearsal cannot be overemphasized. For example, many patients are often told to "relax and take life easier" but few individuals actually know how to do so. In short, they must be taught how to relax. Instruction and practice in muscle relaxation training is one example of how this is done.

Coping with Mucous Colitis

An example of how cognitive coping skills are used clinically has been provided by Youell and McCullough (1975). They applied the technique to a patient who was suffering from mucous colitis, an autonomic nervous system disorder that involves a disturbance in the motor activity and mucous-secreting functions of the colon. It has also been called "spastic colitis," "irritable colon," and "nervous diarrhea." The subjective symptoms associated with a colitis attack were described by the patient in question as follows:

My symptoms are basically the same each time. First I feel the muscles in my abdomen tighten, then relax—then severe cramps occur in my abdomen. Next, my rectum feels like it is jumping up and down, and I usually go to the bathroom at this point. My symptoms are relieved for a brief while but not for long. (1975, p. 740)

The client was initially instructed to keep a record of the frequency of attacks and to note the environmental events that occurred prior to each attack. She reported that the majority of her attacks were precipitated by some form of negative interpersonal encounter that made her feel rejected. The patient was then trained in a form of cognitive hypothesis testing. She was, initially, to approach the individuals who created this feeling of rejection and ask them if that is how they intended her to understand the transaction. For example, in one situation the patient was giving a verbal classroom presentation of a project and became engaged in a debate with her instructor. Afterward she ruminated over the transaction and concluded that the professor was out to get her by making her appear stupid in front of her peers. She was instructed to verify her appraisal of the situation by approaching the instructor, who immediately praised her upon her entry into his office. Later in training, the patient was instructed to engage in cognitive hypothesis testing during the actual interpersonal transaction. The frequency of the patient's attacks during therapy is presented in Figure 7-6. By the 50th week her attacks had diminished to near zero in frequency.

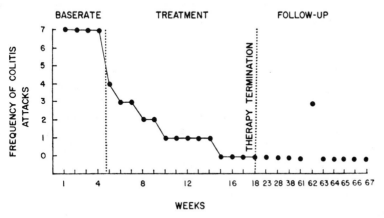

Figure 7-6   Frequency of colitis attacks prior to, during, and following training in cognitive coping (Youell & McCullough, 1975). Copyright 1975 by the American Psychological Association. Reprinted by permission.

Biofeedback

In the early 1970s we were bombarded with claims that many illnesses, from the common cold to cancer, were treatable through the mind-control technique of biofeedback. A representative book from this period bore the title *Your Mind Can Stop the Common Cold* (Freeman, 1973). Biofeedback was offered as a magical solution for the treatment of disorders that had proved resistant to the conventional methods of treatment. Unfortunately, the claims made for this form of treatment were grossly exaggerated. At the same time, however, research continues to explore the possibility that individuals may be able to exert a degree of control of physiological systems that are involved in disorders.

The interest in self-control of physiological responses began largely with interest in the possibility that autonomic nervous system responses in animals could be controlled by operant techniques. Miller and his colleagues demonstrated, in a series of studies, that heart rate (DiCara & Miller, 1968a), blood pressure (DiCara & Miller, 1968b), intestinal contractions (Miller & Banuazizi, 1968), and other autonomic variables could be modified using principles from operant psychology. The general technique used in these studies involved electrical stimulation to the brain as a reward for autonomic nervous system changes in the required direction. The majority of these studies were carried out in rats paralyzed with curare to rule out the possibility that the autonomic changes were simply due to changes in respiration, skeletal-muscle activity, or both. Not only were large autonomic responses produced, but the changes were often quite specific. For example, DiCara and Miller (1968c) found that it was possible to reward differential responses in the two ears of the rat. By only rewarding changes in one ear, it was possible to produce vasodilatation in one ear and either no change or vasoconstriction in the other ear.

Although there have been some very serious difficulties in reproducing any of these early findings (Miller, 1975), clinical investigators were quick to recognize the potential of this work for teaching patients with physiological disorders some control over the disorders. As a result, many researchers and clinicians are currently using biofeedback techniques for assisting patients suffering from headache, hypertension, asthma, epilepsy, and other disorders.

What is biofeedback? *Biofeedback* may be defined as the use of electronic monitoring instruments to record and display physiological processes within the body. The purpose of this procedure is to make this otherwise unavailable information available to the individual. Individuals suffering from muscle-contraction or migraine headache, for example, are often described as being "tense" even though they are unaware of any internal physiological sensations associated with the presumed tension. Using biofeedback techniques, it becomes possible to display to these individuals the moment-to-moment physiological activity that may underlie the psychological tension.

> The general term feedback was coined by the mathematician Norbert Weiner and concisely defined by him as "a method of controlling the system by reinserting into it the results of its past performance." Biofeedback, then, is a special case of this, where the system is a biologic system and where the feedback is artificial, mediated by man-made detection, amplification, and display instruments, rather than being present as an inborn feedback loop inherent within the biologic system. Biologically, then, one should not be so surprised at the efficacy of biofeedback, since, as one reviewer put it, "every animal is a self-regulated system owing its existence, its stability and most of its behavior to feedback controls." Every infant, for example, learns hand-eye coordination (and even the whole concept of space and distance) by means of "visual proprioceptive feedback." By repeated trial-and-error learning, through feedback, eventually the infant comes to be able to control his arm and hand muscles quite precisely, and to reach accurately toward where things are in space, choosing the right direction, distance, angle of approach, and width of grasp on the basis of prior feedback-gained experience. In a way, then, the real surprising thing is not that biofeedback should work at all, but that it was not experimentally looked for and so "discovered" earlier than it was. (Birk, 1973, p. 3)

Unfortunately, the powers of biofeedback were quickly exaggerated and the public began to expect far more than the technique could possibly provide. Some of the early claims for biofeedback are as follows:

- an extraordinary technique which allows you to control the state of your health, happiness and well-being solely through the power of your mind.
- a spectacular scientific theory which has become fact in hospitals and laboratories across the country.
- a revolutionary method of getting quickly in touch with the inner self.
- something Yogis and Zen masters have been doing for centuries to achieve inner peace and joy.
- a visionary technology which places the power for change and con-

trol in the hands of the individual and allows him to control his own
destiny. (Birk, 1973, p. 1)

Although such sensationalistic descriptions have become less frequent
in the past few years, it appears that biofeedback may represent the
beginnings of a new technique and philosophy in medicine, one in
which the patient is required to take an active role in learning not to
become sick.

Clinical Applications

Biofeedback training is described as having three main goals: (a)
the development of increased awareness of the relevant internal
physiological functions or events, (b) the establishment of control over
those functions, and (c) the transfer or generalization of that control
from the laboratory or clinic to other areas of one's life (Budzynski,
1973). An examination of some of the representative clinical biofeedback literature, keeping these goals in mind, should show to what extent the literature suggests that they have been achieved.

Hypertension. Elevated blood pressure is an extremely frequent
and debilitating disorder in the general population. The disorder has
been estimated to occur in 5% to 10% of the general population
(Shapiro & Surwit, 1976), and the presence of the disorder is known
to increase the individual's susceptibility to coronary heart disease and
kidney disease. The majority of individuals suffering from hypertension are diagnosed as *essential hypertensives*, which means their
hypertension has no known physical cause. In these cases it is assumed that psychological and environmental variables play an important role in the etiology of the disorder. If this is true, it seems reasonable to attempt to treat the disorder through self-control techniques.

The efforts to train hypertensive patients to control their blood
pressure levels with biofeedback have not been terribly successful.
Miller (1975) found that a few patients were able to reduce their blood
pressure to some extent, but it began to drift up again after reaching a
plateau. One patient was extremely successful and was able to lower
her diastolic pressure from 97 mm Hg (millimeters of mercury) to 76
mm Hg after 3 months of training. Unfortunately, a series of emotional stresses caused her pressure to rise again and she had to be re-
stored to antihypertensive drugs. To date, no study using biofeedback
has achieved blood pressure changes that would qualify as a "cure" for
the individuals involved.

Even when significant changes in blood pressure occur during biofeedback training, it is difficult to know whether the changes are maintained in the patient's natural environment. Shapiro and Surwit (1976) illustrated the problem of transfer of training with the following example:

> The patient was a 35-year-old mental health worker who was highly motivated and cooperative. He was diagnosed as having essential hypertension with a pressure of 160/110 mm Hg taken during a routine physical examination. The patient was given feedback for reductions in diastolic pressure after six resting control sessions in which he fluctuated from 80 to 105 mm Hg diastolic. Over nine training sessions, he steadily reduced his pressure from over 100 to about 85 mm Hg. A variety of other procedures were then tried, including autogenic phrases and progressive relaxation in addition to feedback, and the patient began oscillating in diastolic pressure between 85 and 95 mm Hg. His systolic pressure, recorded in a final session, ranged from 135 to 130 mm Hg over a 35-minute period. Following these sessions, he returned to his physician for a second examination, and he was recorded again at 160/110. (p. 85)

Although the outcome with this patient is discouraging at the clinical level, the fact that even transient changes were produced is theoretically important, for it supports the hypothesis that, at least for some hypertensive patients, blood pressure is under control of psychobiological mechanisms.

Headache. Biofeedback techniques have been more successful in the treatment of muscle contraction and migraine headaches. Budzynski, Stoyva, Adler, and Mullaney (1973) demonstrated that frontalis EMG biofeedback is effective in reducing the frequency and intensity of muscle contraction headaches. In their study, patients were initially assigned to one of three treatment conditions. One group received 16 sessions of frontalis EMG biofeedback; another group were encouraged to practice relaxation during the treatment sessions while they listened to irrelevant feedback. A third group was simply asked to monitor their headache activity for an identical period of time. The EMG data from the 8 weeks of treatment are presented in Figure 7-7. Patients receiving the direct EMG feedback showed the greatest reduction in frontalis activity and also the greatest reduction in frequency of headaches.

There are several other studies that have found biofeedback of EMG (Hutchings & Reinking, 1976), finger temperatures (Sargent, Green, & Walters, 1973), and even brain waves (McKenzie, Ehrisman, Montgomery, & Barnes, 1974) to be effective in reducing both

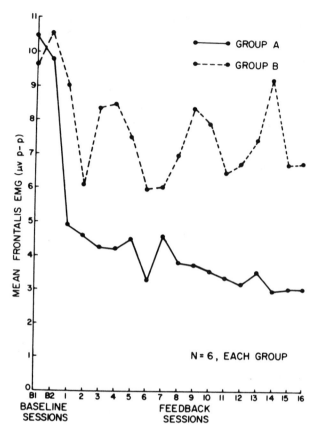

Figure 7-7   Average frontalis EMG levels across training sessions; (Group A) true feedback; (Group B) pseudofeedback (Budzynski, Stoyva, Adler, & Mullaney, 1973). Copyright © 1973 by the American Psychosomatic Society, Inc. Reproduced by permission of the publisher.

muscle-contraction and migraine headaches. Exactly what the subjects are learning in these studies, however, is not clear. It is unlikely that direct control of the relevant physiological variable is being acquired. Examine the data in Figure 7-7 once again. Notice that the great fall in EMG activity occurred during the first session and thereafter very little change occurred. We have noticed the occurrence of a similar phenomenon (Bakal & Kaganov, 1977). If the patients were learning direct control, the curves should be more gradual in decline to indicate that with each session more and more control is being acquired.

Our patients described the sensations associated with the initial decrease in EMG activity as "letting go." This suggests that what patients are learning in biofeedback is to recognize a sensory state that in some patients is associated with a reduction in activity in specific muscles of the head. At the same time it cannot be assumed that the change in sensory awareness will always be related in a neat and simple fashion with the recorded physiological parameter. Epstein and Abel (1977) observed decreases in headaches following EMG biofeedback training in the absence of corresponding decreases in EMG activity. In one patient the decrease in headache activity was correlated with an *increase* in EMG activity.

Epilepsy. Epilepsy is a disorder characterized by irregularly occurring disturbances in consciousness in the form of seizures and convulsions. It is believed to result from spontaneous and massive discharges of brain cells. During an attack the patient often experiences, in a very intense and dramatic fashion, the same behaviors, thoughts, and feelings that are normally mediated by the underlying brain tissue. If motor regions are activated, for example, the patient will spontaneously engage in some kind of physical activity. If visual areas of the brain are involved, he may experience visual hallucinations. Many patients experience an aura or prodromal phase prior to the convulsion. Prodromal symptoms vary from patient to patient depending on the brain structures involved and the patient's attitude toward his disorder. Some patients simply experience a diffuse apprehensiveness, whereas others experience cramps, twitching, or strange odors. Not all epileptics lose consciousness during a seizure.

The possibility of using EEG biofeedback to control epilepsy began with the claim that normal subjects could modify their EEG rhythms (Kamiya, 1969). Sterman and his colleagues (Sterman, 1973; Sterman, Macdonald, & Stone, 1974) pioneered the application of EEG biofeedback training for epileptics. Their work began with the observation that cats could be trained, using milk as a reinforcer, to increase the duration and amplitude of a 12-to-14-Hz EEG rhythm recorded from the sensorimotor cortex (SMR). This particular rhythm occurred primarily when the cats adopted a rigid and motionless posture. In addition, SMR-trained cats were also found to be resistant to drug-induced seizures. They administered a convulsant, monomethylhydrazine, to a group of cats trained in SMR and to a group of cats not trained in SMR. Monomethylhydrazine normally produces convulsions in cats at a dose of 7 milligrams per kilogram. However, the animals trained with SMR biofeedback showed a prolonged latency to seizure at a dose of 9 milligrams per kilogram, and two of the cats failed to convulse at all. The next step was to determine whether the seizure threshold in epileptic patients could be altered with SMR training.

Four epileptic patients were given training in SMR feedback. The patients were given a variety of visual information (lights, interesting slides) as feedback to indicate that their EEG was in the required frequency range of 12 to 14 Hz. All four patients received a minimum of three biofeedback training sessions per week for periods ranging from 6 to 18 months. All patients showed a decrease in the intensity and frequency of their seizures. Three of the patients showed a return of seizure activity when treatment was discontinued, but all three improved with the recommencement of training.

Kaplan (1975) attempted to replicate Sterman's observations and was unable to do so. She found that biofeedback training of 12- to 14-Hz activity in two epileptic patients had no effect on clinical EEGs, seizure incidence, or portion of EEG in the SMR frequency range. She attributed Sterman's success to the possibility that his patients were simply learning to relax rather than to control their brain waves. Finley, Smith, and Etherton (1975) were able to train a 13-year-old epileptic patient to increase the percentage of time spent in SMR from 10% to 65%. The increase in SMR activity coincided with a reduction in the frequency of seizures experienced by the patient.

The biofeedback research with epileptics is promising. We do not know the mode of its effectiveness in terms of whether the patients are actually gaining control over their EEG pattern or are simply learning to relax. We also do not know whether the reduction in seizure activity will be maintained and will be reduced further with continued practice.

Direct or Indirect Control?

Although biofeedback techniques have had a short history in clinical medicine, there are already signs indicating how much can be expected from these techniques. Biofeedback has proved to be more effective with cyclic disorders such as headache than with disorders that are continually present such as hypertension. Accounting for this observation is the fact that most disorders, although exacerbated by emotional and environmental variables, are undoubtedly associated with structural changes in the nervous system. If this is the case, biofeedback techniques may be limited to reducing the frequency and severity of symptoms rather than to reversing these structural changes.

In applying the techniques, one must carefully assess the patient's motivation for treatment. As noted earlier, many headache patients have integrated their symptoms into their lifestyle to such an extent that they are not capable of carrying on any kind of social interaction without discussing their problem. In other words, these patients are being reinforced or are receiving secondary gains from their symptoms. In one sense the symptom has become a vehicle for manipulating others in their environment. In such cases a treatment program must ensure that these patients find other more acceptable means for obtaining social reinforcement from the environment.

Many of the patient's social behaviors might be in conflict with the aims of biofeedback. This is illustrated in a case discussed by Shapiro and Surwit (1976). A patient was treated for essential hypertension and a week of treatment lowered his blood pressure by 20 mm Hg, but over the weekend his pressure would rise again. It was discovered that the patient liked to gamble and was not interested in giving up this antitherapeutic activity. This example suggests where the ultimate value of biofeedback techniques lies.

Although biofeedback has not been proven as a powerful direct technique for gaining control over physiological functions, it might prove to be an extremely useful *indirect* technique for accomplishing this objective. Biofeedback may simply be effective because of its ability to focus the patient on his physiological condition and at the same time focus him away from stress-producing sources of tension. Any technique that teaches the patient to be aware of the debilitating effects of negative thoughts and feelings is likely to possess some therapeutic value. In our own headache research program with biofeedback, the first patient was a tremendous success in that after 12 sessions of forehead-muscle biofeedback training she reported a near-total disappearance of headache. The physiological data indicated that she had gained little or no control over the muscle activity of her forehead. What, then, had happened? Apparently the patient had adopted a new cognitive strategy toward herself and her work situation (which was perceived as quite demanding and stressful). She began to learn to appreciate what she defined as a "feeling of nothingness," which permitted her to cognitively distance herself from previously upsetting work and social situations. Stroebel and Glueck (1973) have summarized the indirect effects of biofeedback as follows:

Biofeedback procedures may prove to be an "ultimate placebo" by squarely placing both the placebo effect and the patient himself in a position of importance in the prevention and treatment of illness. Seen in this light, the placebo component of a biofeedback procedure may assume an importance greater than its potentially active component, particularly in transfer of the active psychophysiologic principle of biofeedback out of the laboratory into daily life, and in eventual persistence of its effects. . . .

An "ultimate placebo" might be defined as a procedure that provides the patient with an effective means of preventing illness and/or potentially curing himself by helping him regulate the pace of his daily life-style, of his thought patterns, of his body processes, his habits, and his perceptual style, hopefully reducing susceptibility to pathological levels of hyperactivation when faced with stressful life events. (p. 20)

Theoretically, it should be possible to achieve these effects without biofeedback machines. For some people, however, the technique has proved very useful in teaching them to be aware of their bodily condition.

Meditation

Meditation is one of the most popular methods being advocated for coping with the stress of living in Western society. Numerous claims are made that meditation is useful not only in every day functioning but also in alleviating disorders such as hypertension, insomnia, headache, asthma, and ulcers. Before looking at its therapeutic value, let us examine the rationale behind the most popular of the meditation techniques: Transcendental Meditation.

Transcendental Meditation, or TM, was introduced to North America in 1959 by Maharishi Mahesh Yogi. The technique is very simple, consisting of sitting comfortably with eyes closed, for 20 minutes twice a day, and thinking to oneself a Sanskrit sound or mantra. The mantras are specifically selected for each individual by the instructor. Advocates of TM believe that the mantra-selection procedure must be carefully done by an expert in order to ensure that a sound congruent with the individual's nervous system is chosen. An improperly selected mantra, they argue, might produce negative effects from meditation (Bloomfield, Cain, Jaffe, & Kory, 1975).

Goleman (1976) claims that the choice of mantra is not critical and that one form of meditation is about as good as another for enhancing the ability to tolerate stress. He provides a short description of how one might experience the essence of the mediation technique:

> Find a quiet place with a straight-back chair. Sit in any comfortable posi-
> tion with your back straight. Close your eyes. Bring your full attention
> to the movement of your breath as it enters and leaves your nostrils.
> Don't follow the breath into your lungs or out into the air. Keep your
> focus at the nostrils, noting the full passage of each in-and-out breath,
> from its beginning to its end. Each time your mind wanders to other
> thoughts, or is caught by background noises, bring your attention back
> to the easy, natural rhythms of your breathing. Don't try to control the
> breath; simply be aware of it. Fast or slow, shallow or deep, the nature
> of the breath does not matter; your total attention to it is what counts. If
> you have trouble keeping your mind on the breath, count each inhala-
> tion and exhalation up to 10, then start over again. Meditate for 20
> minutes; set a timer, or peek at your watch occasionally. Doing so won't
> break your concentration. For the best results, meditate regularly, twice
> a day, in the same time and place. (p. 84)

Goleman and many others believe that meditators are less susceptible to psychosocial stress than nonmeditators. In an experimental
test of this hypothesis, Goleman and Schwartz (Goleman, 1976) confronted both experienced meditators and novice meditators with the
stress-eliciting film of the woodmill accident. The meditators had a
unique pattern of physiological reaction to the film. Just as the accident was about to happen, their heart rates increased and they began
to sweat more than the nonmeditators. As soon as the accident was
over, however, the meditators showed far faster bodily recovery than
the nonmeditators. After the film, they were more relaxed than the
nonmeditators, who still showed signs of tension.

If meditation is indeed effective in reducing stress reactions, how
does it accomplish this change? Wallace and Benson (1972) hypothesized that TM activates an innate physiological mechanism that is antagonistic in function to the sympathetic nervous system fight-flight
reaction. They call this condition the "hypometabolic state" or the "relaxation response." In their original research they found that experienced meditators were capable of producing large-scale changes (in
the range of 10% to 15%) in oxygen consumption, carbon dioxide
production, respiratory rate, the galvanic skin response, and the frequency of alpha waves. In a more recent study, Benson, Steinert,
Greenwood, Klemchuk, and Peterson (1975) found more conserva-
tive changes of 5% in oxygen consumption and 6% in carbon dioxide
elimination during meditation. Both of these physiological measures
are presumed to reflect bodily needs, and because their levels drop-

ped, the authors assumed that this was additional evidence that TM elicits the relaxation response.

Beary and Benson (1974) also reported that the relaxation response can be elicited without meditating. All that is required is that one repeat a constant sound or word while in a passive and relaxed state. Although they found this technique to produce a decrease in oxygen consumption and carbon dioxide elimination, there is some evidence that the technique is no more or less effective than simple relaxation in producing physiological changes. Pollak and Zeiner (1975) had subjects practice the Beary and Benson technique and had another group of subjects simply relax with no special instructions. The physiological changes that occurred were neither profound nor different for the two groups.

Why is the issue of whether profound physiological changes occur during meditation being pressed? Because the answer will help determine whether there is something unique to meditation or whether it is simply another form of relaxation. Glueck and Stroebel (1975) have suggested, for example, that even the mantra might have unique properties. They have observed that the resonance frequencies of the mantras used in TM are very similar to the electrical frequencies that will dampen activity of the limbic system. The possibility that a thought-sound might have such power over one's physiology is intriguing. At the same time, there is considerable evidence that nothing unusual occurs during meditation. Younger, Adriance, and Berger (1975) claim that the EEG patterns of experienced mediators, rather than resembling an altered state of consciousness, are closer in appearance to someone in light sleep. In fact, they have suggested that meditators might actually be spending a fair percentage of the time sleeping.

There is another more practical reason for determining whether meditation has a unique effect on the nervous system. Many claims have been made for its therapeutic value for medical disorders. Wallace, Benson, and Wilson (1971) found that meditators reported fewer minor complaints such as headaches, colds, and insomnia than nonmeditators; yet, the observed effects may have been due less to the direct effects of meditation and more to the lifestyles of meditators. Meditators also reported using less tobacco and alcohol, and these drugs in excess are capable of producing health problems. Benson and Wallace (1972) applied the technique directly on a group of patients suffering from essential hypertension., They measured blood pressure in 22 hypertensive patients before and after the subjects began the regular practice of meditation. Resting-control blood pressures, prior to learning meditation, were 150 ± 17 mm Hg systolic and 94 ± 9 mm Hg diastolic. After learning the TM technique, resting blood pressure outside the meditation period were 141 ± 11 mm Hg systolic and 88 ± 7 mm Hg diastolic. Although the changes were slight, additional changes might have accrued with continued practice of the technique.

In summary, the ultimate benefits of meditation, as with other mind-control techniques, might be more the result of unique lifestyle changes that the technique encourages. For example, a testimonial for TM was once given by a housewife who claimed that her husband was basically an ogre before beginning TM. Now he comes home and behaves like a saint toward her and the children. She attributed the change to TM. Was TM directly responsible for the change? He probably had no justification for behaving in such a negative fashion in the first place. The contact with meditation probably brought this fact to his awareness so "it" did not necessarily change his behavior; he did. This is not a minor issue because the same positive benefits can and should occur without using such techniques as TM. TM is fine, but it should not be viewed as a simple remedy for purifying personality, solving interpersonal difficulties, or curing physiological disorders in some magical way.

Antistress Response

There is a high degree of similarity in the rationales underlying the various self-control techniques. In fact, as of now, there are no convincing data that the techniques differ in terms of their general effectiveness with stress-related psychobiological disorders. Biofeedback, relaxation training, and stress-inoculation procedures in particular all seem to be effective to some degree in providing patients with means of control over their problem.

It has been proposed that self-control techniques share a common pathway in that they promote a pattern of psychobiological responding that is antithetical to the stresses of civilized living. Terms such as *antistress response* and *cultivated low arousal* have been proposed to describe this psychobiological state (Stoyva & Budzynski, 1975). Those who believe in the existence of this mechanism propose that we have all inherited from prehistoric man a *defense-alarm mechanism* that is not suited for coping with the stress and strain of modern living. This mechanism served prehistoric man well because the majority of his potential stressors were physical in nature, such as the sudden appearance of a wild animal or a neighbor with a club in hand. In those times, only one of two responses was possible, either fight or get out of the situation. It made good sense to have an immediate autonomic reaction to provide the bodily resources required to consummate whatever reaction was decided upon. In modern times, the situation has changed. Our neighbors are more subtle; they now send their pets over to urinate on our newly planted shrubs, followed by their children who destroy what the pets miss. We cannot run nor can we fight. All we can do is ruminate. Now the autonomic nervous system responses that occur simply facilitate our destruction.

> Phylogenetically ancient defense mechanisms—originally intended to meet concrete physical dangers in primitive life—have been gradually transferred to the more subtle threat inherent in complex social relations and competitive situations. . . .
>
> Therefore, it is important to realize that civilized man differs from animals, and from very primitive man, in two respects. Firstly, the situations in which mental stress—and its appropriate efferent expressions—is produced have become far more complex, subtle and manifold insofar as socio-economic relationships rather than immediate physical danger provide the most commonly occurring afferent stimuli. Secondly, when in civilized man "defense-alarm" reactions are produced, the somatomotor component is usually more or less effectively suppressed; in other words, *the originally well coordinated somatomotor, visceromotor and hormonal discharge pattern becomes dissociated.*
>
> There are, however, good reasons to assume that the visceromotor and hormonal changes, induced in connection with emotional stress and the defense-alarm reaction, will remain essentially the same. This implies that the mobilization of the cardiovascular and metabolic resources intended to support a violent physical exertion will not be utilized in the natural way. For such reasons the hormonally produced changes of the blood and the chemical environment of the heart and blood-vessels can be expected to be more long-lasting than when a violent muscular exertion ensues. (Charvat, Dell, & Folkor, 1964, p. 130)

The ultimate contribution of self-control techniques, as mentioned earlier, may be their philosophical stance with respect to the individual assuming more responsibility for his health. Such recognition will not come easily but the success to date of these techniques indicates progress is being made.

Multimodal Behavior Therapy

Many patient disorders are controlled by a multitude of factors and cannot be effectively treated simply by using one form of treatment, such as relaxation training, biofeedback, or medication. Poor environmental conditions, interpersonal difficulties, and negative belief systems are all factors that may contribute to the maintenance of a behavioral or physiological disorder. The multitude of variables controlling a disorder partially accounts for the high relapse rates that occur with patients who receive only one form of treatment. In dealing with patients it is important to assess all aspects of their functioning.

How is one to cope with the multitude of variables that influence patient functioning? At first glance, this seems to be an impossible task. Arnold Lazarus (1976) has devised a procedure for this purpose that he calls "BASIC ID." This acronym describes seven important areas of therapeutic intervention: behavior, affect, sensation, imagery, cognition, interpersonal relations, and drugs. Successful treatment requires that intervention take place in as many of these modalities as is necessary.

> Perhaps the plainest way of expressing our major thesis is to stress that comprehensive treatment at the very least calls for the correction of irrational beliefs, deviant behaviors, unpleasant feelings, intrusive images, stressful relationships, negative sensations, and possible biochemical imbalance. To the extent that problem identification (diagnosis) systematically explores each of these modalities, whereupon therapeutic intervention remedies whatever deficits and maladaptive patterns emerge, treatment outcomes will be positive and long lasting. To ignore any of these modalities is to practice a brand of therapy that is incomplete. Of course, not every case requires attention to each modality, but this conclusion can only be reached after each area has been carefully investigated during problem identification (diagnosis). (p. 13)

An immediate advantage of this procedure is that it does not pit one therapeutic philosophy against other philosophies, for example, psychotherapy versus behavior therapy versus chemotherapy. Instead it recognizes that any number of therapeutic procedures may be used to alter the patient's total functioning. In treating depression, for example, Lazarus uses a variety of therapeutic techniques to alter the depressive's environment, cognitions, emotions, interpersonal skills, sensations, and biochemistry. The BASIC ID procedure allows the therapist to be eclectic in theory and at the same time to be systematic in practice. For specific applications of the multimodal procedure, see A. A. Lazarus (1976).

Behavioral Treatment of Chronic Pain

Chapter 5 included a description of the behavioral problems that often develop in chronic-pain patients. A number of pain clinics now incorporate behavioral techniques as part of their treatment program (Fordyce, 1974, 1976; Sternbach, 1974). From the behavioral model, pain-related behaviors involve complaining, grimacing, asking for analgesics, and inactivity. Three essentials are needed to implement a behavioral treatment program for chronic-pain patients:

1. identification of the pain behaviors to be extinguished and the pain-incompatible behaviors to be produced or increased
2. determination of the reinforcers to be used
3. development of an influence or control over the environment sufficient to be able to regulate the consequences of the behavior to be influenced

Patients are fully informed with respect to all aspects of the program.

One of the first environmental changes implemented is to make medication noncontingent on complaints of pain. That is, medication for pain is usually administered following expression of discomfort, which, within the operant framework, reinforces pain behavior by chemotherapeutic relief and by social attention. The problem is solved by shifting the medication prescription from a pain-contingency program to a time-contingency one. Medication is given after a specified time interval that is individually determined for each patient. Medication is never administered following a pain complaint unless the complaint coincides with the lapse of the time interval. It is now possible to carefully reduce the level of active ingredients in the medication vehicle. All treatment staff are instructed to be as neutral and socially unresponsive as possible to pain-related complaints. When the patient is observed participating in any kind of desired activity, the staff is instructed to make a positive effort to be friendly and socially responsive. Pain behavior receives a minimum of social reinforcement, whereas activity is maximally reinforced.

Chronic-pain patients avoid physical activity to avoid pain. Thus, if the patient is engaged in some form of physical exercise and begins to hurt, he is encouraged to rest. Rest unfortunately becomes contingent upon the completion of a pain-incompatible behavior. A simple example of such a behavior is walking. The patient is encouraged to engage in walking by having him walk an agreed-upon distance before returning to his room to rest. Other pain-incompatible activities are reinforced in a similar fashion.

The cooperation of the patient's family is also enlisted to facilitate generalization of the newly acquired behaviors to real-life situations. Family members are instructed to be quietly nonresponsive to inactivity or pain behavior and to be positively responsive toward pain-incompatible behaviors. These procedures must *never* be used with acute-pain patients. Such patients need sympathy and attention for their pain, and hospital personnel need to know when and how much the patients hurt. It is also unethical to manipulate patients' behavior without their knowledge and consent. In Sternbach's program, patients are told what to expect from the nursing staff and why.

The application of these techniques has produced dramatic effects with some patients. Patients that had been bedfast for months were walking a mile a day after a few days in the program. The following case history illustrates the inactivity characteristic of pain patients:

> Mrs. Y. is a 37-year-old white administrator. Since 1948 approximately one year after her marriage, she had had virtually constant low-back pain, and had been decreasingly able to carry out normal homemaking activities. At time of admission to the hospital, she complained of a continuous pain which increased with any activity. She reported her maximum continuous period of activity without an interval of reclining rest as approximately 20 min. Her husband reported she was active in the home an average of less than two hours daily. The remainder of her time was spent reclining; either reading, watching television, or sleeping. During Mrs. Y's 18-year history of back pain, she had undergone four major surgical procedures including removal of a herniated disc and a lumbosacral spine fusion. At the time of admission, Mrs. Y was taking four or five habit-forming analgesic tablets per day when she experienced pain. Physical and radiologic examination revealed a stable spine at the fusion site, with no evidence of neurologic deficit. (Fordyce, Fowler, Lehmann, & DeLateur, 1968, pp. 183–184)

The treatment procedure for this patient consisted of making medication time contingent and reinforcing pain-incompatible behavior such as occupational therapy and walking. Within a few months, the patient became engaged in volunteer work and was managing to walk nearly 2 miles a day. Moreover, the narcotic component of her medication had been completely removed.

Sternbach and his colleagues (Greenhoot & Sternbach, 1974; Ignelzi, Sternbach, & Timmermans, 1977) reported outcome data on 54 pain patients that have completed their behavioral treatment program. In addition to assessing short-term effectiveness, they monitored the patients for a 3-year period following discharge from the program. Some of their patients had also received surgery, so the researchers were able to compare the effectiveness of behavioral treatment alone with behavioral treatment plus surgery. Figure 7-8 illustrates the two groups' changes in pain estimates, activity levels, and

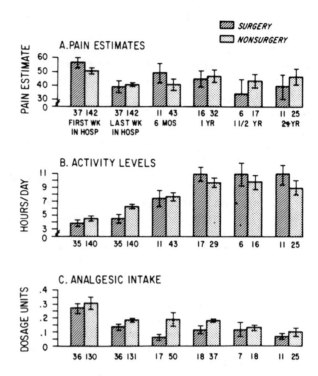

Figure 7-8 Follow-up data on all pain-ward patients at admission, at discharge, and at 6-month intervals thereafter, giving means and
standard errors of pain estimates, activity levels, and analgesic
intake; sample sizes shown beneath histograms (Ignelzi,
Sternbach, and Timmermans, 1977). Copyright © 1977 by
Elsevier/North-Holland Biomedical Press, Amsterdam. Reprinted by permission of the publisher and the author.

analgesic consumption across the 3-year period. Both groups showed
therapeutic gains on all measures. The improvement of the surgery
group did not exceed the improvement of the nonsurgery group.

Tender loving care may actually undermine a patient's rehabilitation. Thus, compassion, concern, and care that are appropriate to
the acute-pain patient do not seem to benefit patients with long-
lasting pain. In a compassionate statement, Sternbach has emphasized
the danger of ignoring this point:

As one who has seen very many pain patients who have been to many
clinics and hospitals, I have had the opportunity to observe how much

harm has been done by well-intentioned doctors who have tried to "comfort the suffering." I have myself, early on, collaborated in the decision to perform the fifty-fifth surgical procedure on a patient with phantom limb pain, a procedure which turned out to be as valueless as the preceding fifty-four. I have seen patients, with totally negative findings on all physical diagnostic tests, so thoroughly addicted to potent narcotics that government agents were investigating the doctors, pharmacists, and patients involved. Clearly, there must be some corollary principle to "comfort the suffering" which will prevent such absurdities. (1974, p. 118)

It is unknown whether the long-term practice of pain-incompatible behaviors will result in the complete disappearance of pain. In fact, the patient may only be learning to avoid attending to and complaining about his pain. Melzack's (1973) gate-control theory of pain predicts that pain can come largely under the control of psychological or central control mechanisms. If this is true, the practice of behaviors incompatible with pain should eliminate the pain. The available data suggests that this is not the case. Patients generally show only a degree of relief from their pretreatment pain levels following behavioral intervention. From a practical standpoint, these gains should not be minimized. Even if behavioral techniques are only partially effective, they may make the difference between unbearable and bearable pain, or between crippled existence and one that allows a normal life.

Groups and Behavior Change

Group therapy represents a useful strategy for implementing attitudes and behaviors conducive to rehabilitation. The traditional mode of treatment in groups has involved psychotherapy, but this method is increasingly being supplemented with techniques and principles from behavior modification. An immediate advantage of the behavioral approach is its requirement that patients formulate their difficulties in behavioral terms. Patients with vague complaints such as "I don't feel well" or "I am depressed" are encouraged to express these complaints in terms of problematic behaviors. Once the problematic behaviors are identified, specific treatment goals are specified and the patient is taught strategies for attaining these goals. Systematic desensitization, modeling, role playing, and a variety of other behavioral techniques are used to assist the group members in attaining the specified goals.

The formation of patient groups can be used to implement programs whereby the patients assume a more active role in their re-habilitation. Many patients enter a hospital or clinic with an extremely passive attitude, believing that their recovery is completely the health professional's responsibility. In the case of chronic illness, patient passivity can seriously undermine all efforts at rehabilitation. Strite (1975) described the reaction of a typical chronic-pain patient upon her discovery that she was expected to take an active role in her rehabilitation:

> My God, this is a hospital, these people are doctors. My pain is worse than when I came in and they expect me to do something about it. The nurse doesn't check on me, I have to get my own medication, make my own bed, walk to my own meals, do sit ups, try to relax, talk to a shrink. They even are suggesting I could have sex! What have I gotten myself into? They are all crazy and I'm getting out of here. (p. 3)

The patient did not leave because, in her terms, she was "either going to die or get well here." Group discussions with other pain patients helped change this patient's initial attitude of passivity.

Group discussions also help patients realize that many of their fears, anxieties, and concerns are shared by other individuals. Patients often function within a state of insulated ignorance about their problems. *Insulated ignorance* is defensiveness that prevents a patient from sharing his concerns with others (Johnson & Matross, 1975). Because of this defensiveness, the patients often operate with a distorted sense of reality. Knowing that others have similar problems often produces considerable relief. Arnold Lazarus (1971) views the advantages of patient-treatment groups as follows:

> Generally the members enjoy the emotional support, the opportunity to release pent-up feelings, the personal reassurance and acceptance, as well as the direct re-educative, explanatory, and insightful experiences. All constructive group encounters provide group members with the chance to see themselves in relation to others, thereby obtaining a realistic appraisal of their adaptive and maladaptive habits, plus specific suggestions and encouragement for remedying the latter. Loss of isolation by discovering that one is not alone in many unusual or disturbing thoughts and feelings, is often exceedingly helpful. When members learn to give to others and help them through trying times, additional gratification and feelings of self-worth often result. (p. 200)

How large should a group be and is it advantageous to restrict participation to patients with similar problems? According to Rose

(1977), therapeutic groups operate best when composed of between six and nine members. Groups with fewer members become sluggish because of a shortage of input, whereas groups with larger numbers are cumbersome. Groups composed of members with the same or similar problems are called homogenous groups. Heterogeneously composed groups are those whose members have diverse problems. An advantage to using homogeneous groups is the ease with which members with common problems can interrelate. In addition, if the members have similar problems, the same techniques of treatment can be used with all members. There are also, however, advantages to using heterogeneous groups. Each member is able to help the other members deal with their specific problems. Moreover, all members acquire experience in learning to cope with a broad range of problems, which may prove useful in the future. Probably the most effective composition of a group is to have the members be similar in some respects and dissimilar in other respects.

Group techniques can also be used to develop and implement effective preventive medicine programs. Durlak (1977) used a behavioral program to alter potential problem behaviors in second graders. The program was conducted in a classroom setting. Initially, teachers rated the children for potential problem behaviors. When present, these behaviors clustered in one of three areas. Some children were shy and withdrawn and seemed to fear social interaction. The target behaviors selected for these children were "talking to others" or "working with others." Other children engaged in considerable disruptive behavior such as fighting, constantly moving about, and exhibiting an inability to work with their classmates. These children were reinforced for "waiting your turn" or "working on your own." Finally, some children manifested learning difficulties, such as an inability to follow directions or to finish a task. These children were reinforced for "working on a task" or "following directions."

The children were told that they would have special tasks to perform in the group, and for these tasks they would receive tokens or poker chips. They could use the chips at a later date to buy items from the "school store." Each child also had a colorful behavioral chart listing his name, his target behavior, and the number of chips earned weekly. Group activities were also designed to allow each child the opportunity to be reinforced for practicing his specific target behavior.

The successfulness of the program was assessed by comparing the behaviors of the experimental group with the behaviors of a control group of children attending a different school. No form of intervention was attempted with the control children. The results showed that, although both groups manifested a similar number of problem behaviors initially, the experimental children had fewer school-adaptation problems than the untreated controls by the end of the program. Moreover, the gains of the experimental group were still present 7 months later. In very young children, the simple reinforcement of adaptive behaviors might establish the beginnings of an adaptive lifestyle that is carried on into adulthood.

In group programs, the role of the health professional becomes that of a consultant. Rather than being expected to cure the patient, the health professional's task is to foster the development of self-reliance in the patient. From the patient's perspective, the group serves to facilitate the attitude transition from "being treated" to "treat thyself" (Strite, 1975). In the long run, this change in attitude creates less of a dependency of the patient on the health professional. When the patient is faced with a similar problem in the future, the patient can attempt to solve it on his own. If unsuccessful, the patient can return to the professional for assistance, but not for a solution.

Epilogue

A New Perspective

Throughout this book, the need for a psychobiological understanding of behavioral and medical disorders had been emphasized. From the psychobiological perspective, physiochemical and psychosocial elements represent equally significant aspects of human functioning. This perspective is hardly new, for a number of theorists, beginning with Freud, have emphasized the role of psychological factors in illness. The present position is simply more encompassing in that the early theorists attempted to separate illnesses that are psychosomatic from those that are organic. This led to countless arguments as to which category a particular illness belonged. Similar discussions can still be found in both psychology and medicine. Many psychologists, for example, believe in the reactive and endogenous categories of depression. Many medical scientists would still like to see the psychosocial aspects of disease separated from the biochemical aspects of disease. The psychobiological perspective avoids the dualism and polarization inherent in these positions by emphasizing that illness does not exist independently of people. There are no illnesses per se but only ill people. From this perspective, all illnesses are the result of environmental, social, psychological, and biological factors. Of course the degree of involvement of the different factors will vary from disease to disease and from person to person. The task facing every health professional is to try and determine the extent to which these various factors operate in every patient.

Early formulations concerning the role of psychological variables in medicine were hampered by a lack of adequate constructs to explain how variables of quite different levels of abstraction, such as psychological and biochemical, interacted to produce illness. The view that specific unconscious conflicts and associated personality traits might lead to specific disorders failed to explain how this came about. Moreover, some 30 years of research failed to provide convincing empirical support for the hypothesized relationships. Conflicts and personality traits involving resentment, frustration, hostility, anxiety, and helplessness have been found across a wide variety of disorders but with their observed prevalence being no greater in one disorder than another disorder. More damaging to the specificity position is the observation that in many instances of disease, the hypothesized psychological antecedents of disease could not be identified.

The psychobiological perspective places less emphasis on the exact content of the psychological components of disease and more emphasis on the psychobiological processes that mediate disease. For example, the split-brain research has provided an explanation of how psychobiological processes outside of awareness may take place. We are by no means suggesting that psychological content is irrelevant, for it is the unique combination of thoughts, feelings, attitudes, and beliefs that ultimately determines the individual's psychobiological transactions with the environment. It is this very observation that has made it impossible to explain emotional and medical disorders solely from a biological perspective. We witnessed the devastating consequences that occurred when psychosurgery was performed on a portion of the brain without due regard for the patient's total psychological makeup. Similar negative outcomes have occurred with patients who have received surgery for pain but who had previously acquired a behavioral pattern that focused on their pain.

In time we may see the emergence of new concepts that encompass the physical and psychological elements of human functioning within one conceptual framework. The fact that many instances of headache, asthma, epilepsy, and other disorders seem to occur in the absence of psychological precipitants does not automatically rule out psychological factors or make them secondary to some more primary biochemical dysfunction. It may be that the critical psychological, or better yet, psychobiological, antecedents have yet to be identified.

Behavior therapy, although a recent innovation in medicine, has already contributed immeasurably to the psychobiological perspective. We now have an array of techniques that can be used to alter a patient's response to events that have been implicated in disease episodes. We must, however, be cautious in our optimism because the successes reported to date have been of a short-term nature and without supporting documentation of any significant long-term changes in the psychobiological status of the patient. The fact that even short-term changes have been achieved is obviously encouraging.

Acceptance of the psychobiological model will also facilitate the health professional's ability to be patient centered rather than disease centered. Countless articles and books have been written that document the importance of interpersonal variables in patient care. Attitudes and communication skills are two areas that have received major attention. Why has this material not had a major impact on patient care? The answer is that many practitioners of technological medicine are not convinced that interpersonal variables are critical to the treatment process. These individuals often refer to interpersonal variables in a mocking fashion, calling them a form of "laying on of hands," which usually means faith healing. It is as if the patient were not really sick in the first place. But what if it is demonstrated in the future that reassurance provided by a health professional is capable of releasing endogenous morphinelike substances within a patient's brain? Without doubt, the phrase "laying on of hands" will acquire a new meaning. The notion is not as far-fetched as it sounds, for it is already known that a patient's mental state can influence the outcome of chemotherapy and surgery.

Patients too will benefit from acquiring a psychobiological understanding of their condition. Physical complaints involving headache or stomach cramps are often viewed by the afflicted individuals as occurring independently from their total psychobiological condition. Consequently they seek out a medication to block the symptoms without realizing that their mode of dealing with the environment actually leads to the symptoms. The symptoms disappear, and the individuals resume a behavior pattern that usually results in the reappearance of the symptoms and the need for additional medication. In time, they may even require surgery. Nothing is more frustrating to the health-professional team than the patient who, after elaborate surgery, returns to the lifestyle that led to his original condition. By learning to recognize that thoughts, feelings, and behaviors have an influence on their physical condition, patients are likely to assume more responsibility for their treatment. Moreover, patients will recognize that health professionals are not miracle workers, that they can only serve as catalysts in the recovery process.

A new perspective on health will also emerge from this model. Health is not merely the absence of disease; it represents a positive psychobiological state that the individual must work toward. It is now recognized that lifestyle variables are probably the most important modifiable factors in health and illness today. In addition to physical risks (tobacco, alcohol, drugs), people also expose themselves to unnecessary emotional and behavioral risks. They ignore the physical consequences of dangerous lifestyles by operating as if they were anesthetized from the neck down. The appearance of bodily danger signs seldom leads them to insight, for they usually turn to medication and fail to realize that lifestyle variables are at the bottom of their condition.

Educational programs are desperately required to emphasize the significance of psychological risks to health, for we now emphasize only the physical risks. Many people, for example, are now jogging to reduce the risk of coronary heart disease. Some of these individuals, however, become so obsessed with running a specific distance within a specific time that one wonders whether their Type A approach to jogging might be doing more harm than good. Possibly the three Rs of education should be expanded to include a fourth R, that of relaxation. It is to be hoped that, by becoming aware of the psychobiological processes operative in illness, individuals will come to understand the necessity of assuming more responsibility for their health.

References

Ackerman, S. H., & Sachar, E. J. The lactate theory of anxiety: A review and reevaluation. *Psychosomatic Medicine*, 1974, *36*, 69–81.

Agras, S., Sylvester, D., & Oliveau, D. The epidemiology of common fears and phobias. *Comprehensive Psychiatry*, 1969, *10*, 151–156.

Akiskal, H. S., & McKinney, W. T. Overview of recent research in depression: Integration of ten conceptual models into a comprehensive clinical frame. *Archives of General Psychiatry*, 1975, *32*, 285–305.

Alexander, F. *Psychosomatic medicine: Its principles and applications.* New York: Norton, 1950.

Alexander, F., French, T. M., & Pollack, G. H. (Eds.). *Psychosomatic specificity* (Vol. 1). Chicago: University of Chicago Press, 1968.

Aman, M. G., & Sprague, R. L. The state-dependent effects of methylphenidate and dextroamphetamine. *The Journal of Nervous and Mental Disease*, 1974, *158*, 268–279.

Andrew, J. M. Recovery from surgery, with and without preparatory instruction, for three coping styles. *Journal of Personality and Social Psychology*, 1970, *15*, 223–226.

Asberg, M., Thoren, P., & Traskman, L. "Serotonin depression"—A biochemical subgroup within the affective disorder? *Science*, 1976, *191*, 478–480.

Asso, D., & Beech, H. R. Susceptibility to the acquisition of a conditioned response in relation to the menstrual cycle. *Journal of Psychosomatic Research*, 1975, *19*, 337–344.

Ax, A. F. The physiological differentiation between fear and anger in humans. *Psychosomatic Medicine*, 1953, *15*, 433–442.

Bakal, D. A. Headache: A biopsychological perspective. *Psychological*

Bulletin, 1975, *82*, 369–382.

Bakal, D. A. Headache. In R. H. Woody (Ed.), *Encyclopedia of clinical assessment*. San Francisco: Jossey-Bass, in press.

Bakal, D. A., & Kaganov, J. A. Muscle contraction and migraine headache: Psychophysiologic comparison. *Headache*, 1977, *17*, 208–215.

Baldessarini, R. J. An overview of the basis for amine hypothesis in affective illness. In J. Mendels (Ed.), *The psychobiology of depression*. New York: Wiley, 1975.

Ban, T. A. Pharmacotherapy of depression—A cricital review. *Psychosomatics*, 1975, *16*, 17–20.

Bandura, A. Influence of model's reinforcement contingencies on the acquisition of imitative responses. *Journal of Personality and Social Psychology*, 1965, *1*, 589–595.

Bandura, A. *Principles of behavior modification*. New York: Holt, Rinehart & Winston, 1969.

Barber, T. X., Spanos, N. P., & Chaves, J. F. *Hypnotism, imagination, and human potentialities*. New York: Pergamon, 1974.

Bardwick, J. M. *Psychology of women: A study of biocultural conflicts*. New York: Harper & Row, 1971.

Barofsky, I. Behavioral therapeutics and the management of therapeutic regimens. In D. L. Sackett & R. B. Haynes (Eds.), *Compliance with therapeutic regimens*. Baltimore: Johns Hopkins University Press, 1976.

Barr, R., & Abernathy, V. Single case study. Conversion reaction. Differential diagnosis in the light of biofeedback research. *The Journal of Nervous and Mental Disease*, 1977, *164*, 287–292.

Beary, J. R., & Benson, H. A simple psychophysiologic technique which elicits the hypometabolic changes of the relaxation response. *Psychosomatic Medicine*, 1974, *36*, 115–120.

Beck, A. T. *Depression: Clinical, experimental, and theoretical aspects*. New York: Harper & Row, 1967.

Beck, A. T. *Depression: Causes and treatment*. Philadelphia: University of Pennsylvania Press, 1972.

Beck, A. T. *Cognitive therapy and the emotional disorders*. New York: International Universities, 1976.

Becker, J. *Depression: Theory and research*. New York: Wiley, 1974.

Becker, J. *Affective disorders*. Morristown, N.J.: Silver Burdett, General Learning, 1977.

Beecher, H. K. *Measurement of subjective responses: Quantitative effects of drugs*. New York: Oxford University Press, 1959.

Beecher, H. K. Quantification of the subjective pain experience. In M.

Weisenberg (Ed.), *Pain: Clinical and experimental perspectives.* Saint Louis: Mosby, 1975.

Benson, H., Steinert, R. F., Greenwood, M. M., Klemchuk, H. M., & Peterson, N. H. Continuous measurement of O_2 consumption and CO_2 elimination during a wakeful hypometabolic state. *Journal of Human Stress*, 1975, *1*, 37–44.

Benson, H., & Wallace, R. K. Decreased blood pressure in hypertensive subjects who practiced meditation. *Circulation*, 1972 (Suppl. II), *15 & 16*, 130.

Bibace, R., & Walsh, M. E. *The development of children's concepts of health and illness.* Paper presented at the meeting of the American Psychological Association, San Francisco, August 1977.

Birk, L. Biofeedback-furor therapeutics. In L. Birk (Ed.), *Biofeedback: Behavioral medicine.* New York: Grune & Stratton, 1973.

Blaney, P. H. Contemporary theories of depression: Critique and comparison. *Journal of Abnormal Psychology*, 1977, *86*, 203–223.

Bloomfield, H. H., Cain, M. P., Jaffe, D. T., & Kory, R. B. *TM—Discovering inner energy and overcoming stress.* New York: Dell, 1975.

Blumetti, A. E., & Modesti, L. M. Psychological predictors of success or failure of surgical intervention for intractable back pain. In J. J. Bonica & D. Albe-Fessard (Eds.), *Advances in pain research and therapy* (Vol. 1). New York: Raven, 1976.

Bogen, J. E. The other side of the brain. I: Dysgraphia and dyscopia following commissurotomy. *Bulletin of the Los Angeles Neurological Societies*, 1969, *34*, 73–105.

Bok, S. The ethics of giving placebos. *Scientific American*, 1974, *231*, 17–23.

Brady, J. V., Porter, R. W., Conrad, D. G., & Mason, J. W. Avoidance behavior and the develpment of gastroduodenal ulcers. *Journal of the Experimental Analysis of Behavior*, 1958, *1*, 69–72.

Breger, L. Dream function: An information processing model. In L. Breger (Ed.), *Clinical-cognitive psychology: Models and integrations.* Englewood Cliffs, N.J.: Prentice-Hall, 1969.

Brooks, J., Ruble, D., & Clark, A. College women's attitudes and expectations concerning menstrual-related changes. *Psychosomatic Medicine*, 1977, *39*, 288–298.

Broughton, R. J. Sleep disorders: Disorders of arousal? *Science*, 1968, *159*, 1070–1078.

Brown, G. W., Harris, I., & Copeland, J. R. Depression and loss. *British Journal of Psychiatry*, 1977, *130*, 1–18.

Bruch, H. Transformation of oral impulses in eating disorders: A conceptual approach. *Psychiatric Quarterly*, 1961, *35*, 458–481.

Budzynski, T. H. Biofeedback procedures in the clinic. In L. Birk (Ed.), *Biofeedback: Behavioral medicine*. New York: Grune & Stratton, 1973.

Budzynski, T. H. Biofeedback and the twilight states of consciousness. In G. E. Schwartz & D. Shapiro (Eds.), *Consciousness and self-regulation: Advances in research* (Vol. 1). New York: Plenum, 1976.

Budzynski, T. H., Stoyva, J. M., Adler, C. S., & Mullaney, D. J. EMG biofeedback and tension headache: A controlled outcome study. *Psychosomatic Medicine*, 1973, *35*, 484–496.

Burnam, M. A., Pennebaker, J. W., & Glass, D. C. Time consciousness, achievement striving, and the Type A coronary-prone behavior pattern. *Journal of Abnormal Psychology*, 1975, *84*, 76–79.

Burstein, S., & Meichenbaum, D. *The work of worrying in children undergoing surgery*. Unpublished manuscript, University of Waterloo, 1974.

Buss, A. H. *Psychopathology*. New York: Wiley, 1966.

Bustamante, J. A., Jordon, A., Vola, M., Gonzalez, A., & Insua, A. State dependent learning in humans. *Physiology and Behavior*, 1970, *5*, 793–796.

Bustamante, J. A., Rossello, A., Jordan, A., Pradera, E., & Insua, A. Learning and drugs. *Physiology and Behavior*, 1968, *3*, 553–555.

Calhoun, L. G., Cheney, T., & Dawes, A. S. Locus of control, self-reported depression, and perceived causes of depression. *Journal of Consulting and Clinical Psychology*, 1974, *42*, 736.

Cannon, W. B. *Bodily changes in pain, hunger, fear and rage*. Washington, D.C.: McGrath, 1929. (Reprinted in 1970.)

Casey, K. L., Keene, J. J., & Morrow, T. J. Bulboreticular and medial thalamic unit activity in relation to aversive behavior and pain. In J. J. Bonica (Ed.), *Advances in neurology (Vol. 4). International symposium on pain*. New York: Raven, 1974.

Cassel, J. Social science theory as a source of hypotheses in epidemiological research. *American Journal of Public Health*, 1964, *54*, 1482–1488.

Charvat, J., Dell, P., & Folkor, B. Mental factors and cardiovascular diseases. *Cardiologia*, 1964, *44*, 124–141.

Cheek, D. B. Surgical memory and reaction to careless conversation. *The American Journal of Clinical Hypnosis*, 1964, *6*, 237–240.

Chertok, L., Michaux, D., & Droin, M. C. Dynamics of hypnotic analgesia: Some new data. *Journal of Nervous and Mental Disease*, 1977, *164*, 88–96.

Chorover, S. L. The pacification of the brain. *Psychology Today*, 1974, 7, 59–69.

Cofer, C. N., & Appley, M. H. *Motivation: Theory and research*. New York: Wiley, 1964.

Cohen, F., & Lazarus, R. S. Active coping processes, coping dispositions, and recovery from surgery. *Psychosomatic Medicine*, 1973, 35, 375–389.

Connelly, J. F., Connelly, J. M., & Phifer, R. Disruption of state-dependent learning (memory retrieval) by emotionally important stimuli. *Psychopharmacologia*, 1975, 41, 139–143.

Cook. R. *The year of the intern*. New York: New American Library, 1972.

Costello, C. G. Electroconvulsive therapy: Is further investigation necessary? *Canadian Psychiatric Association Journal*, 1976, 21, 61–67.

Costello, C. G. A critical review of Seligman's laboratory experiments on learned helplessness and depression in humans. *Journal of Abnormal Psychology*, 1978, 87, 21–31.

Coyne, J. C. Depression and the response of others. *Journal of Abnormal Psychology*, 1976, 85, 186–193.

Dalessio, D. J. *Wolff's headache and other head pain*. New York: Oxford University Press, 1972.

Dalsgaard-Nielsen, T. Migraine and heredity. *Acta Neurologica Scandinavica*, 1965, 41, 287–300.

Dalton, K. Menstruation and crime. *British Medical Journal*, 1961, 2, 1752–1753.

Dalton, K. The influence of mother's menstruation on her child. *Proceedings of the Royal Society of Medicine*, 1966, 59, 1014–1018.

Dana, C. S. The autonomic seat of the emotions: A discussion of the James-Lange theory. *Archives of Neurological Psychiatry*, 1921, 6, 634–639.

Davis, J. M., & Casper, R. Antipsychotic drugs: Clinical pharmacology and therapeutic use. *Drugs*, 1977, 14, 260–282.

Davison, G. C., & Valins, S. Maintenance of self-attributed and drug-attributed behavior change. *Journal of Personality and Social Psychology*, 1969, 11, 25–33.

Delgado, J.M.R., Roberts, W.W., & Miller, N.E. Learning motivated by electrical stimulation of the brain. *American Journal of Physiology*, 1954, 179, 587–593.

De Long, R. D. *Individual differences in patterns of anxiety arousal, stress-relevant information and recovery from surgery*. Unpublished doctoral dissertation, University of California, Los Angeles, 1970.

Dement, W. C. *Some must watch while some must sleep*. Stanford: Stanford Alumni Association, 1972.

Dement, W. C., & Kleitman, N. The relation of eye movements during sleep to dream activity: An objective method for the study of dreaming. *Journal of Experimental Psychology*, 1957, *53*, 339–346.

Dews, P. B. Studies on behavior. 1. Differential sensitivity to pentobarbital of pecking performance in pigeons depending on the schedule of reward. *Journal of Pharmacology and Experimental Therapeutics*, 1955, *113*, 393–401.

DiCara, L. V., & Miller, N. E. Changes in heart rate instrumentally learned by curarized rats as avoidance responses. *Journal of Comparative and Physiological Psychology*, 1968, *65*, 8–12. (a)

DiCara, L. V., & Miller, N. E. Instrumental learning of systolic blood pressure responses by curarized rats: Dissociation of cardiac and vascular changes. *Psychosomatic Medicine*, 1968, *30*, 489–494. (b)

DiCara, L. V., & Miller, N. E. Instrumental learning of vasomotor responses by rats: Learning to respond differentially in two ears. *Science*, 1968, *159*, 1485–1486. (c)

Durlak, J. A. Description and evaluation of a behaviorally oriented school-based preventive mental health program. *Journal of Consulting and Clinical Psychology*, 1977, *45*, 27–33.

Egbert, L. D., Battit, G. E., Turndorf, H., & Beecher, H. K. The value of the preoperative visit by an anesthetist. *Journal of the American Medical Association*, 1963, *185*, 553–555.

Eibl-Eibesfeldt, I. *Ethology: The biology of behavior.* New York: Holt, Rinehart & Winston, 1970.

Ellis, A. Humanistic psychotherapy: The rationale-emotive approach. New York: Julian Press, 1973.

Engel, G. L. "Psychogenic" pain and the pain-prone patient. *American Journal of Medicine*, 1959, *26*, 899–918.

Engel, G. L. Psychophysiological gastrointestinal disorders. 1. Peptic ulcer. In A. M. Freedman, H. I. Kaplan & B. J. Sadock (Eds.), *Comprehensive textbook of psychiatry/II* (Vol. 2). Baltimore: Williams & Wilkins, 1975.

Engel, G. L. The need for a new medical model: A challenge for biomedicine. *Science*, 1977, *196*, 130–136.

English, H. B. Three cases of the "conditioned fear response." *Journal of Abnormal and Social Psychology*, 1929, *34*, 221–225.

Epstein, L. H., & Abel, G. G. An analysis of biofeedback training for tension headache patients. *Behavior Therapy*, 1977, *8*, 37–47.

Evans, F. J. The placebo response in pain reduction. In J. J. Bonica (Ed.), *Advances in neurology (Vol. 4). International symposium on pain.* New York: Raven, 1974.

Fabrega, H., & Manning, P. K. An integrated theory of disease: Ladino-Mestizo views of disease in the Chiapas highlands. *Psychosomatic Medicine*, 1973, *35*, 223–239.

Farquhar, J. W., Wood, P. D., Breitrose, H., Haskell, W. L., Meyer, A. J., Maccoby, N., Alexander, J. K., Brown, B. W., McAlister, A. L., Nash, J. D., & Stern, M. P. Community education for cardiovascular health. *Lancet*, 1977, *1*, 1192–1195.

Fenz, W. D. Strategies for coping with stress. In I. G. Sarason & C. D. Spielberger (Eds.), *Stress and anxiety* (Vol. 2). Washington, D.C.: Hemisphere, 1975.

Ferenczi, S. An attempted explanation of some hysterical stigmata. In S. Ferenczi (Ed.), *Further contributions to the theory and technique of psychoanalysis*. London: Hogarth, 1926.

Finley, W. W., Smith, H. A., & Etherton, M. D. Reduction of seizures and normalization of the EEG in a severe epileptic following sensorimotor biofeedback training: Preliminary study. *Biological Psychology*, 1975, *2*, 189–203.

Fischer, R. Cartography of inner space. In R. K. Siegel & L. J. West (Eds.), *Hallucinations: Behavior, experience, and theory*. New York: Wiley, 1975.

Fisher, C., Kahn, E., Edwards, A., & Davis, D. M. A psychophysiological study of nightmares and night terrors. I. Physiological aspects of the Stage 4 night terror. *Journal of Nervous and Mental Disease*, 1973, *157*, 75–98.

Fisher, C., Kahn, E., Edwards, A., Davis, D. M., & Fine, J. A psychophysiological study of nightmares and night terrors. III. Mental content and recall of Stage 4 night terrors. *Journal of Nervous and Mental Disease*, 1973, *158*, 174–188.

Fordyce, W. E. Treating pain by contingency management. In J. J. Bonica (Ed.), *Advances in neurology (Vol. 4). International symposium on pain*. New York: Raven, 1974.

Fordyce, W. E. *Behavioral methods for chronic pain and illness*. Saint Louis: Mosby, 1976.

Fordyce, W. E., Fowler, R. S., Lehmann, J. F., & DeLateur, B. J. Some implications of learning in problems of chronic pain. *Journal of Chronic Diseases*, 1968, *21*, 179–190.

Frank, R. T. The hormonal causes of premenstrual tension. *Archives of Neurology and Psychiatry*, 1931, *26*, 1053–1057.

Frankl, V. E. Reductionism and nihilism. In A. Koestler & J. R. Smythies (Eds.), *Beyond reductionism*. London: Hutchinson, 1969.

Frazer, A., & Stinnett, J. L. Distribution and metabolism of norepinephrine and serotonin in the central nervous system. In J. Mendels (Ed.), *Biological psychiatry*. New York: Wiley, 1973.

Freeman, L. *Your mind can stop the common cold.* New York: Wyden, 1973.

Friedman, M., & Rosenman, R. H. *Type A behavior and your heart.* New York: Knopf, 1974.

Frost, E. A. M., Kim, Y. I., Hsu, C. Y., & Orkin, L. R. Acupuncture for acute postoperative pain relief. In J. J. Bonica & D. Albe-Fessard (Eds.), *Advances in pain research and therapy* (Vol. 1.). New York: Raven, 1976.

Galin, D. Implications for psychiatry of left and right cerbral specialization. *Archives of General Psychiatry,* 1974, *31,* 572–583. (a)

Galin, D. The two modes of consciousness and the two halves of the brain. In P. R. Lee, R. E. Ornstein, D. Galin, A. Deikman & C. T. Tart (Eds.), *Symposium on consciousness.* New York: Viking, 1974. (b)

Gantt, W. H. Reflexology, schizokinesis, and autokinesis. *Conditional Reflex,* 1966, *1,* 57–68.

Gazzaniga, M. S. The split brain in man. *Scientific American,* 1967, *217,* 24–29.

Glueck, B. C., & Stroebel, C. F. Biofeedback and meditation in the treatment of psychiatric illnesses. *Comprehensive Psychiatry,* 1975, *16,* 303–320.

Goleman, D. Meditation helps break the stress spiral. *Psychology Today,* 1976, *9,* 82–86; 93. (a)

Goleman, D. Radical brain surgery: A case history. *Psychology Today,* 1976, *9,* 51. (b)

Goodell, H., Lewontin, R., & Wolff, H. G. Familial occurrence of migraine headache. *Archives of Neurology and Psychiatry,* 1954, *72,* 325–334.

Greenberg, L., & Roth, S. Differential effects of abrupt versus gradual withdrawal of chlorpromazine in hospitalized chronic schizophrenic patients. *American Journal of Psychiatry,* 1966, *123,* 221–226.

Greenhoot, J. H., & Sternbach, R. A. Conjoint treatment of chronic pain. In J.J. Bonica (Ed.), *Advances in neurology (Vol. 4). International symposium on pain.* New York: Raven, 1974.

Grosz, H. G., & Farmer, B. B. Blood lactate in the development of anxiety symptoms: A critical examination of Pitts and McClure's hypothesis and experimental study. *Archives of General Psychiatry,* 1969, *21,* 611–619.

Gurel, L. *A ten year perspective on outcome in functional psychosis* (VA Rep. 1B11-14). Houston, April 1970.

Harlem, O. K. *Communication in medicine: A challenge to the profession.* New York: S. Karger, 1977.

Harvey, J. A. *Behavioral analysis of drug action*. Glenview, Ill.: Scott, Foresman, 1971.

Haughton, E., & Ayllon, T. Production and elimination of symptomatic behavior. In L. P. Ullmann & L. Krasner (Eds.), *Case studies in behavior modification*. New York: Holt, Rinehart & Winston, 1965.

Heistad, G. T. A bio-psychological approach to somatic treatments in psychiatry. *American Journal of Psychiatry*, 1957, *114*, 540–545.

Hendin, H. Student suicide: Death as a life style. *Journal of Nervous and Mental Disease*, 1975, *160*, 204–219.

Hilgard, E. R. The alleviation of pain by hypnosis. *Pain*, 1975, *1*, 213–231.

Hilgard, E. R., & Hilgard, J. R. *Hypnosis in the relief of pain*. Los Altos: William Kaufmann, 1975.

Hohmann, G. W. Some effects of spinal cord lesions on experienced emotional feelings. *Psychophysiology*, 1966, *3*, 143–156.

Hughes, J., Smith, T. W., Kosterlitz, H. W., Fothergill, L. A., Morgan, B. A., & Morris, H. R. Identification of two related pentapeptides from the brain with potent opiate agonist activity. *Nature*, 1975, *258*, 577–579.

Hutchings, D. F., & Reinking, R. H. Tension headaches: What form of therapy is most effective? *Biofeedback and Self-Regulation*, 1976, *1*, 183–190.

Ignelzi, R. J., Sternbach, R. A., & Timmermans, G. The pain ward follow-up analyses. *Pain*, 1977, *3*, 277–280.

Jaffe, J. H. Drug addiction and drug abuse. In L. S. Goodman & A. G. Gilman (Eds.), *The pharmacological basis of therapeutics* (5th ed.). New York: Macmillan, 1975.

James, W. *The principles of psychology*. New York: Henry Holt, 1890.

Janis, I. *Psychological stress*. New York: Academic, 1958.

Jarvik, M. E. The psychopharmacological revolution. *Psychology Today*, 1967, *1*, 51–59.

Jenkins, C. D. Psychologic and social precursors of coronary disease. *New England Journal of Medicine*, 1971, *284*, 244–255 (Pt. 1); 307–317 (Pt. 2).

Jenkins, C. D. Recent evidence supporting psychologic and social risk factors for coronary disease. *New England Journal of Medicine*, 1976, *294*, 987–994 (Pt. 1); 1033–1038 (Pt. 2).

Jenkins, C. D., Zyzanski, S. J., & Rosenman, R. H. Progress toward validation of a computer-scored test for the Type A coronary-prone behavior pattern. *Psychosomatic Medicine*, 1971, *33*, 193–202.

John, E. R. Switchboard versus statistical theories of learning and memory. *Science*, 1972, *177*, 850–864.

Johnson, A. Recent trends in sex mortality differentials in the United States. *Journal of Human Stress*, 1977, *3*, 22–32.

Johnson, D. W., & Matross, R. P. Attitude modification methods. In F. H. Kanfer & A. P. Goldstein (Eds.), *Helping people change*. New York: Pergamon, 1975.

Jones, M. C. The elimination of children's fears. *Journal of Experimental Psychology*, 1924, *7*, 382–390.

Julien, R. M. *A Primer of drug action*. San Francisco: W. H. Freeman, 1975.

Kamiya, J. Operant control of the EEG alpha rhythm and some of its reported effects on consciousness. In C. T. Tart (Ed.), *Altered states of consciousness*. New York: Wiley, 1969.

Kaplan, B. J. Biofeedback in epileptics: Equivocal relationship of reinforced EEG frequency to seizure reduction. *Epilepsia*, 1975, *16*, 477–485.

Katz, R. L., Kao, C. Y., Spiegel, H., & Katz, G. J. Pain, acupuncture, hypnosis. In J. J. Bonica (Ed.), *Advances in neurology (Vol. 4). International symposium on pain*. New York: Raven, 1974.

Kaufman, I. C., & Rosenblum, L. A. The reaction to separation in infant monkeys: Anaclitic depression and conservation-withdrawal. *Psychosomatic Medicine*, 1967, *29*, 648–675.

Kelman, H. C. Was deception justified—and was it necessary? Comments on "self-control techniques as an alternative to pain medication." *Journal of Abnormal Psychology*, 1975, *84*, 172–174.

Kepes, E. R., Chen, M., & Schapira, M. A Critical evaluation of acupuncture in the treatment of chronic pain. In J. J. Bonica & D. Albe-Fessard (Eds.), *Advances in pain research and therapy* (Vol. 1). New York: Raven, 1976.

Kety, S. S. A biologist examines the mind and behavior. *Science*, 1960, *132*, 1861–1870.

Klein, D. F. Endogenomorphic depression: A conceptual and terminological revision. *Archives of General Psychiatry*, 1974, *31*, 447–454.

Koelle, G. B. Drugs at synaptic and neuroeffector junctional sites. In L. S. Goodman & A. G. Gilman (Eds.), *The pharmacological basis of therapeutics* (5th ed.). New York: Macmillan, 1975.

Koeske, R. Culture and the curse, *Time*, February 23, 1976, pp. 50–57.

Kushner, M. Faradic aversive controls in clinical practice. In C. Neuringer & J. L. Michael (Eds.), *Behavior modification in clinical psychology*. New York: Appleton-Century-Crofts, 1970.

Lacey, J. I. Psychophysiological approaches to the evaluation of psychotherapeutic process and outcome. In E. A. Rubinstein & M. B. Parloff (Eds.), *Research in psychotherapy*. Washington, D.C.: American Psychological Association, 1959.

Lachman, S. J. *Psychosomatic disorders: A behavioristic interpretation*. New York: Wiley, 1972.

Lader, M., & Tyrer, P. Vegetative system and emotion. In L. Levi (Ed.), *Emotions—Their parameters and measurement*. New York: Raven, 1975.

Lang, P. J., & Melamed, B. G. Case report: Avoidance conditioning therapy of an infant with chronic ruminative vomiting. *Journal of Abnormal Psychology*, 1969, *74*, 1–8.

Lazarus. A. A. *Behavior therapy and beyond*. New York: McGraw-Hill, 1971.

Lazarus, A. A. *Multimodal behavior therapy*. New York: Springer, 1976.

Lazarus, R. S. *Psychological stress and the coping process*. New York: McGraw-Hill, 1966.

Lazarus, R. S. A cognitively oriented psychologist looks at biofeedback. *American Psychologist*, 1975, *30*, 553–561. (a)

Lazarus, R. S. The self-regulation of emotion. In L. Levi (Ed.), *Emotions—Their parameters and measurement*. New York: Raven, 1975. (b)

Lazarus, R. S., Opton, E. M., Nomikos, M. S., & Rankin, N. O. The principle of short-circuiting of threat: Further evidence. *Journal of Personality*, 1965, *33*, 622–635.

Leavitt, F. *Drugs and behavior*. Philadelphia: Saunders, 1974.

Lee, P. R., & Petrocelli, F. Can consciousness make a difference? In P. R. Lee, R. E. Ornstein, D. Galin, A. Deikman, & C. T. Tart (Eds.), *Symposium on consciousness*. New York: Viking, 1974.

Lele, P. P., & Weddell, G. The relationship between neurohistology and corneal sensibility. *Brain*, 1956, *79*, 119–154.

Lennox, W. G. *Epilepsy and related disorders* (Vol. 1). Boston: Little, Brown, 1960.

Lester, G., & Lester, D. *Suicide: The gamble with death*. Englewood Cliffs, N.J.: Prentice-Hall, 1971.

Levendusky, P., & Pankratz, L. Self-control techniques as an alternative to pain medication. *Journal of Abnormal Psychology*, 1975, *84*, 165–168.

Levi, L. Psychosocial stress and disease: A conceptual model. In E. K. Gunderson & R. H. Rahe (Eds.), *Life stress and illness*. Springfield, Ill.: Thomas, 1974.

Levine, J. D., Gormley, J., & Fields, H. L. Observations on the analgesic effects of needle puncture (acupuncture). *Pain*, 1976, *2*, 149–159.

Levine, R. R. *Pharmacology: Drug actions and reactions.* Boston: Little, Brown, 1973.

Levitt, E. E., & Lubin, B. *Depression: Concepts, controversies and some new facts.* New York: Springer, 1975.

Lewinsohn, P. M. A behavioral approach to depression. In R. J. Friedman & M. M. Katz (Eds.), *The psychology of depression: Contemporary theory and research.* New York: Wiley, 1974.

Lewinsohn, P. M., Zeiss, A. M., Zeiss, R. A., & Haller, R. Endogeneity and reactivity as orthogonal dimensions in depression. *Journal of Nervous and Mental Disease,* 1977, *164,* 327–332.

Li, C. H., Chung, D., & Doneen, B. A. Isolation, characterization and opiate activity of B-endorphin from human pituitary glands. *Biochemical and Biophysical Research Communications,* 1976, *72,* 1542–1547.

Liddell, H. S. The conditioned reflex. In F. A. Moss (Ed.), *Comparative psychology.* Englewood Cliffs, N.J.: Prentice-Hall, 1934.

Liebeskind, J. C., & Paul, L. A. Psychological and physiological mechanisms of pain. *Annual Review of Psychology,* 1977, *28,* 41–60.

Lief, H. I., & Fox, R. C. Training for "detached concern" in medical students. In H. I. Lief & V. F. Lief (Eds.), *The psychological basis of medical practice.* New York: Harper & Row, 1963.

Lipowski, Z. J. Psychosomatic medicine in the seventies: An overview. *American Journal of Psychiatry,* 1977, *134,* 233–244.

Locke, E. A. Purpose without consciousness: A contradiction. *Psychological Reports,* 1969, *25,* 991–1009.

Long, D. M. Use of peripheral and spinal cord stimulation in the relief of chronic pain. In J. J. Bonica & D. Albe-Fessard (Eds.), *Advances in pain research and therapy* (Vol. 1). New York: Raven, 1976.

Luborsky, L., Docherty, J. P., & Penick, S. Onset conditions for psychosomatic symptoms: A comparative review of immediate observation with restrospective research. *Psychosomatic Medicine,* 1973, *35,* 187–203.

Luce, G. *Biological rhythms in psychiatry and medicine* (National Institute of Mental Health, No. 2088). Washington, D.C., 1970.

Ludwig, L. D. Elation-depression and skill as determinants of desire for excitement. *Journal of Personality,* 1975, *43,* 1–22.

Lynch, J. J., & Fertziger, A. P. Drug addiction: Light at the end of the tunnel? An editorial. *Journal of Nervous and Mental Disease,* 1977, *164,* 229–230.

Lynch, J. J., Stein, E. A., & Fertziger, A. P. An analysis of 70 years of morphine classical conditioning: Implications for clinical treatment of narcotic addiction. *Journal of Nervous and Mental*

Disease, 1976, *163*, 47–58.

Lynch, J. J., Thomas, S. A., Mills, M. E., Malinow, K., & Katcher, A. H. The effects of human contact on cardiac arrhythmia in coronary care patients. *Journal of Nervous and Mental Disease*, 1974, *158*, 88–99.

MacLean, P. D. The brain in relation to empathy and medical education. *Journal of Nervous and Mental Disease*, 1967, *144*, 374–382.

Maddi, S. R. The existential neuroses. *Journal of Abnormal Psychology*, 1967, *72*, 311–325.

Maddi, S. R. *Personality theories: A comparative analysis* (3rd ed.). Homewood, Ill.: Dorsey, 1976.

Mahoney, M. J., Kazdin, A. E., & Lesswing, N. J. Behavior modification: Delusion or deliverance. In C. M. Franks & G. T. Wilson (Eds.), *Annual review of behavior therapy, theory and practice*. New York: Brunner/Mazel, 1974.

Malmo, R. B. Emotions and muscle tension: The story of Anne. *Psychology Today*, 1970, *3*, 64–67; 83.

Malmo, R. B., & Shagass, C. Physiologic study of symptom mechanisms in psychiatric patients under stress. *Psychosomatic Medicine*, 1949, *11*, 25–29.

Malmo, R. B., Shagass, C., & Davis, F. H. Symptom specificity and bodily reactions during psychiatric interview. *Psychosomatic Medicine*, 1950, *12*, 362–276.

Mandell, A., & Mandell, M. Suicide and the menstrual cycle. *Journal of the American Medical Association*, 1967, *200*, 792–793.

Marcus, M. G. Cancer and character. *Psychology Today*, 1976, *10*, 52–59; 85.

Mason, J. W. A historical view of the stress field. *Journal of Human Stress*, 1975, *1*, 22–36.

Mayer, D. J., Price, D. D., Barber, J., & Rafii, A. Acupuncture analgesia: Evidence for activation of a pain inhibitory system as a mechanism of action. In J. J. Bonica & D. Albe-Fessard (Eds.), *Advances in pain research and therapy* (Vol. 1). New York: Raven, 1976.

McKenzie, R. E., Ehrisman, W. J., Montgomery, P. S., & Barnes, R. H. The treatment of headache by means of electroencephalographic biofeedback. *Headache*, 1974, *13*, 164–172.

McLean, P. Therapeutic decision-making in the behavioral treatment of depression. In P. O. Davidson (Ed.), *The behavioral management of anxiety, depression and pain*. New York: Bruner/Mazel, 1976.

Mechanic, D. *Politics, medicine, and social science*. New York: Wiley, 1974.

Mefferd, R. B., & Pokorny, A. D. Individual variability reexamined with standard clinical measures. *American Journal of Clinical Pathology*, 1967, *48*, 325–331.

Meichenbaum, D. Examination of model characteristics in reducing avoidance behavior. *Journal of Personality and Social Psychology*, 1971, *17*, 298–307.

Meichenbaum, D. Toward a cognitive theory of self-control. In G. E. Schwartz & D. Shapiro (Eds.), *Consciousness and self-regulation: Advances in research* (Vol. 1). New York: Plenum, 1976.

Melamed, B. G., & Siegel, L. J. Reduction of anxiety in children facing hospitalization and surgery by use of filmed modeling. *Journal of Consulting and Clinical Psychology*, 1975, *43*, 511–521.

Melzack, R. *The puzzle of pain*. Harmondsworth: Penguin, 1973.

Melzack, R. Central neural mechanisms in phantom limb pain. In J. J. Bonica (Ed.), *Advances in neurology (Vol. 4). International symposium on pain*. New York: Raven, 1974.

Melzack, R. Prolonged relief of pain by brief, intense, transcutaneous somatic stimulation. *Pain*, 1975, *1*, 357–373.

Melzack, R, & Scott, T. H. The effects of early experience on the response to pain. *Journal of Comparative and Physiological Psychology*, 1957, *50*, 155–161.

Melzack, R., & Wall, P. D. Pain mechanisms: A new theory. *Science*, 1965, *150*, 971–979.

Mendels, J., & Frazer, A. Brain biogenic amine depletion and mood. *Archives of General Psychiatry*, 1974, *30*, 447–451.

Merskey, H., & Spear, F. G. *Pain: Psychological and psychiatric aspects*. London: Ballière, Tindall, 1967.

Meyer, V., & Crisp, A. H. Phobias. In C. G. Costello (Ed.), *Symptoms of psychopathology: A handbook*. New York: Wiley, 1970.

Mikulic, M. A. Reinforcement of independent and dependent patient behaviors by nursing personnel: An exploratory study. *Nursing Research*, 1971, *20*, 162–165.

Miles, C. P. Conditions predisposing to suicide: A review. *Journal of Nervous and Mental Disease*, 1977, *164*, 231–246.

Miller, N. E. Applications of learning and biofeedback to psychiatry and medicine. In A. M. Freedman, H. I. Kaplan, & B. J. Sadock (Eds.), *Comprehensive textbook of psychiatry/II* (Vol. 1). Baltimore: Williams & Wilkins, 1975.

Miller, N. E. Biofeedback and visceral learning. *Annual Review of Psychology*, 1978, *29*, 373–404.

Miller, N. E., & Banuazizi, A. Instrumental learning by curarized rats of a specific visceral response, intestinal or cardiac. *Journal of Comparative and Physiological Psychology*, 1968, *65*, 1–7.

Mintz, I. A note on the addictive personality: Addiction to placebos.

American Journal of Psychiatry, 1977, *134*, 327.

Mintz, R. S. Basic considerations in the psychotherapy of the depressed suicidal patient. *American Journal of Psychotherapy*, 1971, *25*, 56–73.

Moffett, A. M., Swash, M., & Scott, D. F. Effect of chocolate in migraine: A double-blind study. *Journal of Neurology, Neurosurgery and Psychiatry*, 1974, *37*, 445–448.

Moos, R. The development of a menstrual distress questionnaire. *Psychosomatic Medicine*, 1968, *30*, 853–867.

Moos, R. H., Kopell, B. S., Melges, F. T., Yalom, I. D., Lunde, D. T., Clayton, R. B., & Hamburg, D. A. Fluctuations in symptoms and moods during the menstrual cycle. *Journal of Psychosomatic Research*, 1969, *13*, 37–44.

Morris, D. *The naked ape*. New York: McGraw-Hill, 1967.

Morris, J. B., & Beck, A. T. The efficacy of antidepressant drugs: A review of research (1958 to 1972). *Archives of General Psychiatry*, 1974, *30*, 667–674.

Morrow, T. J., & Casey, K. L. Analgesia produced by mesencephalic stimulation: Effect on bulboreticular neurons. In J. J. Bonica & D. Albe-Fessard (Eds.), *Advances in pain research and therapy* (Vol. 1). New York: Raven, 1976.

Murphy, T. M. Subjective and objective follow-up assessment of acupuncture therapy without suggestion in 100 chronic pain patients. In J. J. Bonica & D. Albe-Fessard (Eds.), *Advances in pain research and therapy* (Vol. 1). New York: Raven, 1976.

Nathan, P. W. The gate-control theory of pain: A critical review. *Brain*, 1976, *99*, 123–158.

Neisworth, J. T., & Moore, F. Operant treatment of asthmatic responding with the parent as therapist. *Behavior Therapy*, 1972, *3*, 95–99.

Nemiah, J. C. Hysterical neurosis, conversion type. In A. M. Freidman, H. I. Kaplan, & B. J. Sadock (Eds.), *Comprehensive textbook of psychiatry/II* (Vol. 1). Baltimore: Williams & Wilkins, 1975.

Nordquist, V. M. The modification of a child's enuresis: Some response-response relationships. *Journal of Applied Behavior Analysis*, 1971, *4*, 241–247.

Olds, J., & Milner, P. Positive reinforcement produced by electrical stimulation of septal area and other regions of rat brain. *Journal of Comparative and Physiological Psychology*, 1954, *47*, 419–427.

O'Neil, S. The application and methodological implications of behavior modification in nursing research. In M. Batey (Ed.), *Communicating nursing research: The many sources of nursing know-*

ledge (Vol. 5). Boulder: WICHE, 1972.

Ornstein, R. E. *The Psychology of consciousness.* San Francisco: W. H. Freeman, 1972.

Overton, D. A. State-dependent or "dissociated" learning produced with pentobarbital. *Journal of Comparative and Physiological Psychology,* 1964, *57*, 3–12.

Park, L. C., & Covi, L. Nonblind placebo trial. *Archives of General Psychiatry,* 1965, *12*, 336–345.

Pavlov, I. P. *Conditioned reflexes.* Oxford: Milford, 1927.

Paykel, E. S. Life stress, depression and attempted suicide. *Journal of Human Stress,* 1976, *2*, 3–12.

Pearce, J. P. Migraine: A psychosomatic disorder. *Headache,* 1977, *17*, 125–128.

Penfield W., & Roberts, L. Speech and brain-mechanisms. New York: Atheneum, 1966.

Phillips, D. P. Motor vehicle fatalities increase just after publicized suicide stories. *Science,* 1977, *196*, 1464–1465.

Pitts, F. N. The biochemistry of anxiety. *Scientific American,* 1969, *220*, 69–75.

Pitts, F. N., & McClure, J. N. Lactate metabolism in anxiety neurosis. *New England Journal of Medicine,* 1967, *277*, 1329–1336.

Pollak, M. H., & Zeiner, A. *Physiological correlates of Bensonian relaxation training with controls for relaxation and sitting.* Paper presented at the meeting of the Society for Psychophysiological Research, Toronto, October 1975.

Pribram, K. H. Self-consciousness and intentionality. In G. E. Schwartz & D. Shapiro (Eds.), *Consciousness and self-regulation: Advances in research* (Vol. 1). New York: Plenum, 1976.

Prien, R. F., Caffey, E. M., & Klett, C. J. *Pharmacotherapy in chronic schizophrenia.* Washington, D.C.: Veterans' Administration, Department of Medicine and Surgery, May 1973.

Prien, R. F., & Klett, C. J. An appraisal of the long-term use of tranquilizing medication with hospitalized chronic schizophrenics. *Schizophrenia Bulletin,* 1972, *64*, 64–73.

Purcell, K., Weiss, J., & Hahn, W. Certain psychosomatic disorders. In B. B. Wolman (Ed.), *Manual of child psychopathology.* New York: McGraw-Hill, 1972.

Rahe, R. H. Life changes and near-future illness reports. In L. Levi (Ed.), *Emotions—Their parameters and measurement.* New York: Raven, 1975.

Rardin, M. Treatment of a phobia by partial self-desensitization. *Journal of Consulting and Clinical Psychology,* 1969, *33*, 125–126.

Rechtschaffen, A. The psychophysiology of mental activity during sleep. In F. J. McGuigan & R. A. Schoonover (Eds.), *The psychophysiology of thinking: Studies of covert processes*. New York: Academic, 1973.

Refsum, S. Genetic aspects of migraine. In P. J. Vinken & G. W. Bruyn (Eds.), *Handbook of clinical neurology* (Vol. 5). New York: Wiley, 1968.

Richter, C. P. On the phenomenon of sudden death in animals and man. *Psychosomatic Medicine*, 1957, *19*, 191–198.

Richter, C. P. *Biological clocks in medicine and psychiatry*. Springfield, Ill.: Thomas, 1965.

Rippere, V. Comments on Seligman's theory of helplessness. *Behavior Research and Therapy*, 1977, *15*, 207–209.

Rose, S. D. *Group therapy: A behavioral approach*. Englewood Cliffs, N.J.: Prentice-Hall, 1977.

Rosenman, R. H., Brand, R. J., Jenkins, C. D., Friedman, M., Straus, R., & Wurm, M. Coronary heart disease in the Western Collaborative Group Study: Final follow-up experience of 8½ years. *Journal of the American Medical Association*, 1975, *233*, 872–877.

Rosenman, R. H., Friedman, M., Straus, R., Jenkins, C. D., Zyzanski, S. J., & Wurm, M. Coronary heart disease in the Western Collaborative Group Study: A follow-up experience of 4½ years. *Journal of Chronic Disease*, 1970, *23*, 173–190.

Rosenman, R. H., Friedman, M., Straus, R., Wurm, M., Jenkins, C. D., & Messinger, H. B. Coronary heart disease in the Western Collaborative Group Study: A follow-up experience of two years. *Journal of the American Medical Association*, 1966, *195*, 86–92.

Rowland, K. F., & Sokol, B. A review of research examining the coronary-prone behavior pattern. *Journal of Human Stress*, 1977, *3*, 26–33.

Russek, H. I., & Russek, L. G. Is emotional stress an etiologic factor in coronary heart disease? *Psychosomatics*, 1976, *17*, 63–67.

Ryan, V. L., & Gizynski, M. N. Behavior therapy in retrospect: Patients' feelings about their behavior therapies. *Journal of Consulting and Clinical Psychology*, 1971, *37*, 1–9.

Sackeim, H. A., Packer, I. K., & Gur, R. C. Hemisphericity, cognitive set, and susceptibility to subliminal perception. *Journal of Abnormal Psychology*, 1977, *86*, 624–630.

Sackett, D. L. The magnitude of compliance and noncompliance. In D. L. Sackett & R. B. Haynes (Eds.), *Compliance with therapeutic regimens*. Baltimore: Johns Hopkins University Press, 1976.

Sargent, J. D., Green, E. E., & Walters, E. D. Preliminary report on the use of autogenic feedback training in the treatment of migraine and tension headaches. *Psychosomatic Medicine,* 1973, *35,* 129–135.

Schachter, S. The assumption of identity and peripheralist-centralist controversies in motivation and emotion. In M. B. Arnold (Ed.), *Feelings and emotions: The Loyola symposium.* New York: Academic, 1970.

Schachter, S., & Singer, J. E. Cognitive, social, and physiological determinants of emotional state. *Psychological Review,* 1962, *69,* 379–399.

Schildkraut, J. J. The catecholamine hypothesis of affective disorders: A review of supporting evidence. *American Journal of Psychiatry,* 1965, *122,* 509–522.

Schildkraut, J. J., & Kety, S. S. Biogenic amines and emotion. *Science,* 1967, *156,* 21–30.

Schmale, A. H. Somatic expressions and consequences of conversion reactions. *New York State Journal of Medicine,* 1969, *69,* 1878–1883.

Schulz, R. Effects of control and predictability on the physical and psychological well-being of the institutionalized aged. *Journal of Personality and Social Psychology,* 1976, *33,* 563–573.

Schwab, J. J., Fennell, E. B., & Warheit, G. J. The epidemiology of psychosomatic disorders. *Psychosomatics,* 1974, *15,* 88–93.

Schwartz, G. E. Biofeedback, self-regulation, and the patterning of physiological process. *American Scientist,* 1975, *63,* 314–324.

Schwartz, G. E., Davidson, R. J., & Maer, F. Right-hemisphere lateralization for emotion in the human brain: Interactions with cognition. *Science,* 1975, *190,* 286–288.

Schwartz, G. E., Fair, P. L., Salt, P., Mandel, M. R., & Klerman, G. L. Facial expression and imagery in depression: An electromyographic study. *Psychosomatic Medicine,* 1976, *38,* 337–347.

Seligman, M. E. P. Depression and learned helplessness. In R. J. Friedman & M. M. Katz (Eds.), *The psychology of depression: Contemporary theory and research.* New York: Wiley, 1974.

Seligman, M. E. P. *Helplessness: On depression, development, and death.* San Francisco: W. H. Freeman, 1975.

Seligman, M. E. P., Klein, D. C., & Miller, W. R. Depression. In H. Leitenberg (Ed.), *Handbook of behavior modification and behavior therapy.* Englewood Cliffs, N.J.: Prentice-Hall, 1976.

Selye, H. *The stress of life.* New York: McGraw-Hill, 1956.

Selye, H. *Stress without distress.* Scarborough: New American Library of Canada, 1974.

Shaffer, J. W., Schmidt, C. W., Zlotowitz, H. I., & Fisher, R. S. Biorhythms and highway crashes. *Archives of General Psychiatry,* 1978, *35,* 41–46.

Shapiro, A. K. Placebo effects in medicine, psychotherapy, and psychoanalysis. In A. E. Bergin & S. L. Garfield (Eds.), *Handbook of psychotherapy and behavior change*. New York: Wiley, 1971.

Shapiro, A. K. Psychotherapy. In R. G. Grenell & S. Gabay (Eds.), *Biological foundations of psychiatry*. New York: Raven, 1976.

Shapiro, D., & Surwit, R. S. Learned control of physiological function and disease. In H. Leitenberg (Ed.), *Handbook of behavior modification and behavior therapy*. Englewood Cliffs, N.J.: Prentice-Hall, 1976.

Shorkey, C., & Himle, D. P. Systematic desensitization treatment of a recurring nightmare and related insomnia. *Journal of Behavior Therapy and Experimental Psychiatry*, 1974, *5*, 97–98.

Sicuteri, F. Migraine, a central biochemical dysnociception. *Headache*, 1976, *16*, 145–159.

Singer, J. E. Historical background. In H. London & R. E. Nisbett (Eds.), *Thought and feeling: Cognitive alteration of feeling states*. Chicago: Aldine, 1974.

Singer, J. L. *The inner world of daydreaming*. New York: Harper & Row, 1975.

Sjoerdsma, A., Engelman, K., & Spector, S. Inhibition of catecholamine synthesis in man with alpha methyl tyrosine, an inhibitor of tyrosine hydroxylase. *Lancet*, 1965, *2*, 1092–1094.

Snyder, S. H. *Madness and the brain*. New York: McGraw-Hill, 1974.

Spanos, N. P., Barber, T. X., & Lang, G. Cognition and self-control: Cognitive control of painful sensory input. In H. London & R. E. Nisbett (Eds.), *Thought and feeling: Cognitive alteration of feeling states*. Chicago: Aldine, 1974.

Speisman, J. C., Lazarus, R. S., Mordkoff, A. M., & Davison, L. A. The experimental reduction of stress based on ego-defense theory. *Journal of Abnormal and Social Psychology*, 1964, *68*, 367–380.

Sperry, R. W., Gazzaniga, M. S., & Bogen, J. E. Interhemispheric relationships: The neocortical commissures; syndromes of hemisphere disconnection. In P. J. Vinken & G. W. Bruyn (Eds.), *Handbook of clinical neurology* (Vol. 4). Amsterdam: North-Holland, 1969.

Spitz, R. A. Anaclitic depression. *Psychoanalytic Study of the Child*, 1946, *2*, 313–342.

Starker, S., & Hasenfeld, R. Daydream styles and sleep disturbance. *Journal of Nervous and Mental Disease*, 1976, *163*, 391–400.

Sterman, M. B. Neurophysiologic and clinical studies of sensorimotor EEG biofeedback training: Some effects on epilepsy. In L. Birk (Ed.), *Biofeedback: Behavioral medicine*. New York: Grune & Stratton, 1973.

Sterman, M. B., Macdonald, L. R., & Stone, R. K. Biofeedback training of the sensorimotor electroencephalogram rhythm in man: Effects on epilepsy. *Epilepsy*, 1974, *15*, 395–416.

Stern, D. B. Handedness and the lateral distribution of conversion reactions. *Journal of Nervous and Mental Disease*, 1977, *164*, 122–128.

Sternbach, R. A. The effects of instructional sets on autonomic responsivity. *Psychophysiology*, 1964, *1*, 67–72.

Sternbach, R. A. *Principles of psychophysiology.* New York: Academic, 1966.

Sternbach, R. A. *Pain: A psychophysiological analysis.* New York: Academic, 1968.

Sternbach, R. A. *Pain patients: Traits and treatment.* New York: Academic, 1974.

Sternbach, R. A., Wolf, S. R., Murphy, R. W., & Akeson, W. H. Aspects of chronic low back pain. *Psychosomatics*, 1973, *14*, 52–56. (a)

Sternbach, R. A., Wolf, S. R., Murphy, R. W., & Akeson, W. H. Traits of pain patients: The low-back "loser." *Psychosomatics*, 1973, *14*, 226–229. (b)

Stoyva, J. M., & Budzynski, T. H. Cultivated low arousal—An antistress response? In L. V. DiCara, T. X. Barber, J. Kamiya, N. E. Miller, D. Shapiro, & J. M. Stoyva (Eds.), *Biofeedback and self-control: 1974.* Chicago: Aldine, 1975.

Strite, L. C. *Overview of patient-treatment interactions in chronic back pain management.* Paper presented at the meeting of the American Psychological Association, Chicago, August 1975.

Stroebel, C. F. Psychophysiological pharmacology. In N. S. Greenfield & R. A. Sternback (Eds.), *Handbook of Psychophysiology.* New York: Holt, Rinehart & Winston, 1972.

Stroebel, C. F. Chronopsychophysiology. In A. M. Friedman, H. I. Kaplan & B. J. Sadock (Eds.), *Comprehensive textbook of psychiatry/II* (Vol. 1). Baltimore: Williams & Wilkins, 1975.

Stroebel, C. F., & Glueck, B. C. Biofeedback treatment in medicine and psychiatry: An ultimate placebo? In L. Birk (Ed.), *Biofeedback: Behavioral medicine.* New York: Grune & Stratton, 1973.

Stunkard, A. Obesity and the denial of hunger. *Psychosomatic Medicine*, 1959, *21*, 281–289.

Suinn, R. M. Behavior therapy for cardiac patients. *Behavior Therapy*, 1974, *5*, 569–571.

Symington, T., Currie, A. R., Curran, R. S., & Davidson, J. N. The reaction of the adrenal cortex in conditions of stress. In *Ciba Foundations Colloquia on Endocrinology* (Vol. 8). *The human adrenal cortex.* Boston: Little, Brown, 1955.

Szasz, T. S. The psychology of persistent pain: A portrait of l'homme douloureux. In A. Soulairac, J. Cahn, & J. Charpentier (Eds.), *Pain*. New York, Academic, 1968.

Taub, A. Acupuncture "anesthesia": A critical view. In J. J. Bonica & D. Albe-Fessard (Eds.), *Advances in pain research and therapy* (Vol. 1). New York: Raven, 1976.

Taulbee, E. S., & Wright, H. W. A psycho-social-behavioral model for therapeutic intervention. In C. D. Spielberger (Ed.), *Current topics in clinical and community psychology* (Vol. 3). New York: Academic, 1971.

Tyrer, P. *The role of bodily feelings in anxiety*. London: Oxford University Press, 1976.

Ullmann, L. P., & Krasner, L. *A psychological approach to abnormal behavior*. Englewood Cliffs, N. J.: Prentice-Hall, 1969.

Valenstein, E. S. *Brain control: A critical examination of brain stimulation and psychosurgery*. New York: Wiley, 1973.

Valenstein, E. S. The practice of psychosurgery: A survey of the literature (1971–1976). In *Appendix: Psychosurgery* (The National Commission for the Protection of Human Subjects of Biomedical and Behavioral Research, HEW Publication No. [OS] 77-002). Washington, D.C.: U.S. Government Printing Office, 1977.

van Pragg, H., Korf, J., & Schut, D. Cerebral monoamines and depression: An investigation with the probenecid technique. *Archives of General Psychiatry*, 1973, *28*, 827–831.

Volicer, B. J., Isenberg, M. A., & Burns, M. W. Medical-surgical differences in hospital stress factors. *Journal of Human Stress*, 1977, *3*, 3–13.

Wadsworth, M. Health and sickness: The choice of treatment. *Journal of Psychosomatic Research*, 1974, *18*, 271–276.

Waldron, I. Why do women live longer than men? (Pt. I). *Journal of Human Stress*, 1976, *2*, 2–13.

Waldron, I., & Johnston, S. Why do women live longer than men? (Pt. II). *Journal of Human Stress*, 1976, *2*, 19–30.

Wall, P. An eye on the needle. *New Scientist*, 1972, *55*, 129–131.

Wallace, R. K., & Benson, H. The physiology of meditation. *Scientific American*, 1972, *226*, 84–90.

Wallace, R. K., Benson, H., & Wilson, A. F. A wakeful hypometabolic physiologic state. *American Journal of Physiology*, 1971, *221*, 795–799.

Waters, W. E. Migraine: Intelligence, social class and familial prevalence. *British Medical Journal*, 1971, *2*, 77–78.

Watson, J. B., & Rayner, R. Conditioned emotional reactions. *Journal of Experimental Psychology*, 1920, *3*, 1–14.

Webb, W. B., & Cartwright, R. D. Sleep and Dreams. *Annual Review of Psychology*, 1978, *29*, 223–252.

Weiner, H. On the inter-relationship of emotional and physiological factors in peptic ulcer disease. In A. E. Lindner (Ed.), *Emotional factors in gastrointestinal illness.* New York: American Elsevier, 1973.

Weiner, I. W. The effectiveness of a suicide prevention program. *Mental Hygiene*, 1969, *53*, 357–363.

Weisenberg, M. Cultural and racial reactions to pain. In M. Weisenberg (Ed.), *The control of pain.* New York: Psychological Dimensions, 1977. (a)

Weisenberg, M. Pain and pain control. *Psychological Bulletin*, 1977, *84*, 1008–1004. (b)

Weiss, J. M. Influence of psychological variables on stress-induced pathology. In R. Porter & J. Knight (Eds.), *Physiology, emotion and psychosomatic illness* (Ciba Foundation Symposium 8). New York: American Elsevier, 1972.

Weissman, M. M., Klerman, G. L., Paykel, E. S., Prusoff, B., & Hanson, B. Treatment effects on the social adjustment of depressed patients. *Archives of General Psychiatry*, 1974, *30*, 771–778.

Whitehead, G. C. Methadone pseudowithdrawal syndrome: Paradigm for a psychopharmacological mode of opiate addiction. *Psychosomatic Medicine*, 1974, *36*, 189–198.

Williams, J. G. L., Jones, J. R., Workhoven, M. N., & Williams, B. The psychological control of preoperative anxiety. *Psychophysiology*, 1975, *12*, 50–54.

Williams, R. J. *You are extraordinary.* New York: Random House, 1967.

Wolf, S., & Wolff, H. G. *Human gastric function* (2nd ed.). New York: Oxford University Press, 1947.

Wolpe, J. *Psychotherapy by reciprocal inhibition.* Stanford: Stanford University Press, 1958.

Wolpe, J., & Lazarus, A. A. *Behavior therapy techniques.* Oxford: Pergamon, 1966.

Youell, K. J., & McCullough, J. P. Behavioral treatment of mucous colitis. *Journal of Consulting and Clinical Psychology.* 1975, *43*, 740–745.

Younger, J., Adriance, W., & Berger, R. J. Sleep during transcendental meditation. *Perceptual and Motor Skills*, 1975, *40*, 953–954.

Zifferblatt, S. M. Increasing patient compliance through the applied analysis of behavior. *Preventive Medicine*, 1975, *4*, 173–182.

Index